Music and Political Imprisonment in Pinochet's Chile

Currents in Latin American & Iberian Music

Alejandro L. Madrid, Series Editor
Walter Aaron Clark, Founding Series Editor

Nor-tec Rifa!
Electronic Dance Music from Tijuana to the World
Alejandro L. Madrid

From Serra to Sancho:
Music and Pageantry in the California Missions
Craig H. Russell

Colonial Counterpoint:
Music in Early Modern Manila
D. R. M. Irving

Embodying Mexico:
Tourism, Nationalism & Performance
Ruth Hellier-Tinoco

Silent Music:
Medieval Song and the Construction of History in Eighteenth-Century Spain
Susan Boynton

Whose Spain?
Negotiating "Spanish Music" in Paris, 1908–1929
Samuel Llano

Federico Moreno Torroba:
A Musical Life in Three Acts
Walter Aaron Clark and William Craig Krause

Representing the Good Neighbor:
Music, Difference, and the Pan American Dream
Carol A. Hess

Danzón:
Circum-Caribbean Dialogues in Music and Dance
Alejandro L. Madrid and Robin D. Moore

Agustín Lara:
A Cultural Biography
Andrew Grant Wood

Music and Youth Culture in Latin America:
Identity Construction Processes from New York to Buenos Aires
Pablo Vila

In Search of Julián Carrillo and Sonido 13
Alejandro L. Madrid

Tracing Tangueros:
Argentine Tango Instrumental Music
Kacey Link and Kristin Wendland

Playing in the Cathedral:
Music, Race, and Status in New Spain
Jesús A. Ramos-Kittrell

Entertaining Lisbon:
Music, Theater, and Modern Life in the Late 19th Century
Joao Silva

Music Criticism and Music Critics in Early Francoist Spain
Eva Moreda Rodríguez

Discordant Notes:
Marginality and Social Control in Madrid, 1850–1930
Samuel Llano

Carmen *and the Staging of Spain:*
Recasting Bizet's Opera in the Belle Epoque
Michael Christoforidis
Elizabeth Kertesz

Rites, Rights and Rhythms:
A Genealogy of Musical Meaning in Colombia's Black Pacific
Michael Birenbaum Quintero

Sonidos Negros:
On the Blackness of Flamenco
K. Meira Goldberg

Opera in the Tropics:
Music and Theater in Early Modern Brazil
Rogério Budasz

Sound-Politics in São Paulo
Leonardo Cardoso

Bossa Mundo:
Brazilian Music in Transnational Media Industries
K. E. Goldschmitt

After the Dance, the Drums Are Heavy:
Carnival, Politics and Musical Engagement in Haiti
Rebecca Dirksen

The Invention of Latin American Music:
A Transnational History
Pablo Palomino

Latin Jazz:
The Other Jazz
Christopher Washburne

Elite Art Worlds:
Philanthropy, Latin Americanism, and Avant-garde Music
Eduardo Herrera

Panpipes & Ponchos:
Musical Folklorization and the Rise of the Andean Conjunto Tradition in La Paz, Bolivia
Fernando Rios

Música Típica:
Cumbia and the Rise of Musical Nationalism in Panama
Sean Bellaviti

The Sweet Penance of Music:
Musical Life in Colonial Santiago de Chile
Alejandro Vera

Text, Liturgy, and Music in the Hispanic Rite:
The Vespertinus Genre
Raquel Rojo Carrillo

Africanness in Action:
Essentialism and Musical Imaginations of Africa in Brazil
Juan Diego Díaz

Inventing the Recording:
The Phonograph and National Culture in Spain, 1877–1914
Eva Moreda Rodríguez

Inca Music Reimagined:
Indigenist Discourses in Latin American Art Music, 1910–1930
Vera Wolkowicz

Coros y Danzas:
Folk Music and Spanish Nationalism in the Early Franco Regime (1939–1953)
Daniel David Jordan

Silvestre Revueltas:
Sounds of a Political Passion
Roberto Kolb-Neuhaus

Cuban Music Counterpoints:
Vanguardia Musical in Global Networks
Marysol Quevedo

Mario Lavista:
Mirrors of Sounds
Ana R. Alonso-Minutti

Indigenous Audibilities:
Music, Heritage, and Collections in the Americas
Amanda Minks

Immaculate Sounds:
The Musical Lives of Nuns in New Spain
Cesar D. Favila

Music and Cosmopolitanism:
Rio de Janeiro at the Turn of the 20th Century
Cristina Magaldi

Mexican Canto Nuevo:
Music, Politics, and Resistance
Claudio Palomares-Salas

Music and Political Imprisonment in Pinochet's Chile
Katia Chornik

Music and Political Imprisonment in Pinochet's Chile

KATIA CHORNIK

OXFORD
UNIVERSITY PRESS

OXFORD
UNIVERSITY PRESS

Oxford University Press is a department of the University of Oxford.
It furthers the University's objective of excellence in research, scholarship,
and education by publishing worldwide. Oxford is a registered trade mark of
Oxford University Press in the UK and in certain other countries.

Published in the United States of America by Oxford University Press
198 Madison Avenue, New York, NY 10016, United States of America.

CIP data is on file at the Library of Congress

ISBN 9780190052263 (pbk.)
ISBN 9780190052256 (hbk.)

DOI: 10.1093/9780190052294.001.0001

Paperback printed by Marquis Book Printing, Canada
Hardback printed by Lightning Source, Inc., United States of America

The manufacturer's authorized representative in the EU for product safety is
Oxford University Press España S.A. of Parque Empresarial San Fernando de Henares,
Avenida de Castilla, 2 – 28830 Madrid (www.oup.es/en or product.safety@oup.com).
OUP España S.A. also acts as importer into Spain of products made by the manufacturer.

FSC www.fsc.org
MIX
Paper | Supporting
responsible forestry
FSC® C103567

Contents

Figures

Cover

"Manuel Flores," watercolour by Francisco Aedo Carrasco (Chacabuco, 1974). María Cristina González Benedetti collection. Museo de la Memoria y los Derechos Humanos.

The artist and his model were political prisoners at Chacabuco concentration camp in the Atacama Desert during the Pinochet dictatorship. The artist is among the disappeared.

Prologue by Michelle Bachelet Jeria

The document you hold in your hands is an invaluable contribution to understanding one of the most complex aspects of Chile's recent history: the role of music in contexts of political repression and imprisonment during Augusto Pinochet's dictatorship. Within these pages, the narratives of victims and survivors are not only recounted but interwoven with the cultural, emotional, and social dimensions of a phenomenon that profoundly shaped our society.

Through rigorous and sensitive analysis, this work invites us to reflect on how music, as a cultural expression, can acquire radically different meanings depending on its context. For some, it was a tool of resistance and hope amid darkness. For others, it was weaponized as an instrument of dehumanization and suffering. This duality, far from being contradictory, highlights the complexity of experiences lived in political detention centers.

This document delves into broader questions that transcend Chile's specific case. How do we construct collective memory around episodes of mass human rights violations? What role do art and culture play in healing the social wounds of such events? And how can we ensure that the lessons of the past are passed down to future generations to prevent the recurrence of these tragedies?

A key strength of this document is its focus on diverse perspectives and lived realities. While the voices of survivors take center stage, the text also incorporates testimonies from other actors and contexts. This approach enriches our understanding and underscores the importance of inclusive memory—which encompasses both the heroic and the heartbreaking. By doing so, it paints a fuller, more nuanced picture of a harrowing period.

For Chile, this work serves as a vital tool for deepening our understanding of our history and reinforcing our permanent commitment to justice and human rights. Yet its relevance extends far beyond our borders. In a world where democracies are increasingly under threat, the lessons drawn from these pages can inspire other societies to value memory, truth, and reconciliation as essential pillars of coexistence.

Throughout history, music has been a powerful tool of expression. These pages demonstrate that even in the most oppressive circumstances, music became a form of resistance and resilience. Songs hummed under one's breath or shared in whispers acted as acts of defiance, preserving identity and solidarity among prisoners. These stories remind us that the human spirit seeks expression and connection, even in the darkest times.

This text also examines the ethical complexities of memory. Whose voices do we amplify? How do we navigate the tension between celebrating resilience and confronting complicity? The testimonies shared here are raw and multifaceted, reflecting both the courage of resistance and the unsettling ways in which music was weaponized by oppressors.

The broader cultural perspective offered by this document sheds light on how art and music contribute to collective memory. Chile's history is often recounted through the lens of political events and social movements. However, this work reminds us that cultural practices, including music, are equally central to our national narrative. They reveal emotions, hopes, and humanity in ways that official records often cannot capture.

I want to congratulate the author on this essential contribution. This work documents historical facts and invites deep reflection on the transformative power of music and memory. The meticulous research, ethical commitment, and profound empathy embedded in every page ensure that the voices of those silenced are preserved and honored.

I also would like to highlight the project *Cantos Cautivos*, which you will get to know through these pages. I celebrate all the efforts that add to the collective memory of the dictatorship. Memory is a powerful tool when we seek to keep alive the flame of freedom, democracy, and justice. *Cantos Cautivos*, as the author establishes, preserves cultural heritage by collecting and disseminating it throughout Latin America, amplifying the voices and stories of those who experienced human rights violations, thereby making a valuable contribution.

To the readers, I encourage you to approach this book with an open heart and a reflective mind. Allow the stories to move you, challenge your perspectives, and deepen your understanding of resilience and the human spirit. This is not only a journey into the past but also an opportunity to reflect on our present and build a more just and compassionate world for everyone.

As we look to the future, let us draw inspiration from the courage and creativity of those who resisted oppression through music. Their stories remind us of the enduring power of art and humanity to confront even the darkest forces. May we honor their legacy by committing ourselves to a world where every voice is heard, every story is valued, and every person is treated with dignity and respect.

Michelle Bachelet Jeria
Former President of Chile, 2006–2010, 2014–2018
Former Executive Director of UN Women, 2010–2013
Former UN High Commissioner for Human Rights, 2018–2022

Preface

My interest in the topic of music in incarceration centers started in the early 2000s, when I was studying for a master's degree at the Royal Academy of Music in London and a biography of the noted Austrian violinist Alma Rosé fell into my hands. Born in 1906, she was the daughter of Arnold Rosé, concertmaster of the Vienna Philharmonic Orchestra, and the niece of composer Gustav Mahler. Before Hitler's ascent to power, she directed the hugely successful women's orchestra Die Wiener Walzermädeln. In 1942, due to her Jewish ancestry, she was arrested in France, held at the internment camp of Drancy, and subsequently transferred to Auschwitz, where she directed the women's orchestra Das Mädchenorchester von Auschwitz. She died in the camp in April 1944.

Reading Rosé's biography made me think about my Ukrainian paternal ancestors. Escaping anti-Jewish pogroms in Imperial Russia at the turn of the twentieth century, they emigrated to Argentina and subsequently settled in Chile. My grandmother, a violinist, was among the first women to become a professional musician in Chile and in her youth played in an all-women orchestra in Santiago. Although there was a gap of almost half a century between the events causing my relatives' escape to South America and the events leading to the imprisonment and death of Alma Rosé, it somehow felt as if I had inherited her story. I was vividly experiencing events that neither my relatives nor I personally lived. At one point, I realized that I was subconsciously trying to reach another story with which I did have a direct connection: the story of political imprisonment in Pinochet's Chile.

As a child, I had scant knowledge of Chile's political situation and recent history. We lived abroad, and my parents, who were political exiles, told me little. It was only as a teenager in the 1990s, after we returned to Chile, that I began to comprehend the magnitude of what happened in the detention centers of Pinochet's regime. After watching a television report about the publication of the long-awaited report of the first truth commission, I obtained a copy and read it without my parents' knowledge. It was very tough reading.

Around this time, I learned about the rediscovery of a former torture house on Irán Street in south-east Santiago and that a memorial service would take place on the outside. I went to the service against my parents' wishes. They had been imprisoned there, and this was their first time back. Standing outside on a gray evening, the emotion of that experience can hardly be described. An otherwise unremarkable two-floor house, it was used to detain, torture, and exterminate political opponents. The widespread use of sexual violence against prisoners, always blindfolded, prompted its macabre name of Venda Sexy (Sexy Blindfold), allegedly coined by agents of the DINA secret police. Venda Sexy is also always known as La Discotheque due to Pinochet's agents' practice of blasting loud music. Three decades after its rediscovery, Venda Sexy would become known worldwide through Hugo Covarrubias's 2021 animated short film *Bestia* (Beast), which tells the story of Ingrid Olderöck, a DINA agent who committed horrific acts in that house. *Bestia* won numerous national and international film prizes and was shortlisted for the Oscars.

For survivor Beatriz Bataszew, the loud, constant music at Venda Sexy "was noise, except for one song that is engraved in my mind." The song was "Hoy canto por cantar" (Today I Sing Just for the Sake of Singing), popularized by Puerto Rican singer Nydia Caro. "The officers from the DINA secret police amused themselves with it," Bataszew recalls. "They would say to us 'sing' because singing also means grassing on someone." Prisoners at Venda Sexy also used music as a form of communication and self-expression. Such was the case of Ana María Arenas who, after being tortured, sang a Christmas carol and a Mexican *bolero* to let fellow prisoners know she was there and to have something to share safely.[1]

Attending the service outside Venda Sexy as a teenager and getting to know other survivors had a profound impact on me. At that time, I was studying the violin, and learning that music was so prominent at Venda Sexy—as a backdrop to and even an aspect of torture—shocked me. Decades later, I started researching music in political imprisonment centers as a method to understand my family history by deduction, gathering information from people who were not my parents but who had lived similar experiences. Gradually, I began to realize that this was a topic of interest and importance above and beyond the circle of survivors and their families.

Some of the people featured in this book took an active role in implementing the massacre against opponents and have been convicted of human rights violations. It is important for me to clarify that I condemn the views and actions of these individuals. In a country in which most cases of disappearances, executions, and torture committed by agents of the state remain unresolved, it is my firm belief that those who were responsible must be accountable for these acts. This book also features people who were, and in some cases still are, members or sympathizers of leftist political parties and movements with whom I do not share views or affinity. While many left-wing activists who in the past were associated with movements promoting the armed struggle have, over time, softened their stance, moved toward the center, or retired from political activity, others have not shifted their views. I want to make it clear that I wholly reject doctrines, acts, and opinions promoting, praising, or justifying violence coming from any sector of the political spectrum. In all disagreements between my views and those of people featured in this book, I have done my best to minimize my biases and remain as open-minded as possible.

I completed the core of the research and writing of this book in early 2023. Thus, only a few brief references to the commemorations of the fiftieth anniversary of the Pinochet coup are included.

Introduction

In October 2019, millions of Chileans turned to the streets to protest social inequality. The social uprising, known as *el estallido social*, was started by secondary school students following an increase of 30 Chilean pesos in the metro fare (around 3 U.S. cents). The outcry quickly spread throughout the country and included broader demands such as better and equal access to education and healthcare as well as fairer salaries and pensions. These demands were rooted in a long-standing dissatisfaction with the neoliberal transformation of the economy and the state, which began under the dictatorship led by General Augusto Pinochet (1973–1990) and continued under civilian-led governments. Against a backdrop of arson, widespread violence, arbitrary detentions, and serious human rights violations reminiscent of the Pinochet years, the song "El derecho de vivir en paz" (The Right to Live in Peace) became especially resonant. The song was originally a response to the Vietnam War and was written by the Chilean singer-songwriter and theater director Víctor Jara (1932–1973), one of the most emblematic victims of the Pinochet regime.

Víctor Jara was a visible figure in the Nueva Canción Chilena (Chilean New Song) movement, which came to prominence in the 1960s and became closely identified with the campaign and subsequent government of the Unidad Popular (Popular Unity) coalition from 1970 to 1973. On September 11, 1973, the day of the coup, Jara was detained at the Universidad Técnica del Estado (Technical State University), where he was due to sing at the opening of an exhibition about the horrors of civil war and fascism. He was taken to the Estadio Chile in Santiago, an indoor sports complex repurposed by the military to hold and torture hundreds of political prisoners. Shortly before his execution, Jara left a moving testimony of his captivity through an untitled poem known as "Somos cinco mil" (We Are Five Thousand), "Estadio Chile," or "Canto qué mal me sales" (How Hard It Is to Sing). Jara's poem reads: "There are five thousand of us here / in this small part of the city / We are five thousand / I wonder how many we are in all / in the cities and in the whole country?" (Jara 1998: 242). Jara's poem was smuggled to Argentina

Music and Political Imprisonment in Pinochet's Chile. Katia Chornik, Oxford University Press.
 DOI: 10.1093/9780190052294.003.0001

and France and was set to music by Isabel Parra. Since 2010, it has been permanently displayed by the main entrance to the Museum of Memory and Human Rights in Santiago, Chile, in a mural titled "Al mismo tiempo, en el mismo lugar," created by the Chilean artist Jorge Tacla (see Figure I.1).

FIGURE I.1 Mural "Al mismo tiempo, en el mismo lugar" by Jorge Tacla, depicting Victor Jara's poem known as "Somos cinco mil." Museo de la Memoria y los Derechos Humanos. Photograph by Katia Chornik, 2024.

During the social uprising that began in October 2019, Jara's "El derecho de vivir en paz" became viral when a group of musicians from Valparaíso city plotted an online protest against President Sebastián Piñera's use of martial law and public declaration that Chile was "at war."[1] Their call was to play Jara's song at full volume on musical instruments, CD players, mobiles, smart TVs, and turntables at the exact time when the curfew would begin. The call had a vast following—even the National Opera House of Santiago played a recording on loudspeakers. During the uprising, the collective Mil Guitarras para Víctor Jara (A Thousand Guitars for Víctor Jara) convened hundreds to sing Jara's song outside the National Library as part of a massive demonstration held on October 25, 2019 (see Figure I.2).

FIGURE I.2 Mil Guitarras para Víctor Jara performing "El derecho de vivir en paz." Screenshot from microdocumental by José Tomás Urrutia et al. *Mil Guitarras por la Paz y Víctor Jara*. Santiago, Chile: Museo del Estallido Social.

"El derecho de vivir en paz," along with other iconic Chilean protest songs of the 1970s and 1980s, reached top spots on streaming platforms in 2019. "El derecho de vivir en paz" had an equally important presence in the streets, from solo performances to multitudinous demonstrations throughout Chile and in the diaspora. Yet Jara's song was also appropriated by opponents to the political and social reforms demanded by protesters. In 2020, in the run-up to a referendum to decide if Pinochet's Constitution should be replaced, the far-right Unión Demócrata Independiente (UDI) party used Jara's song in their social media campaign to reject the proposed change. As UDI has consistently endorsed the legacy of Pinochet's government, its use of a song written by a man assassinated by the dictatorship was condemned by vast sectors of Chilean society as an opportunistic and insensitive decision.[2]

Jara's cultural activism and tragic death in a political detention center have undoubtedly played a part in the pivotal role that his music has had in the collective memory of Chileans and in the globalization of his story and music. But unlike the story of Víctor Jara, the musical experiences of tens of thousands, including non-musicians, who set foot in the political imprisonment centers of Pinochet's dictatorship are not widely known. This research contributes to filling this gap, collecting, documenting, and interpreting memories of musical experiences and the repertoire of music composed, sung, played, and listened to in the over 1,000 political imprisonment and torture centers of the dictatorship. I posit that remembering through music, possibly the most subjective and affective cultural form, enables witnesses to address difficult experiences, facilitating, engaging with, and contributing to memory processes, as well as opening previously closed spaces. Thus, music is a possible answer to the question posed by Michael Lazzara (2006: 13) regarding Chile's past: "When a nation has suffered a traumatic and scarring episode, in what 'languages' is it possible to convey the experience?"

Historical Overview

The Pinochet dictatorship was preceded by the presidency of Salvador Allende (1970–1973) (see Figure I.3).[3] Allende was the first socialist president to be democratically elected and the first to attempt a transition to socialism through peaceful means, known as "the Chilean road to socialism." Allende was backed by the Unidad Popular coalition of left-wing parties, initially formed in 1969 by the Partido Comunista de Chile and the Partido Socialista de Chile. Five other parties subsequently joined the Unidad Popular—the Movimiento de Acción Popular Unitario, the Acción Popular

FIGURE I.3 President Salvador Allende speaking at the port of Talcahuano in April 1973. Photograph by Armindo Cardoso, "Presidente Allende se dirige a los presentes." Archivo Fotográfico, Biblioteca Nacional de Chile.

Independiente, the Partido Social Demócrata, the Partido Izquierda Radical, and the Izquierda Cristiana. The Movimiento de Izquierda Revolucionaria (MIR) represented the radical, extra-parliamentary left that promoted the armed struggle to defeat capitalism; the MIR did not belong to the Unidad Popular, yet it supported Allende's government once in office.

Allende set an ambitious program of social, economic, and political changes in motion. He deepened the agrarian reform process initiated by previous administrations and expropriated and bought shares of a considerable number of strategic businesses. Social spending caused a growing deficit in public funds, generating an inflationary process aggravated by severe supply issues, hoarding, corporate sabotage, and strike actions in various sectors of the economy.

Allende should have remained in office until 1976. The opposition hoped for a constitutional impeachment to remove him earlier. Yet the results of the parliamentary elections of March 1973, which achieved high support for the Unidad Popular, meant that it would not be possible to secure more than two-thirds of the Congress votes needed for impeachment. In June 1973, a military coup attempt known as *el tanquetazo*, supported by some sectors of the opposition, was thwarted. Allende subsequently planned to call a referendum on his permanence in office. Yet, the idea could not come to fruition, as the armed forces overthrew Allende's government on September 11, 1973.

The coup was a historical rupture that would have consequences for many generations. It was led by General and Commander-in-Chief of the Army Augusto Pinochet (see Figure I.4), with support from the U.S. government and the CIA. Allende retreated with his followers to La Moneda, the presidential palace, where he killed himself as troops stormed. A military junta constituted by Augusto Pinochet, José Toribio Merino, Gustavo Leigh, and César Mendoza served as the new government's executive and legislative branch.

In June 1974, Pinochet was appointed Supreme Chief of the Nation and, in December of the same year, President of the Republic. Using the National Security Doctrine and the nationalistic concept of *chilenidad* (Chileanness) as ideological base, Pinochet's government was characterized by human rights violations, the breakdown of the democratic system, the dissolution of the Congress, the banning of political parties and unions, the restriction of civil rights, massive dismissals, and military discipline in workplaces and educational institutions. Human rights violations under Pinochet included

FIGURE I.4 General Augusto Pinochet in August 1988 at the Diego Portales building (headquarters of the military junta) during his nomination as a presidential candidate for the October 1988 referendum. ©José Giribás M.

political incarceration, torture, murder, disappearance, and forced exile of thousands of people.[4]

Taking direct advice from a group of young Chilean economists called the Chicago Boys, who studied at the University of Chicago under Milton Friedman, Pinochet radically changed the economy, turning Chile into the first country where the neoliberalist doctrine was tested and applied on a massive scale. These steps resulted in massive privatizations, unemployment, and low wages. The paramilitary group Frente Patriótico Manuel Rodríguez (FPMR) made a failed attempt to assassinate Pinochet in 1986. Mass protests coupled with mounting international pressure forced Pinochet to hold a referendum in October 1988, which he lost, leading to the presidential and parliamentary elections in December 1989.

Pinochet remained in command of the Army for another ten years, spanning the presidencies of Patricio Aylwin and Eduardo Frei Ruiz-Tagle. In October 1998, during a visit to London, Pinochet was arrested by the British Metropolitan Police after an international warrant was issued for extradition to Spain, indicting him for human rights violations. After 503 days under arrest at a London clinic and later at a rented house in Virginia Water (Southeast England), the British government released Pinochet on the grounds of fragile health and let him return to Chile. In 2005, the Chilean Supreme Court voted to remove his immunity and considered him fit to stand trial for fraud and embezzlement of public funds. Yet Pinochet never faced the courts or served a prison sentence. He died in 2006.

Music Overview

Chilean popular music has been influenced by tradition and foreign currents.[5] In the 1920s and 1930s, folk genres like *cueca*, *tonada*, and *vals* were widely disseminated by *música típica* ensembles like Los Cuatro Huasos, Los Huasos Quincheros, and Los Provincianos. These ensembles impersonated the *huaso* (horseman), an archetypical figure symbolizing the farms of central Chile and the tradition of those lands. Chilean folk music genres such as *cueca*, *tonada*, *vals*, *pericona*, *sirilla*, *refalosa*, *cachimbo*, *mapuchina*, and *trote* were popularized in the 1960s and 1970s by the Neofolklore, Nueva Canción, and Canto Nuevo movements. Genres from Cuba and Mexico had wide circulation in Chile, particularly the *rumba*, *conga*, and *guaracha* in the 1930s, the *mambo* and *chachachá* in the 1950s, and the *cumbia* in the 1960s. Genres originating in Argentina (*tango*), Brazil (*maxixe* and *samba*), Mexico (*corrido*, *bolero*, and *ranchera*), and the USA (foxtrot, jazz, and rock and roll) also exerted a strong influence on Chilean popular music from the 1950s onward. Various Chilean ensembles performing tropical music, swing, and foxtrots emerged in that decade, inspired by films, records, and touring ensembles from abroad.

Chile's first response to the international boom of rock and roll was the Nueva Ola Chilena (Chilean New Wave), which emerged in the late 1950s and saw young Chilean artists performing covers of English-language songs in Spanish translation. Nueva Ola was tightly linked with radio and television, starting with Peter Rock in 1958 and crowning with The Ramblers' "El rock del mundial" single for the 1962 FIFA World Cup finals. Other well-known Nueva Ola artists were Los Carr Twins, Cecilia Pantoja, Buddy Richard, Los Red Junior, Luis Dimas, Fresia Soto, Gloria Aguirre, Alan y sus Bates, and Los Rockets. Toward the late 1960s, under the hippie movement's influence, the mellow rock of Nueva Ola gave way to a psychedelic sound and countercultural movement represented by bands like Los Jockers. Chilean rock developed its own identity in the 1970s with Los Jaivas and Congreso, which began amalgamating Chilean and Latin American instruments and rhythms with elements of English-language rock. Other well-known Chilean bands of the 1960s and 1970s are Aguaturbia, Los Blops, and Los Mac's. In the 1980s, rock musicians overtly criticized Pinochet's repressive regime, with Los Prisioneros being the most influential band of this period.

Nueva Canción Chilena (New Chilean Song) was a mass-mediated movement that built creative bridges between different music traditions. It emerged in the 1960s during a period of political struggle across Latin America, denouncing injustices through socially conscious lyrics and expressing aspirations of social movements from below. Its origins are found in the work of Violeta Parra, who revitalized traditional Chilean genres as well as folk music from across Latin America. In 1965, Violeta Parra's children Ángel and Isabel Parra founded La Peña de los Parra, a folk meetup that established the sound of Nueva Canción and found an audience for future luminaries like Víctor Jara, Rolando Alarcón, and Patricio Manns. Many Nueva Canción artists actively participated in the campaign and the subsequent government of Salvador Allende, bestowing the movement with an explicit political militancy. During the 1960s and 1970s, some groups worked with composers of the so-called classic tradition—most notably Quilapayún's and Inti-Illimani's collaborations with Sergio Ortega and Luis Advis.[6] Nueva Canción emerged almost simultaneously in Chile and other countries under different names: Argentina (Nuevo Cancionero), Uruguay (Canto Popular), Cuba (Nueva Trova), and Catalonia (Nova Cançó); it later spread to other countries in the region.

In the name of *chilenidad*, the Pinochet regime banned folk music and Andean instruments such as the *quena*, the *zampoña*, and the *charango*, and viewed Nueva Canción as "un-Chilean." The regime officialized *cueca* as the national music genre and dance through Decree 23 (1979), imposing a type associated with landowners and cleansed of indigenous elements to wipe out any memories of Nueva Canción musicians, who were particularly targeted. Víctor Jara, Ángel Parra, and Ernesto Parra (not related) became political prisoners. Víctor Jara was killed. Many others, including Isabel and Ángel Parra, Patricio Manns, Osvaldo "Gitano" Rodríguez, and members of Quilapayún, Inti-Illimani, Illapu, Tiemponuevo, and Amerindios, were exiled. Exiled musicians performed worldwide and contributed to raising awareness of human rights violations in Chile and developing international opposition to the dictatorship.

In the mid-1970s, a new movement called Canto Nuevo (its name meaning roughly the same as Nueva Canción, showing the links between these movements) emerged in Chile as a response to the dictatorship's cultural and political repression. Some Canto Nuevo musicians, such as Osvaldo Torres (an early member of Illapu), Payo Grondona, and Nano Acevedo, were formerly associated with Nueva Canción. Other prominent Canto Nuevo groups and soloists were Barroco Andino, Ortiga, Aquelarre, Santiago del Nuevo Extremo, Abril, Schwenke y Nilo, Eduardo Peralta, Hugo Moraga, Isabel Aldunate, Cristina González, and Juan Carlos Pérez. The sound of Canto Nuevo incorporated elements of Nueva Canción, jazz, bossa nova, rock, and baroque music; its lyrics were symbolic, coded, and metaphorical to circumvent censorship.

Besides Mil Guitarras para Víctor Jara, a notable contemporary initiative commemorating Jara is the band and dance troupe Los Diablos Rojos de Víctor Jara (The Red Devils of Víctor Jara). Its origin traces back to the 2009 funeral and reburial of Jara's remains at Chile's largest cemetery, the Cementerio General de Santiago. Jara's body had been exhumed so that a court could clarify the circumstances of his death.[7] Los Diablos Rojos was among the various groups that responded to an open call for artists to accompany the funeral procession. Since then, Los Diablos Rojos have participated in annual marches marking Pinochet's coup and sporadically in events at former political imprisonment centers. In a previous publication (Chornik 2019), I discuss Los Diablos Rojos de Víctor Jara as a revival initiative. I examine their borrowings, adaptations, and decontextualizations of musical, dance, and costume elements from Andean religious festivities in Chile, Bolivia, Peru, and Ecuador, transferences from Banda Conmoción, a well-known fusion band based in Santiago. I posit that Los Diablos Rojos have not only appropriated and recontextualized Andean elements in nonreligious contexts but have also exerted aesthetic transformations of Jara's music and political legacy. In doing so, they recode and update Jara's work to contemporary circumstances, keep alive the memory of victims of the dictatorship, and challenge attempts to criminalize social protests. In Los Diablos Rojos, the figure of the devil, through time and cultures seen as a representation of evil, embraces that of Víctor Jara, who, over decades, has become a martyr figure. I find certain subversion in the association of devils with Jara, as in the party-like way Los Diablos Rojos mark anniversaries of the Pinochet coup, which brought so many human casualties, including Jara's.[8]

Another influential figure who has been the center of recent commemorations is the composer, conductor, and pedagogue Jorge Peña Hen. Based in the northern city of La Serena, in the 1950s and 60s, Peña Hen founded the Regional Conservatory, the Children's Symphony Orchestra, and the Experimental School of Music. He sought to provide instrumental tuition to children who did not have the financial means to study music, combining pedagogical and social aspects. In September 1973, Peña Hen was detained at the Cárcel de La Serena and subsequently assassinated at the Regimiento Arica of that city by the Caravan of Death, an army death squad that executed over seventy political opponents.[9]

Soon after Jorge Peña Hen's tragic death, his legacy influenced the emerging youth orchestras movement in Venezuela. It did so through three Chilean musicians who had worked closely with Peña Hen and settled in the city of Carora (center-western Venezuela), where they co-founded and coached the children's orchestra. The Carora orchestra developed in parallel to, and fed into, El Sistema program, which would become world famous in subsequent years.[10] Peña Hen's would have resonance in Chile's youth orchestras program, the Fundación de Orquestas Juveniles e Infantiles (FOJI), established in 1992 and influenced by El Sistema too. The increased visibility of Peña Hen's legacy in Chile has been aided by the broader dissemination of concert music through multitudinous events in public spaces and the use of orchestral instruments in popular music. In 2023, coinciding with the fiftieth anniversary of the coup and Peña Hen's death, there was further impetus to commemorate his work, with initiatives like the production of a film and a concert attended by over two thousand people.[11]

Political Violence and Human Rights Violations

Chile has a long history of torture and other maltreatment by state agents. The most serious cases, due to their massiveness, gravity, and systematicity, happened during Pinochet's dictatorship and the *estallido social*, which took place under democracy (Comité para la Prevención de la Tortura 2021; Centro de Derechos Humanos 2022).

Five government-sponsored truth commissions documented the political violence and human rights violations occurring during the dictatorship. These were the Comisión de Verdad y Reconciliación (1990–1991, also known as Comisión Rettig), the Corporación Nacional de Reparación y Reconciliación (1992–1994), the Mesa de Diálogo (1999–2001), the Comisión Nacional sobre Prisión Política y Tortura (2003–2004, hereafter CNPPT, also known as Comisión Valech), and the Comisión Asesora

Presidencial para la Calificación de Detenidos Desaparecidos, Ejecutados, Prisión Política y Tortura (2010–2011).[12] The commissions counted a total of 41,481 victims of human rights violations and political violence committed during the dictatorship, including political imprisonment, torture, forced disappearances, and executions, as follows:

2,130 victims of serious human rights violations and 168 victims of political violence (Comisión Nacional de Verdad y Reconciliación 1991)	644 victims of serious human rights violations and 255 victims of political violence (Corporación Nacional de Reparación y Reconciliación 1996)
28,459 victims of political imprisonment (27,153 adults and 102 minors) with over 94% suffering torture (Comisión Nacional sobre Prisión Política y Tortura 2004)	9,795 new victims of political imprisonment and torture, and thirty new cases of detained-disappeared and executed for political reasons (Comisión Presidencial para la Calificación de Detenidos Desaparecidos, Ejecutados, Prisión Política y Tortura 2011)

In addition, at least 200,000 individuals (roughly 2% of Chile's population at the time) were exiled (Wright and Oñate Zúñiga 2007: 31).[13] The total number of people affected by human rights violations is expected to be substantially higher than the official figures. First, truth commissions were open to receive testimonies for limited time periods. Lack of time and a range of barriers (logistic, financial, and access, among others) may have prevented people from giving testimonies. Second, the commissions qualifying political imprisonment and torture accepted testimonies of living people only, meaning that those who survived human rights violations and political violence under Pinochet but died before the commissions started operating were not counted. Third, trauma and distrust in the process may have deterred some survivors and relatives of victims from giving evidence. To the present day, survivors have demanded a permanent qualifying process. Many cases of human rights violations are still waiting for truth, justice, and reparation to be served (Collins et al. 2020: 497–98).

For Chile's CNPPT (2004: 24), imprisonment and torture were considered political when state agents gave political reasons, such as national security, when ordering or performing these actions.[14] Of all survivors who gave testimony to this commission, 87.5% were men and 12.5% were women, and 58% were under the age of thirty at the time of imprisonment. On average, each person was incarcerated in 2.9 different centers. Among those who declared membership in a union or a territorial, social, or political organization, 72.3% were grassroots militants and 20.5% held a position of responsibility within their organization (CNPPT 2004: 568–70).

Political imprisonment and torture were also commonplace in dictatorial regimes of other Southern Cone countries in the second half of the twentieth century: Paraguay (1954–1989, under Stroessner), Bolivia (1964–1982, under Barrientos, Ovando, Torres, and Banzer), Brazil (1964–1983, under Castelo Branco, Silva, Médici, Geisel, and Figueiredo), Uruguay (1973–1985, under Bordaberry, Demicheli, Méndez, and Conrado), and Argentina (1976–1983, under Videla, Viola, Galtieri, and Bignone). Together with Chile, these countries were core members of Operation Condor, a CIA-backed secret program of cooperation between their intelligence services; subsequently, Ecuador and Peru joined in a peripheral role. The Condor network began in 1973–1974 and was institutionalized in 1975. Condor operatives carried out covert disappearance, torture, and extrajudicial executions across borders. Special death squads also targeted leading opposition figures exiled in Latin America, Europe, and the USA (McSherry 2005; Lessa 2015).[15]

In Chile, a total of 1,132 centers for political imprisonment and torture were recognized by the CNPPT (2004: 261), including prisons, camps, clandestine houses, stadiums, and commissariats. Some of these facilities were run by the armed forces, the secret police services Dirección de Inteligencia Nacional (DINA) and Central Nacional de Informaciones (CNI), or Carabineros (the militarized police force). Other centers were administered by Gendarmería (the prison service) and collaborators such as the nuns of Buen Pastor (Good Shepherd) and the members of Colonia Dignidad (a colony of German settlers). In recent years, media outlets have mentioned the existence of 1,168 centers, yet it is unclear how this latter figure came about. The exact number of facilities might never be known, as José Santos Herceg (2019: 25) points out in his study of political imprisonment centers in Pinochet's Chile, which uses over 100 testimonial books written by survivors as primary sources. Many of these centers have been dismantled, destroyed, or converted into other buildings since the end of the dictatorship. Following decades of campaigning by associations of survivors and victims' relatives, fifty-three memory sites have been denominated as Historical National Monuments by the National Monuments Council.[16] Yet this official status has, for some memory sites, not guaranteed preservation or public access.

Such is the case of the Cuartel Central Borgoño in Santiago, the most important imprisonment and torture center of the CNI secret police. With the arrival of democracy in 1990, the CNI was dissolved, and Borgoño was ceded to Chile's investigative police, the Policía de Investigaciones (PDI). Borgoño was partly demolished in 1998, and a new PDI building was built on the site (Santos Herceg 2019: 186–87). Despite a decree stating that, "its preservation over time is a contribution to the promotion, protection, and education of human rights of society at large," its remains have been neglected, upsetting survivors and victims' relatives.[17]

Another notable case is that of Venda Sexy. From the end of the Pinochet era until 2024, it was in private hands and used as a family home. Although the property was granted Historical National Monument status in 2016, it was not accessible to the public for years, as the state could not acquire it or prevent a murky private sale in 2019. When the news of the sale became public, activists organized protests outside Venda Sexy, displaying placards reading "La memoria no se vende" (Memory is not for sale). Survivors believed that those doing business with Venda Sexy were seeking to prevent it from becoming a public site of memory. They also feared that the property would be demolished, as with other notorious centers such as Villa Grimaldi and José Domingo Cañas 1367, erasing not only an important site of memory but also a key to understanding the origins of the ongoing gendered violence carried out by the state against political opponents in present-day Chile. In July 2024, the state could finally expropriate Venda Sexy.[18]

More than 94% of survivors who gave testimony to the CNPPT (2004: 191) suffered torture. Common methods included beatings, injuries, hangings, forced positions, application of electricity, confinement in subhuman conditions, deprivation of nourishment and sleep, asphyxia, exposure to extreme temperatures, mock executions, witnessing torture and executions of others, stripping, sexual assault, threats, humiliation, and abuse (CNPPT 2004: 255–97). A Ministry of Health report concluded that of the estimated 800,000 people directly affected by state terrorism under Pinochet, many have suffered from extreme traumatization, with severe consequences for their physical and psychological health (Ministerio de Salud 2006: 4). The directly affected population comprises family groups in which one or more members were victims of repressive actions of the state.

Users of the PRAIS health program, offered by the state to those directly affected by the dictatorship, exhibit substantial polytraumatization, with

49% of families suffering more than one traumatic experience (Ministerio de Salud 2006: 47). Around half of all diagnoses of PRAIS users relate to mental disorders, particularly of neurotic type, followed by adaptation reactions, personality disorders, and psychoses. The most frequent reasons for PRAIS mental health consultations are anxiety and depression syndromes as well as interpersonal conflicts. Regarding physical health, most consultations relate to musculoskeletal, circulatory, and respiratory problems, as well as psychosomatic symptoms that appear to relate to re-traumatization situations (Ministerio de Salud 2006: 60).[19]

Psychologist Valeria Moscoso Urzúa (2013) has evaluated the effects of post-traumatic stress disorder (PTSD) in people affected by state repression in Chile. She has found that, in addition to psychopathological syndromes, these populations display adaptive responses to conflict situations. Moscoso Urzúa notes that while individual psychological trauma is seen as something that "has already happened," psychosocial trauma constitutes something that "continues to happen;" she argues that the non-recognition of the damage or the breach of state reparation promises can be even more traumatic than the repression itself (Moscoso Urzúa 2013: 107–8). Psychologists and psychiatrists Madariaga (2020), Matamala (2021), and Faúndez et al. (2014), among others, have demonstrated that trauma does not stop at the generation who suffered the repression directly, but it is also transmitted to children and grandchildren of victims. In particular, the extreme violence committed by the Chilean state during the social uprising that began in October 2019 revived the wounds of the dictatorship.

Working with Memories

Pierre Nora (2002) noted that the worldwide memory upsurge since the 1980s has seen countries and social, ethnic, and family groups profoundly change their relationship with the past through critiques of official histories, commemorative events, new museums, and increasing attachment to heritage. This observation certainly holds regarding Chileans' relationship with the Pinochet past. Steve Stern (2004) has identified four emblematic memories of the military coup and the ensuing dictatorship:

- Memory as rupture: seen as an unresolved, open, and profound wound that destroyed lives due to death and torture.

- Memory as persecution and awakening: defined by struggle, commitment, and self-discovery experienced by people who did not conform to the regime.
- Memory as salvation: the coup and dictatorship viewed as the salvation of a country in ruins during the Unidad Popular.
- Memory as a closed box: the coup and dictatorship seen as something divisive and troubling that need to be forgotten.

As noted by Adam Sharman et al. (2017: 7), in Chile and Argentina, "memory" has come to be a metonym for memory of dictatorships, and it is in that sense that I mostly use the word in this book. As it may be expected here of a study dealing with political imprisonment, my research has paid substantial attention to ex-prisoners and others who directly suffered the consequences of state terrorism. Their memories and music often draw on canonical narratives of resistance and struggles against oppression that relate to the emblematic memories of rupture and of persecution and awakening identified by Stern. My work has also featured ex-members of the secret services—their music and memories drawing on emblematic memories of salvation, following Stern—as well as people who, without being prisoners or state agents, were present in centers for political imprisonment.

In this book, I propose the term memory cacophony to describe the discordant kaleidoscope of testimonial voices, emblematic and non-emblematic memories of musical happenings, music repertoire, and commemorative music practices that have emerged when researching music phenomena under political imprisonment. Memory sources relating to traumatic historical events like the Pinochet coup and dictatorship are not cacophonic *per se* when considered individually or within a homogeneous set. Yet when clashing types are combined and juxtaposed, noises emerge at individual, group, and societal levels, which can be disturbing and unpleasant. The metaphor of cacophony thus embodies the noises, disturbances, and unpleasantness of these memory discordances, which I have deliberately chosen not to resolve. I understand memory cacophony as an expansive framework that is both theoretical and methodological. I favored the metaphor of cacophony over dissonance, as the latter can certainly be resolved in music. Outside music, dissonances may also resolve. For example, in social psychology, cognitive dissonance theory proposes that individuals encountering dissonances—understood as the discrepancies between mutually incompatible cognitions—elicit a drive to reduce them (Fiedler and Salmen 2021).

Further on sonic metaphors, polyphony of memory and polyphonic memory are terms frequently used in memory scholarship, as exemplified by the works of Mario Panico (2019), Angelos Theocharis (2019), and Alessandro Achilli (2020). The term polyphony became widespread in literary studies after Mikhail Bakhtin began to use it. As Peter Dayan (2011: 107–8) notes, literary scholars commonly use the term when referring to the multiplicity of voices in literature, in contrast to music scholars, who understand it as the plurality of equal voices. However, Bakhtin used two different Russian words that have been indifferently translated as polyphony: one that could be transcribed as *polifonija* and corresponds to polyphony in the music sense, and a different one that could be transcribed as *raznogolosie* and may be translated as heterophony, a linguistic concept evoking a multiplicity of different voices (Dayan 2011: 107–8). Thus, using the terms polyphony of memory and polyphonic memories to refer to the diversity of memories is problematic, as memories have different hierarchies depending on their content and features and the person who recalls them.

Regarding memory's relationships with history, I follow two of three broad approaches used by humanities and social sciences scholars, identified by Elizabeth Jelin (2002: 63). First, memory as a research tool to obtain and construct data about the past, and second, memory as an object of historical study or research. (The third research approach recognized by Jelin [2002: 63] is the use of historical research to "correct" erroneous or false memories.)

I chose to conduct interviews, observations, and online crowdsourcing rather than basing my research on existing testimonial writings containing references to music in political imprisonment centers, like Hernán Valdés (1974), Sheila Cassidy (1977), Claudio Durán Pardo (2003), Ana María Jiménez and Teresa Izquierdo (2015), and Luis Cifuentes Seves (2020).[20] I opted for these methodological approaches for three reasons. First, the number of people who experienced music during their imprisonment is considerably larger than the number of people who have been able to write and publish their memories. Second, ethnographic methods allow probing questions that texts and other cultural production of survivors may not touch upon. Third, I find personal interaction with survivors and other witnesses enriching.

The kinds of memories that are valued and transmitted do change with time. In a 2015 testimony, ex-prisoner Rosalía Martínez, herself an ethnomusicologist and human rights activist, recounts that until the time of

Pinochet's arrest in London, survivors would often self-censor memories of their personal experiences, as only testimonies shedding light on judicial investigations were valued:

> When Pinochet was arrested in London in 1998, I had been working intensively in Paris for several years with a team of fellow former political prisoners, collecting hundreds of testimonies for use in the judicial processes in London and Madrid. At that point, we became aware that many people had never talked about what they had lived through, not even to their families, or partners, or children. Many individual and collective reasons explain this silence, but two were particularly common. The first was that there had been self-censorship regarding the importance of each individual's own experience. How could a person who had survived worry about what they had lived through if this meant nothing compared to the fate of the missing and the executed? The second reason had to do with the ineffectiveness of testifying at that time. In 1998, providing a testimony had no legal or political consequences. The only situation in which people testified and revealed details of their experience was when they were called upon to say something about a missing person. Since then, much water has flowed under the bridge. And I think the most important thing is that a collective memory has now been set in motion, the construction of a collective memory that materializes in many different forms, one of which is this project. It is a memory that transcends us and goes beyond each of us.[21]

The project referred to above is *Cantos Cautivos* (Captive Songs, www.cantoscautivos.org), a digital project I created and led for a decade, which compiles a repertoire of music written, sung, played, and listened to under imprisonment, and testimonies of musical experiences in these contexts. I first developed the *Cantos Cautivos* project in 2015 in partnership with Chile's Museo de la Memoria and networks of ex-prisoners. Its name is an adaptation of *Canto Cautivo*, the title of a web project and radio series I developed for the BBC World Service in 2005. The *Cantos Cautivos* project serves the purpose of collecting memories before they are lost; it calls for recognition of the importance of archival and documentary work, aligning with the ethos of initiatives seeking to generate politically and socially productive public records, such as the oral archives of Villa Grimaldi (Chile) and Memoria Abierta (Argentina).

Jesse Freedman (2022) asserts that this project facilitates an expansive consideration of memory beyond trauma and victimhood, giving participants space to testify and experience empowerment, as opposed to more official projects that foreground notions such as victimhood. Freedman considers how *Cantos Cautivos* works with and against the "official" memories of the Chilean government and other memories in this virtual archival space, and how it simultaneously approaches conceptual aspects of public-facing archives and private testimonies. For Freedman, the infrastructure of the project website facilitates the production of *intramemories* (dialogues across geography and generations) and *intermemories* (dialogues between website content with other spaces and external memory projects).

Jonathan Ritter (2012) addressed narratives and discourses of remembrance relating to human rights abuses committed in Peru by state forces and insurgents between 1980 and 2000. He compares narratives and discourses presented within the work of the Peruvian Truth and Reconciliation Commission (2001–2003) with those of hundreds of testimonial songs (*canciones testimoniales* or *canción social ayacuchana*), written in response to events of Peru's "dirty war." Ritter finds similarities between these memory instances in their ability to make public statements about violence—what he terms "public speakability"—and how "speaking the unspeakable" came to form a sort of mantra and mandate in discourses surrounding each. The "public speakability" of remembrance initiatives involving music is also found in post-dictatorial Chile, as will be discussed in Chapter 4 of this book.

Memories are complex sources to work with. Cognitive neuroscience and neuroimaging have shown that memories associated with traumatic experiences are encoded and recalled differently than everyday memories: they can be fragmented, associated with intense arousal, readily primed and triggered, and poorly contextualized (Department of Justice 2019). Jelin (2002: 64) notes that the process of remembering and mediating subjectivities raises questions about the reliability or trust of the information collected in this way, including voluntary or involuntary mistakes in the recalling and transmission of memories. Shirli Gilbert (2005: 121) explains, in reference to Holocaust survivors, that discrepancies and inconsistencies in their narratives may be due to a common difficulty in apprehending and describing the larger context within which their experiences were situated. Caroline Bithell and Juniper Hill (2014: 13), in turn, highlight the refinements that stories about the past undergo: "corrections are made and new errors introduced, facts are forgotten and elaborations added, inconvenient details are erased and rough edges smoothed off."

In the case of post-traumatic testimonials, Meg Jensen (2019: 33) observes that there is no primary evidence or unmediated witness statements; this is unlike first-person testimonies for legal purposes (focusing on evidential facts, time, place, and incident), oral history (looking for factual evidence and context or "feel" for the events), and trauma psychology (listening for lapses, repetitions, and connections with other autobiographical narratives). As Evelyn Hevia Jordán (2020: 121) notes regarding survivors of state terrorism under Pinochet, biographical narratives are influenced by the changing conditions of truth and justice at the time of the interviews. These narratives are also shaped by the gap between the time of the experiences and the time of recalling, as well as the age and health conditions of those sharing their stories. Most of the memories I discuss in this book date from 2013 onward, that is, four decades or more after the onset of Pinochet's dictatorship. Several of those who participated in my research have passed away.[22]

Music in Torture Contexts

Examples of music in torture contexts go back at least to the Middle Ages and have been found in different regions of the world to the present day (Fifer et al. 2022: 323–82; Grant and Papaeti 2013a; 2013b). The scholarly interest in this topic is relatively recent and has been amplified by press outlets, particularly after *Al Jazeera*'s 2007 investigation into U.S. Forces' uses of music in Guantanamo Base and other centers of the so-called War on Terror.

Lawyer Manfred Nowak (2022), who was the United Nations' Special Rapporteur on Torture in 2004–2010 and part of a team investigating torture practices in sixty-six countries, noted that the subjection to noise and use of loud music in imprisonment centers were associated with "enhanced interrogation methods" employed during the period of George W. Bush's administration. These techniques were at least partly based on the five "deep interrogation techniques" used by British security forces in Northern Ireland in the 1970s and on the Israeli guidelines prepared by the Landau Commission in the 1990s (Nowak 2022: 328). Musicologist Suzanne Cusick (2006) previously linked the use of music in "enhanced interrogation methods" to the "no-touch torture" techniques codified in the CIA's *Kubark Counterintelligence Interrogation Manual* (1963). Scholars have argued about possible effects of prisoners being subjected to loud music and in close relationships with torture. While Cusick (2013) points toward the destruction of subjectivity and alterability of consciousness, Morag Grant (2013) highlights physical effort and loss of sleep, but notes that psychological damage is difficult to predict.

Drawing on Cusick's work, in 2007, the Society for Ethnomusicology (SEM) issued a position statement against the use of music as part of torture practices; in 2008, the American Musicological Society (AMS) also condemned the use of music in torture.[23] In the U.K., no academic organization made a statement, yet the Musicians Union, the lobbying group UK Music, and the NGO Reprieve organized campaigns against unethical music practices. Jeff Todd Titon, who drafted the SEM statement against torture, reflected on its significance for the organization in his Introduction to the OUP *Handbook of Applied Ethnomusicology*: "[It] was a significant step in SEM's evolution. It recognizes that ethnomusicologists are citizens of the world with social responsibilities, and that our professional organization has not only the right but also the duty to represent the profession's ethical beliefs and act upon them" (Pettan and Titon 2015: 28–29).

Reasons for scholars' involvement in memory work concerning the soundscapes of political incarceration centers are debated by Anna Papaeti (2020), whose research focuses on Greece under the Military Junta (1967–1974). Papaeti makes an impassioned call to researchers, as witnesses, to account for the sounds and music of resistance and terror, warning that failure to do so brings the risk of reproducing the soundscapes of power and oppression. For Papaeti, ethical imperative calls researchers to interpret and respond to these stories. While I agree about the importance of preserving life stories of political prisoners, including stories dealing with music, I do not share the proposal that not reporting on the sounds and music of resistance and terror may result in the reproduction of abuse. I posit that in memory projects, survivors and relatives of victims and survivors should have a central role in the discussion of these questions and the implementation of resulting agreements. As highlighted by Hevia Jordán (2020: 122), there is a need to reflect on why we are creating these memory archives and to whom we are hoping to bequeath and transmit those memories.

For over a decade since I wrote a master's dissertation at the Royal Academy of Music (2003), I was alone in researching music in political imprisonment centers in Pinochet's Chile. Since then, several scholars and undergraduate and postgraduate students in Chile and abroad have taken up the topic. Besides the aforementioned study by Freedman (2022), undergraduate and master's theses in social anthropology, musicology, digital humanities, and music pedagogy have discussed music and political incarceration in Pinochet's Chile, with several drawing on the *Cantos Cautivos* platform.

The theses of Rebecca Waxman (2020) and Francisca Cornejo Ulloa (2020), as well as Cornejo Ulloa's book (2023), focus on female ex-prisoners' musical and sound memories. While Waxman discusses musical happenings, genres of music sung, and how music-making was organized, Cornejo Ulloa focuses on how sound acts as a social framework for memories associated with places and socio-affective dynamics. Maxim Karagodin's (2019) thesis deals with digital practices concerning cultural memory and human rights crimes in Latin America used by the Chilean diaspora.

The theses of Cabaluz Gómez and Sosa Valenzuela (2021) and Carmona Estay et al. (2021) propose using testimonial materials in secondary school-level education in music. Both devise classroom plans centered around music and political imprisonment during the Pinochet dictatorship, grounded on pedagogy of memory and other theoretical literature, and tying in with the Chilean national school curriculum. Cabaluz Gómez and Sosa Valenzuela aim to develop students' critical thinking around social justice through engagement with testimonies from former prisoners singing in the Voces de la Rebeldía choir. For their part, Carmona Estay et al. highlight the value of archives containing artistic production of inmates during the dictatorship's early years and promote their use as patrimonial sources.[24]

Regarding research on music and imprisonment in other late twentieth-century dictatorships in the Southern Cone, a paper by Victoria Polti (2014) analyzes aspects of social memory of experiences in Club Atlético, a clandestine incarceration and torture center in Buenos Aires. Polti posits that listening to sounds allowed prisoners to maintain a connection with the environment and was fundamental for communication and survival. Also focusing on the soundscapes of Buenos Aires imprisonment centers are Raúl Minsburg's (2015) study of the role of sound images as memory devices and Analía Lutowicz's (2012) examination of the ways in which survivors construct meaning from their experiences.

Abel Gilbert's (2021) book *Satisfaction en la ESMA: música y sonido durante la dictadura (1976–1983)* takes its title from two short testimonial references to the Rolling Stones's song "Satisfaction" played on record at the ESMA center in Buenos Aires. Gilbert's book provides a comprehensive analysis of modes of listening under the last dictatorship in Argentina and of music works that account for these experiences. Some of the discussions of music and sound in torture centers are weakened by recurrent references to *A Clockwork Orange*, a novel by Burgess and film adaptation by Kubrick set in a dystopian Britain, which are juxtaposed with survivor testimonies from non-fictional Argentina. The mixture of radically different types of sources raises methodological questions, including some about the validity of linking and extrapolating from "Ludovico's technique" (an aversion treatment involving music and applied to the protagonist of *A Clockwork Orange*, a delinquent who commits rape and theft) to draw conclusions about the experiences suffered by real-life political prisoners in Argentina.

Scholarship dealing with music in prison contexts and the broader area of trauma has developed fast during the last decades, engaging researchers and practitioners not only in music and sound studies but also in other disciplines in the arts and humanities, social sciences, medicine, psychology, and allied health.[25] As expected in an interdisciplinary area, researchers working in the interface of music, sound, and trauma use a range of angles and methods. Many scholars do not use face-to-face and other direct-contact methods for collecting primary sources. Much of the scholarship in the last decades that deals with music during the Holocaust (e.g., Pavlovic 2013; Brauer 2016) and other non-recent periods examines sources published by survivors or collected from survivors by previous researchers.

Research on cultural responses and interpretations of trauma in literature, theater, the visual and performing arts, architecture, religion, and mythmaking tends to use methods that do not involve direct contact with people who have experienced trauma. Such is the case of the works of Cathy Caruth (2014), Yochai Ataria et al. (2016), Colin Davis and Hanna Meretoja (2020), and Maria Cizmic (2021).[26] Scholars in health disciplines tend to do case studies on people who have experienced or recovered from trauma, using methods such as observations, interviews, music-making, and reflective practice. These professionals would have typically undergone long, specialist training and are, therefore, well-equipped to deal with trauma when it emerges during the research process. An influential volume focused on clinical work is *Music, Music Therapy and Trauma* (Sutton 2002), with chapters dealing with developmental aspects, single events, and war. Other relevant studies on therapeutic uses of music include Atarah Fisher and Avi Gilboa (2016, on Holocaust survivors), Susanne Bauer (2009, on settlers of the Colonia Dignidad sect in Chile), and Jude Boyles and Christine Adcock (2013, on torture survivors living in Manchester, U.K.).

An increasing number of music scholars are using qualitative research methods and working directly with people who have experienced trauma. It is paramount to reflect on risks and expertise. Qualitative research requiring data collection from living people is riskier than other types of research. The personal nature of qualitative data collection brings with it the complexities associated with cultural norms, beliefs, values, and behaviors (Mertens 2018: 33), and clearly, additional levels of complexity are involved in research dealing with trauma. Qualitative research expertise appears on occasions to be taken for granted, even at the institutional ethical approval stage. Julie Mooney-Somers and Anna Olsen (2016: 136) notice that qualitative competence is rarely discussed as an ethical issue by committees, and often it is not assessed, or the criteria are unclear. They highlight two main issues around research competence in ethical reviews. First, the rare inclusion of claims about qualitative skills and experience in research applications involving qualitative research, and second, ethical review committees do not always appear to have members with sufficient qualitative expertise to make such judgments (Mooney-Somers and Olsen 2016: 130).

Beyond the requirements of formal ethical approval processes and ethics guidelines, when could music scholars conducting qualitative research with people who have been exposed to trauma feel confident in their approach? Firstly, being aware of our own limitations and acting accordingly should be central to scholars' research integrity. In my case, while I have substantial knowledge and experience of conducting qualitative research, I am not a trained mental health professional and would therefore be unqualified to deal with a serious situation should it happen when or after interacting with participants. Although my study is not clinical and the information sheet given to prospective participants explicitly requests that those with PTSD or other conditions that could be aggravated by interviews do not take part, some may not be aware that they have had these conditions.[27] Furthermore, psychology research on event centrality (the extent to which traumatic or stressful events are perceived to be integral to a person's life) has shown that individuals who do not match clinical criteria for PTSD but have nevertheless been exposed to stressful or traumatic events in their past may still display a range of other symptoms (Garcia da Silva et al. 2016; Gehrta et al. 2018).

Secondly, in my interactions with survivors, I have taken an extremely cautious approach, not insisting beyond the experiences they can and want to share. Consequently, some years ago, I declined to take on the comments made by an anonymous reviewer of an article I had written and submitted to a reputed music journal. Among other things, the reviewer queried whether I had asked survivors questions about musical and acoustic torture or not, whether I had asked them the reason for not discussing that aspect of their experience, and how they accounted for the ease with which they could talk about their own agential use of music in torture centers. In my view, the reviewer's comments do not suggest full awareness of the risks that asking such questions may pose.

Thirdly, the ways in which interviews with survivors are conducted are critical. Hevia Jordán (2020: 116–17) posits that in biographical interviews, interviewers should avoid asking the type of questions that interviewees have had to answer to truth commissions or in judicial processes. Interviewers should not ask questions that "test the story" being recounted or look for details that validate the accuracy of facts. For example, if the interviewee says, "They put me on the *parrilla*" (a metal frame bed used for electric torture), it would not be appropriate to ask questions such as, "How many times were you on the *parrilla*?" or "Do you remember how many hours?" or "What did they do to you?." For Hevia Jordán, asking these types of questions suggests to the interviewee that their truth is being called into question.

In biographical interviews, notes Hevia Jordán, there is a subjective exchange between the biography of the person being interviewed and the biography of the person conducting the interview. The latter operates as a "biographical resonance box" that allows the construction of the interviewee's biographical narrative. Stories about experiences of political imprisonment and torture are difficult to narrate but also difficult to listen to, and the interviewer should do self-work around their relationship with violence, as well as their own apprehensions and limitations around the subject. Therefore, if the interviewer has had a childhood experience of violence, it might be very challenging for them to ask the interviewee about violence (Hevia Jordán 2020: 98, 115).

Hevia Jordán's views echo my own regarding the kind of questions that should not be asked to survivors, and they also explain my sensitivity toward certain topics due to my positionality as a daughter of survivors of political imprisonment and torture. Although my research participants have been explicitly summoned to share their experiences of music in political imprisonment centers, I wish not to steer conversations to focus on torture experiences only. Through personal and professional experience, I know how extremely difficult it is to recall and discuss the maltreatment that political prisoners have been subjected to.

Most survivors who have contributed to my research have focused on agential uses of music. Anna Papaeti (2013: 68) observed similar responses when interviewing ex-detainees of the Greek Junta (1967–1974), suggesting that these occur because "reconstructing the abuse of music by the regime requires brushing against the grain of coherently constructed narratives [of music as resistance]," which have been consistently transmitted for decades. While survivors appear to favor positive memories—and this is consistent with psychology research findings that autobiographical memory is normally biased toward positive events, supporting positive views of self and the past (Gehrta et al. 2018: 57)—it is also possible that their less forthcoming attitude to discussing music directly linked with torture and other forms of mistreatment could signal stress. In the case of my interviews with former agents of the DINA and CNI secret police, I purposely did not ask questions about torture, assassination, and disappearance of political prisoners.

Finally, at various stages of research, publication, and dissemination processes, music researchers can seek advice and feedback from others with professional expertise in trauma—I have consulted clinical psychologists on multiple occasions concerning this research. Lived experience is also a valuable source of knowledge and can be used, for example, to test interview questions. In my case, I have instinctively learned what can and cannot be asked through decades of dinner table conversations and informal gatherings with relatives and close friends affected by political violence.

Some of the studies on music in prison and torture contexts mentioned above draw on very small samples and put forward totalizing conclusions not just regarding the specific facilities referred to in the sources examined but sometimes across prisons of a given regime. The expectation that scholarly research should make general conclusions, extrapolating from a few examples to wider phenomena, is problematic, as experiences were significantly varied. Some people I have talked to have vivid recollections about experiencing music in a particular detention center, but others who were imprisoned in the same facility at the same time have assured me there was no music at all. Each person will have different memories, and these are individual and unique truths. Thus, it is challenging to elucidate patterns or make overarching conclusions that neatly encapsulate the eclectic ways music functioned in political imprisonment centers and the assorted forms in which it has been remembered.

In a similar vein, Santos Herceg (2019: 11), after studying over 100 testimonial books written by survivors of political imprisonment and torture in

Pinochet's Chile, concluded that differences are the most prominent aspect of this corpus. Content, says Santos Herceg, differs hugely: experiences varied from person to person, and when they were similar, they were described in different and, at times, contradictory ways. Like Jorge Montealegre Iturra (2018: 410), I posit that the stories of those who experienced political imprisonment first-hand, accounting for the atmosphere, mood, and actions of common histories lived in different places and moments, have an invaluable affect, and I have included in this book a plethora of testimony excerpts.

Throughout the book, I often use the term "survivor" when referring to former political prisoners. I tend to employ the term "victim" when referring to people who died or are presumed dead as a result of serious violations of human rights and political violence (tying in with truth commissions' understanding of this term), but sometimes I use it more broadly to include both those who died and those who survived. Regarding the generic term "perpetrator," I use it sparsely throughout the book: when citing survivors or scholars who employ the term in that way and when alluding to a collective of individuals implicated in gross human rights violations, be they convicted or not. I use "convicted perpetrators" for those who have been sentenced.[28]

Being acutely aware of the disbalance in epistemic power between the Global North and the Global South and being wholly supportive of efforts to decolonize academia, where possible, I give preference to critical texts by Latin American authors.[29] All English translations of quotations from testimonies and song lyrics are mine or from other members of the *Cantos Cautivos* team. When quoting from *Cantos Cautivos* materials, I have taken the license to tweak the British spelling and punctuation of texts found on the website, so that they are consistent with the U.S. spelling and punctuation I use throughout this book. Some of the interview materials I discuss in the book are not available on the *Cantos Cautivos* platform. The book incorporates and develops sections from articles published in the *Journal of Latin American Cultural Studies*, *The Routledge Companion to Music and Human Rights*, *The Guardian*, *Open Democracy*, and *Diagonal*.

Chapter Summary

In Chapter 1, I explore a selection of memories of singing and listening experiences linked to torture and other cruel, inhuman, and degrading treatment, as well as experiences of comforting others and recovering through music. My probing of these memories finds some overlaps between the views of music held by prisoners and state agents. First, the linking of musical taste to political activism. Second, the perception that certain music genres and musicians are apolitical. And third, the repurpose of songs via elements of song lyrics. Although these connections are subtle and may appear non-central to overall experiences of political imprisonment, my findings challenge the established belief that the worldviews of political prisoners and those of state agents have nothing in common whatsoever. Next, the chapter addresses challenges around disclosing music experiences threaded into mistreatment and the need to consider legal typology, survivors' histories of testifying, and changing needs to discuss torture. I show that while music can sensitize audiences and allow survivors to address extreme experiences, focusing exclusively on, and going public about, music used for harmful purposes has the potential risks of producing unintended consequences, including the fetishization of mistreatment.

Chapter 2 centers around Álvaro Corbalán, a convicted perpetrator and prolific singer-songwriter, formerly Head of Operations of the CNI police and commander of Cuartel Borgoño, one of the most notorious torture centers of the dictatorship. Addressing contentions about engaging with perpetrators' stories and identities, I assert that paying attention to these does not justify, relativize, or validate perpetrators' crimes and stain the memory of victims, and that music and other art forms do not necessarily imply good moral values. Next, the chapter reviews Corbalán's biographical milestones and the circumstances, dilemmas, and dynamics around interviewing him at Punta Peuco prison, where he serves manifold sentences. I then explore the features and themes of a selection of his songs and writings, his performance style, musical taste, and elusive memories of his time as a CNI agent. Lastly, I reflect on how Corbalán's music might be judged morally and aesthetically, as well as the ethics and legality of recording and disseminating it.

Chapter 3 discusses memories of musical happenings, pieces, and voices that are unconventional in testimonies of political imprisonment. These include stories about a disastrous gig of the Spanish superstar Julio Iglesias at Valparaíso Jail (featuring and narrated by ex-detainees, the presenter of the event, and Iglesias himself), festive musical events, and humorous songs written and sung by political prisoners to satirize their situation. I contend that the dictatorship's archive admits more stories than those about exertion and defiance of power, and that the more diverse the voices and stories we preserve, the richer the cultural legacy for present and future generations will be. These unconventional materials, however, beg for strong historical contextualization, given common societal knowledge gaps and attitudes of denial about the dictatorship, as well as music's potential to be viewed as relativizing or even negating human rights violations.

Chapter 4 investigates matters of activism, revival, and commemoration by tracing the history of a nameless choir operating in 1976 at Tres Álamos camp, as well as its contemporary iteration, the choir Voces de la Rebeldía (Voices of Rebellion), formed in 2013 by ex-political prisoners. I scrutinize the eclectic song repertoire at Tres Álamos, showing how it became inmates' shared heritage through a process of repurposing. When adopted by Voces de la Rebeldía, this repertoire has undergone a second repurposing process and has added new songs. I suggest that the choir's repertoire expansion, together with its alliances with well-known activists and artists, signals a wish to engage with current socio-political struggles of broader remit and may be influenced by a process of generational replacement in the membership. Next, the chapter examines drivers and barriers around participation and motivation, including the long-term effects of political violence, illness, old age, and loss. Despite its heterogeneous membership, the choir publicly emphasizes survivors' centrality, thus affirming their legitimacy and authenticity as a choir of ex-political prisoners. Memory activism and the desire for change appear central to members' motivation to sing, and I argue that by revealing violations and commemorating survival through performances, Voces de la Rebeldía is an instance of self-reparation.

Chapter 5 focuses on *Cantos Cautivos* (www.cantoscautivos.org), a born-digital, open-access archival project I devised. Bilingual in Spanish and English, it compiles over 160 testimonies on music activities under political imprisonment. These testimonies refer to an eclectic repertoire originating in nineteen countries, mainly from popular music and music of folk traditions. I discuss the project's trajectory, trends and peculiarities of its archival content and contributors, its web structure and technicalities, use of participatory methodologies, collaborations with traditional institutions and grassroots movements, and roles of the press and social media to harness contributions and reach audiences beyond those directly affected by human rights violations. The chapter outlines the relevance of *Cantos Cautivos*, as a public history project, in preserving cultural patrimony and promoting human rights through public dissemination and education, proposing that it contributes to addressing current knowledge gaps about the dictatorship and denials of human rights violations. Furthermore, as many remembrance sites have been dismantled, destroyed, or repurposed, or are not open to the public, digital projects such as *Cantos Cautivos* have an important role in making these places known.

The Coda sketches out the various contributions of this book. First, it rearticulates the importance of "memory cacophony" as both a theoretical and methodological framework through recognizing a discordant kaleidoscope of testimonial voices, music memories, and repertoire, and extending and contrasting dominant memory discourses. Second, it outlines the contributions to ongoing debates about representation, inclusivity, extractivism, and co-production of research and public and community engagement, exposing the tension between the growing scholarly interest in music in contexts of imprisonment, torture, and trauma, and, on the other hand, the risks of conducting and disseminating work on such areas. Third, it considers the personal effects of working on these topics as well as conundrums, feelings, and unachieved objectives. Fourth, it highlights how the research has added to the material legacy of the dictatorship, particularly through the *Cantos Cautivos* project. Finally, it outlines avenues for further research.

Places

Of the 1,132 political imprisonment and torture centers recognized by the CNPPT (2004), the *Cantos Cautivos* platform holds records relating to forty-one centers located in all sixteen current regions of Chile (see Figure I.5), as follows:

Arica y Parinacota Region

- Cárcel Pública de Arica

Tarapacá Region

- Campamento de Prisioneros de Pisagua

Antofagasta Region

- Campamento de Prisioneros Chacabuco

Coquimbo Region

- Cárcel de la Serena
- Cárcel de Mujeres Buen Pastor, La Serena

FIGURE I.5 Location of political imprisonment centers relating to testimonial materials on the Cantos Cautivos platform.

Atacama Region

- Regimiento de Infantería Motorizada Nº 23, Copiapó

Valparaíso Region

- Campamento de Prisioneros Melinka-Puchuncaví
- Campamento de Prisoneros Ritoque
- Regimiento de Infantería Nº 2 Maipo/Regimiento Playa Ancha/Fiscalía Militar
- Academia de Guerra Naval
- Cárcel de Valparaíso
- Regimiento de Ingenieros de Tejas Verdes

Metropolitana de Santiago Region

- Recinto CNI, Cuartel Central Borgoño
- Cárcel de Santiago
- Campamento de Prisioneros Cuatro Álamos
- Anexo Cárcel Capuchinos
- Cárcel de Menores Blas Cañas / Centro de Reinserción Abierto Manuel Rodríguez
- Recinto DINA, José Domingo Cañas Nº 1367
- Villa Grimaldi
- Campamento de Prisioneros, Estadio Nacional
- Penitenciaría de Santiago (Centro de Detención Preventiva Santiago Sur)
- Calle Irán Nº 3037/Venda Sexy/La Discotheque
- Campamento de Prisioneros, Tres Álamos
- Tenencia de Carabineros Nueva España, Población San Gregorio

O'Higgins Region

- Cárcel de Rancagua
- Intendencia de Rancagua

Maule Region

- Colonia Dignidad

Ñuble Region

- Cárcel de Mujeres Buen Pastor, Chillán

Biobío Region
- Cárcel de Concepción/Cárcel El Manzano
- Campamento Prisioneros Estadio Regional
- Comisaría de Concepción
- Cárcel de Coronel
- Regimiento de Infantería Reforzada Nº 3, Los Ángeles
- Cárcel de Los Ángeles

Araucanía Region
- Cárcel de Temuco
- Comisaría de Carabineros N° 2, Temuco

Los Ríos Region
- Cárcel de Valdivia / Cárcel de Isla Teja
- Recinto CNI calle Pérez Rosales 764, Valdivia

Los Lagos Region
- Cárcel de Río Negro

Aysén Region
- Campamento de Prisioneros Las Bandurrias

Magallanes y la Antártica Chilena Region
- Campamento de Prisioneros Isla Dawson

Below are brief descriptions of a few imprisonment centers discussed in the ensuing chapters of this book, based on the report of the CNPPT (2004), the *Memoria Viva* digital archive (www.memoriaviva.com), and Santos Herceg's book *Lugares espectrales: topología testimonial de la prisión política en Chile* (2019). I have included only a few general details of torture practices. Those interested in knowing more about political imprisonment centers in Pinochet's Chile should consult the sources mentioned above and other publications dealing with the repression.

Calle Irán Nº 3037/Venda Sexy/La Discotheque (Sexy Blindfold)

A two-story house located in southeast Santiago, used by the DINA police as a torture center. It was run by agents during the daytime and by guards at night.

Prisoners always remained blindfolded. There was permanent background music at high volume, which is why this house was known as La Discoteque. Prisoners were continuously subjected to interrogation, harassment, manipulation, and torture. In this enclosure, sexual abuse was practiced with particular emphasis. After spending up to about a month in this center, detainees were transferred to facilities such as Villa Grimaldi, Cuatro Álamos, and Tres Álamos.

Campamento de Prisioneros Isla Dawson (Dawson Island Prisoners' Camp)

A concentration camp on Dawson Island, located in Patagonia and extending over 2,000 square kilometers. The camp, run by the Navy, was built a few days before the coup d'état and operated from 1973 to 1974. It had a capacity for 1,500 prisoners and was divided into two sections: Compingin and Río Chico. Inmates included ministers and friends of the deposed president Salvador Allende. Prisoners had to do forced labor, military exercises, and marching. They were regularly subjected to torture and intimidation.

Campamento de Prisioneros, Tres Álamos (Tres Álamos Prisoners' Camp)

A camp in south Santiago used between 1974 and 1976 as a transit place for men and women. Officially, it was under the command of the Carabineros police, but in practice, the DINA police ran it. Tres Álamos held approximately 400 detainees at any given time. Detainees first arrived at an adjacent facility called Cuatro Álamos, run by the DINA, where they were held incommunicado, subjected to interrogations, and sometimes taken out to torture centers. Prisoners at Tres Álamos were not tortured, but were subjected to strict military discipline and violent treatment. They lived in overcrowded conditions and were frequently punished by the arbitrary suspension of visits and food parcels from relatives. From this place, many detainees were expelled from the country.

Cárcel de Mujeres Buen Pastor, La Serena (Women's Jail of Buen Pastor, La Serena)

A women's prison located in the northern city of La Serena. It was administered by the nuns of Buen Pastor (Good Shepherd), a Catholic religious order operating in Chile since the nineteenth century. Political prisoners were held incommunicado for long periods, were poorly fed, and lived in permanent fear and anguish; they were interrogated and tortured elsewhere, at the Arica regiment. During the Pinochet dictatorship, the nuns of Buen Pastor administered nineteen other political imprisonment centers throughout Chile, located in the cities of Arica, Iquique, Antofagasta, Copiapó, Quillota, San Felipe, Valparaíso, Rancagua, San Fernando, Constitución, Curicó, Linares, Chillán, Concepción, Los Ángeles, Temuco, Santiago, Talca, and Los Ángeles.

Cárcel de Valparaíso (Valparaíso Jail)

The main prison of the Valparaíso region in central Chile, run by Gendarmería (the prison service). Political prisoners, held on the jail's top floor, were often subjected to long periods of solitary confinement and were tortured by prison staff, the Carabineros police, the Navy, and the secret services. Political inmates were discriminated against the rest of the prison population, were denied visits, and were permanently subjected to abuse and mistreatment.

Campamento de Prisioneros Chacabuco (Chacabuco Prisoners' Camp)

Located in the Atacama Desert and run by the Army, the Air Force, and the Carabineros police, Chacabuco was one of the largest concentration camps in the country, occupying an area of thirty-six hectares. The facilities were first built in the 1920s as a nitrate town but were abandoned the following decade when the nitrate boom halted. From 1973 to 1975, the camp held hundreds of male political prisoners who had often been tortured in previous imprisonment centers and during the journey to Chacabuco. Detainees at Chacabuco were routinely subjected to abuse, intense military-type exercise, forced labor, a demeaning diet, and exposure to extreme temperatures outdoors, day and night. Some were continuously interrogated and tortured.

Campamento de Prisioneros, Estadio Nacional (National Stadium Prisoners' Camp)

Located in the east of Santiago, the Estadio Nacional is the largest stadium in Chile. The Army ran it as a prisoners' camp between September and November 1973. It held female and male detainees, mostly from Santiago and surrounding areas. On September 22, 1973, according to a report from the International Red Cross, there were 7,000 detainees, including between 200 and 300 foreigners. Detainees were interrogated and tortured in the velodrome or the dressing rooms and were in deplorable condition. Dressing rooms, also used for sleeping, were overcrowded, with precarious shelter and hygienic conditions. Men had to spend long periods in the football field stands, while women remained in the pool area of the stadium. Pregnant women were tortured without regard to their condition. Family visits or lawyers were not permitted. Many prisoners were transferred to Chacabuco and other imprisonment centers, while others regained their freedom.

Campamento de Prisioneros Melinka-Puchuncaví (Melinka-Puchuncaví Prisoners' Camp)

Located north of Valparaíso and run by the Navy. Before the dictatorship, the camp was a holiday resort for members of the Central Única de Trabajadores (CUT), the national network of unions. Between 1973 and 1976, the camp was used for the mass imprisonment of male political prisoners, who arrived in terrible physical and psychological conditions, having been tortured in previous facilities. The first detainees had to install barbed wire fences and erect watchtowers. From this facility, detainees were released, transferred to other centers, or expelled from the country.

Campamento de Prisoneros Ritoque (Ritoque Prisoners' Camp)

Located north of Valparaíso and run by the Army, this camp was also a former holiday resort for workers who were members of the CUT. Between

1974 and 1975, it held male prisoners who had previously been detained in torture centers and camps in surrounding areas, Santiago, and the far north and far south of Chile (as Melinka-Puchuncaví Camp). Prisoners lived in barracks that were frequently raided. They were subjected to punishments, threats, beatings, intimidation, and exhausting days of physical exercise.

Colonia Dignidad (Dignity Colony)

A German sect in the south of Chile, it was founded in 1961 and led by Paul Schäfer (1921–2010), a pedophile and former Nazi who had been a member of the Hitler Youth during the Second World War. The colony projected an image of harmony, collective work, and order to the outside world. However, those who lived there suffered inhuman treatment and sexual abuse and had to undertake forced labor. During the Pinochet dictatorship, Colonia Dignidad functioned as an imprisonment and torture center for political detainees, in collaboration with the DINA police. Some were taken to Colonia Dignidad immediately after being arrested, while others came from other imprisonment centers. Colonia Dignidad had technical equipment that included microphones and loudspeakers for interrogation, which was conducted in soundproofed underground cells and under torture. Survivors also recall the deafening sound of fans during torture sessions.

Cuartel Central Borgoño (Central Borgoño Cartel)

Located in central Santiago and known as *la casa de la risa* (the house of laughter), Cuartel Borgoño was the main facility of the CNI police and one of the longest-lasting political detention centers, operating between 1977 and 1989. Scores of political prisoners were tortured and assassinated there, mostly between 1984 and 1986. Political detainees spent most of their time in a basement, where they were photographed, fingerprinted, interrogated, tortured, and medically examined. Prisoners were subjected to conditions that produced disorientation in space-time. A light bulb that was lit day and night, preventing them from sleeping. Upstairs, there was a soundproof room containing sound and video equipment, where detainees were taken to be filmed and photographed.

Cuartel Villa Grimaldi (Villa Grimaldi Cartel)

Located in the east of Santiago, Villa Grimaldi was formerly a restaurant. Expropriated in 1974, it became the headquarters of the Brigada de Inteligencia Metropolitana (Metropolitan Intelligence Brigade) and was used until 1977 by the DINA and later by the CNI. During the dictatorship, Villa Grimaldi was known as Cuartel Terranova. Until 1978, Villa Grimaldi was the DINA's main center for kidnapping, torture, and extermination. There were several constructions on the property, including the so-called Casas Corvi (tiny rooms where the detainees were "softened"), the Casas Chile (rooms where detainees were placed after torture), and La Torre (a tower with tiny niches where prisoners were locked up in absolute isolation). Prisoners were always blindfolded and subjected to interrogations and torture throughout their stay. The Villa Grimaldi buildings were demolished by the military in 1989, just before the first democratic government took office. Since 1997, it has been a Park for Peace and, since 2004, a National Monument.

Dirección General de Investigaciones (Directorate-General for Investigations)

A cartel of the Policía de Investigaciones (PDI, Investigations Police), located in central Santiago. Political prisoners were tortured and kept in overcrowded conditions in the dungeons, deprived of food, water, and sleep. In 1980, this cartel was the headquarters of an integrated command formed by the PDI and Carabineros police and the CNI (COVEMA). On occasions, political prisoners were transferred to DINA or CNI facilities, released, or sent to other regions.

1

Music Threaded into Torture and Other Mistreatment

Music linked to torture is swiftly mentioned in the reports of truth commissions of several Southern Cone countries under dictatorship in the second half of the twentieth century: Paraguay's Comisión de Verdad y Justicia (2008), Brazil's Comissão Nacional da Verdade (2014), Chile's Comisión Nacional sobre Prisión Política y Tortura (2004), and Argentina's Comisión Nacional sobre la Desaparición de Personas (1984). These reports state that music was employed as a background to torture, with little detail and analysis. In the case of Chile, music is only noted in relation to five DINA and CNI centers—Calle Azola (Arica), Londres 38 and Venda Sexy (Santiago), Piscicultura de Curicó (Maule Region), and Pedro de Valdivia 710 (Concepción)— and three facilities from the Armed Forces—Academia de Guerra Aérea (Santiago), Regimiento de Infantería 19 Colchagua (San Fernando), Regimiento La Concepción (Lautaro) (CNPPT 2004: 317, 390, 415, 444, 445, 453, 517, 529).

This chapter adds further evidence of music experiences threaded into mistreatment, obtained from in-depth interviews I conducted in September 2013 in Santiago with survivors Luis Cifuentes, Ernesto Parra, and Ana María Jiménez. In these interviews, survivors shared a variety of recollections about music during their imprisonment, mainly relating to positive experiences. This chapter thus focuses on what they talked less about. In what follows, I explore how music was part of interrogation sessions and how agents' practices and detainees' responses threaded matters of musical taste, activism, and the perceived political and apolitical nature of certain music genres and artists. I then discuss survivors' experiences of comforting others through singing as well as listening to specific songs on the radio to prepare for and recover from torture. Finally, I discuss the challenges around disclosures of torture and other mistreatment and reflect on the reasons for and risks of conducting and disseminating research focused on misuses of music.

Music and Political Imprisonment in Pinochet's Chile. Katia Chornik, Oxford University Press.
 DOI: 10.1093/9780190052294.003.0002

A brief biographical note about my interviewees. Ana María Jiménez trained as a music teacher and pianist. Aged twenty-three, she was arrested in 1975 and taken to the torture and detention complex of Villa Grimaldi, after which she was imprisoned in Cuatro Álamos and Tres Álamos camps. In Tres Álamos, she ran music workshops and founded and directed a choir of prisoners, which she revived in 2013 (the choirs' history is explored in detail in Chapter 4). After imprisonment, Jiménez was exiled to Cuba.

Luis Cifuentes is a retired professor of electrometallurgy at the Universidad de Chile. He is also a musician and writer. He was an early member of the Nueva Canción group Inti-Illimani before it was known by that name. Cifuentes was imprisoned at the Estadio Chile and Estadio Nacional, and at the Campamento de Prisioneros Chacabuco. At Chacabuco, he was a member of the prisoners' music group Los de Chacabuco, playing guitar and various stringed, percussion, and wind folkloric instruments. After imprisonment, Cifuentes was exiled to Germany and England.

Ernesto Parra is a guitarist and conductor. Before the coup, he studied biology pedagogy and was a founding member of the Nueva Canción groups Los de la Peña and Curacas. Parra was imprisoned in various centers in Santiago (Comisaría de Carabineros N°1, Dirección General de Investigaciones, Estadio Chile, and Estadio Nacional) and the Campamento de Prisioneros Chacabuco. At Chacabuco, he was one of the leaders of Los de Chacabuco group. After detention, he was exiled to Germany. In the last two decades, Parra has led various youth orchestra programs in Santiago.

Music During Interrogation

During interrogation sessions at Villa Grimaldi, agents often made Jiménez listen to the song "Un millón de amigos" (A Million Friends) by the Brazilian singer-songwriter Roberto Carlos. "Un millón de amigos" is Roberto Carlos's Spanish version of his own song "Eu quero apenas," first released in Portuguese in 1974. The lyrics praise friendship and generosity, imagine a future of peace and happiness, and call to sing together: "I want to have a million friends / and with them I will be able to sing louder." Another song frequently played during interrogation was "Gigi l'amoroso" by Jacqueline Misrahi, Lana, and Paul Sebastian. "Gigi l'amoroso" was recorded by the Italian-French singer Dalida in multiple languages and popularized in Chile in the Spanish version ("Gigi el amoroso"). The lyrics narrate the story of an

Italian man who, thanks to his sex appeal and singing talent, has conquered all the women of his town: "We love you Gigi l'amoroso / the greatest Italian lover since man discovered fire / Gigi l'amoroso, if you only knew what you make us do / with your songs of desire."

Jiménez describes her experience:

> At Villa Grimaldi, they made you listen to recorded music, which was insufferable. You heard it day and night. I physically felt the music. It was Kafkaesque: you heard the screams of the inmates and, amid all that, the music and commentary of the guards. You lived a permanent torture session because if they weren't torturing you, you were listening to the torture of others, which was absolutely unbearable. And with music the whole time. The two songs that were most often heard were "Un millón de amigos" and "Gigi l'amoroso." When they would come to torture you, they said: "here comes Gigi l'amoroso." They sang the song, and they loved to feel like they were Gigi. They used to put that song on at full blast while they performed the torture.

Jiménez's memories reveal that agents repurposed "Un millón de amigos" and "Gigi l'amoroso" to the context of Villa Grimaldi via elements of song lyrics, showing several levels of linguistic connections to aspects of interrogation and torture. Singing, a central theme of both songs, suggests an interrogation-specific meaning of the verb "to sing," which in Spanish and other languages means to confess or grass on someone, usually under pressure.[1] "Gigi," the name of the subject featured in "Gigi l'amoroso," suggests a wordplay on *gigí*, a slang term employed by agents to refer to a device for administering electric shocks to prisoners. The term *gigí* was used by personnel operating at the clandestine torture house on Simón Bolívar Street in Santiago too (Rebolledo 2012: 129). It is likely that the term was employed in other imprisonment facilities, given that Pinochet's agents often operated in several centers simultaneously. It is possible that the *gigí* term, in turn, originated from the French argot *gégène* (short for *génératrice*), to denote a magnetic torture device. As Darius Rejali (2009: 144) explains, in the late 1950s, the term *gégène* became notorious in France and Algeria; the word *gégéneur* (the person operating the *gégène*) was used as a synonym for torturer. This device was later exported to the U.S. School of the Americas, where Latin American dictatorships sent thousands of agents to be trained.[2]

Villa Grimaldi agents show gross cruelty when telling the prisoner, "Here comes Gigi l'amoroso" ("aquí viene Gigi el amoroso"), as remembered by Jiménez. This phrase performs a double function—Gigi is both the subject of the song and the impersonation of the torturers, linking the conquering prowess of Gigi to the subjugation that torturers exerted over political prisoners. Furthermore, the word *amoroso*, found in the title and verses, is unusual and ambiguous in the original Italian language of the song—it is not often used in common-day language and may translate as being loving or affectionate, or being a seducer. In Spanish, however, the word *amoroso* is frequently used and is understood as loving or caring. I would suggest that the torturers' announcement, "here comes Gigi l'amoroso," in any of the possible meanings of the word *amoroso*, could have also been a euphemism for sexual torture to which female political prisoners were systematically subjected.

The following excerpts from Cifuentes's memories render an account of how music featured in questions from his interrogators at the Estadio Nacional and how he repurposed a song to the context in which he found himself. Cifuentes recalled that during an interrogation session, agents asked him: "What music do you like?" The question was not casual, indicating that agents knew that left-wing militants tended to prefer music associated with their own political organization. Confessing a taste for Quilapayún or Inti-Illimani, groups that were connected to the Communist Party and participated in Allende's campaign and government, could suggest being a militant or supporter of the Communist Party or another party affiliated with the Unidad Popular; those in the Movimiento de Izquierda Revolucionaria (MIR) would often tune in to the songs of Patricio Manns, who was linked to that organization.[3]

Cifuentes replied to the interrogators: "I like Vivaldi, Bach, and Leo Dan." He was referring to a line from the 1969 song "Ding dong, las cosas del amor" (Ding, Dong, Matters of Love). This song was written by the Argentine singer-songwriter, actor, and director Leonardo Favio, a precursor of the Latin American romantic ballad genre that emerged in the 1960s. In the song, Favio impersonates a young man trying to seduce a schoolgirl (performed by Carola Leyton) he has met in the street. Through singing and spoken dialogue, the pair reveals opposite musical tastes. By the end of the song, however, they discover they both like the popular Argentine singer-songwriter Leo Dan, himself a close collaborator of Favio: "Ding dong ding dong, there is no agreement in love / if she says The Bee Gees, I tell her The Tremeloes / if she says Los Beatles, I tell her The Rolling Stones."

Cifuentes's quotation from Favio's song lyrics is remarkably witty and shows how he played with various levels of meanings. In response to his interrogator's demand for musical taste disclosure to uncover his political militancy, he invokes the song's play on musical taste to define personalities. Irony is generated in the incongruence between the themes of the song and the context in which Cifuentes recalls it. Irony is also produced at the expense of the agents, who, according to Cifuentes, did not understand the meaning of his response.

In this excerpt from Parra's memories, focused on his experience of having to listen to his torturer at the Dirección General de Investigaciones sing, it is also possible to see a link between musical taste and political belonging:

> At one point, I lifted the blindfold a little bit and saw that he was an enormous fat guy in a grey suit. He was singing a song. I came to the conclusion that this guy did this [the torture] as a job. His singing was sort of commonplace. And he sang every time, so naturally. I used to think, "What's this scumbag thinking about? He's beating the shit out of me and singing as if it were nothing, as if it were so normal." I've never been able to remember what song it was, but it was a well-known song of the time that wasn't popular in our crowd. It was some type of *bolero*, *cumbia* or *ranchera*. You'd be so immersed in another type of music that you couldn't even identify what he was singing.

For Parra, the torturer's singing is felt as something deplorable and irremediably alien. It is possible that his distancing from the song is caused not by its genre or the naturality of the torturer's singing but by it being sung in conjunction with grievous harm. The torturer's singing is also disturbing as it normalizes the act of torture, transforming it into an ordinary occupation.

Parra's dichotomy between the torturer's song and the music of his own crowd points to the divisions between left and right in society that existed at the time in Chile. As a political activist and member of the music groups Los de la Peña and Curacas, Parra and his social group were immersed in the world of Nueva Canción. While people on the left regarded Nueva Canción as their own because it denunciated injustices and communicated their hopes for a fairer future, counterinsurgent forces within the military considered it subversive as it was associated with their ideological enemies (McSherry 2015). Looking at the broader Cold War context helps to understand the framing of these opposite worldviews, as it structured politics and perceptions of politics, both domestic and international.

In the quote above, Parra associates the torture's song with a *bolero*, *cumbia*, or *ranchera*, seeming to hint at a perception of these popular music genres as devoid of meaningful and political content. These genres (originating, respectively, in Cuba, Colombia, and Mexico) have been widely popular in Chile and have been adopted by local musicians. Although numerous songs in these genres have no overtly political lyrics and have been performed in Chile primarily or exclusively for non-political purposes, some undercurrents challenge the perception of these genres as apolitical.

For example, the well-known Colombian *cumbia* "El africano" (written by Calixto Ochoa and recorded in 1983 by Calixto Ochoa y su Conjunto) became an emblematic protest song against Pinochet. Its light-hearted lyrics voice a woman's description of the suggestive behavior of a man, repeatedly asking in the chorus, "Mami ¿qué será lo que quiere el negro?" (Mommy, what would the Black man want?). "El africano" became fashionable in Chile via a cover of the Orquesta Cubanacán, a well-known Chilean tropical music band of the time. When the cumbia was played at parties, partakers would sing a new line, "que se vaya Pinochet" (that Pinochet goes), in response to the chorus question, "Mami ¿qué será lo que quiere el negro?" The Orquesta Cubanacán, believed to be Pinochet supporters, paradoxically decided to play "El africano" at the 1986 Festival Internacional de la Canción de Viña del Mar (the oldest and largest international song contest in Latin America); they did so despite organizers had asked them not to. Not surprisingly, the audience roared "que se vaya Pinochet" in response (Karmy Bolton et al. 2011).[4] Later in this chapter, we shall see how a Villa Grimaldi agent used a contraposition between, on one hand, *cumbias* and songs by Roberto Carlos, and, on the other hand, songs of Argentina's Nuevo Cancionero movement.

The lyrics of Roberto Carlos's songs have no political content and are primarily concerned with romantic love. However, the persona of Roberto Carlos is not politically neutral, as exemplified by an explicit statement of political support for Pinochet he made during his 1975 performance at the Festival de Viña del Mar, attended by the dictator himself: "For me, the presence of a country's president is a pride. Thanks very much, Mr. President, thanks very much, Sir Augusto Pinochet."[5]

Furthermore, one may argue that the setting of these pieces in *political* imprisonment centers—with state agents having a *political* motivation to order or action the torture and imprisonment of people—adds a new political dimension. One may also suggest that any music has the potential to have political connotations due to its capacity to convene, unite, and spur people to action. As we shall explore in other chapters, political prisoners organized themselves to make music, and these activities were empowering for them.

Singing to Comfort Others

One of the episodes Jiménez remembered vividly from her time at Villa Grimaldi was when a DINA agent demanded she sing. The agent had asked if someone was a musician during a winter night, when all the prisoners were formed up on the patio. After Jiménez identified herself, the agent said: "We're all bored here and it's such a cold night, so you are going to sing to keep us entertained." The agent threatened Jiménez that if she did not obey, all the prisoners would have "a rough time." Jiménez recalled: "Despite the fear I felt, I decided that my small act of rebellion would be not to sing. Plus, I really thought that I wasn't going to be able to sing and was afraid that they would take me back for electric shocks."

But when the agent briefly left to obtain cigarettes, another detainee persuaded Jiménez to sing, not to please the agent but to comfort another prisoner, Cedomil Lausic, who, after a brutal torture session, was suffering in solitary confinement at some distance. When the agent returned, Jiménez sang "Zamba para no morir" (Zamba so as Not to Die), a song written by Hamlet Quintana, Norberto Ambrós, and Héctor Rosales and popularized by Mercedes Sosa. Jiménez often sang that song before being detained. The song's subject, in death throes, voices feelings of solitude and hope for transcendence: "My voice will ring through the afternoon, until the echo of yesterday / in the end, I am left alone, dying of thirst, tired of walking / but I continue to grow in the sun . . . I live."[6]

Jiménez chose "Zamba para no morir" hoping it would lend some strength to Lausic. Singing at the top of her lungs, she saw that "all of my comrades had tears rolling down their faces and I don't know where I got the strength, but my voice began to lift up as I sang, like it was in flight." The agent abruptly stopped her and told her not to overstep her bounds "with cute little political songs and to instead sing a *cumbia* or a song by Roberto Carlos." As Jiménez did not comply, she was made to spend the entire night in the rain. She recalled: "I was cold and afraid, but I felt I had performed a minimal act of resistance." She later learned that her rendering of "Zamba para no morir" was the last thing Lausic heard before passing away.[7]

Although Jiménez identified physical and psychological damage resulting from Villa Grimaldi agents using music in the ways she described, she did not recognize that these may be classed as torture or other forms of cruel, inhuman, and degrading treatment. Furthermore, when I asked her if she had ever included her experiences with music in testimonies that she gave to various truth commissions and court cases against state agents, she gave a negative answer. She also told me that she still likes Roberto Carlos's songs. Likewise, as we shall explore in Chapter 3, two survivors of Colonia Dignidad continue to love a song by Julio Iglesias that a guard sang to them during their imprisonment. This is despite the fact they suffered horrific torture and psychological distress when listening to the guard singing.

Music Listening to Build Courage and Recover

Cifuentes and Parra shared experiences of listening to specific songs to prepare for and recover from torture. Both men used portable radio receivers that circulated clandestinely in imprisonment centers. Some of these devices were in prisoners' pockets at the time of arrest and were not found and confiscated by the authorities; other devices were secretly manufactured in prison. Detainees would tune in to local and international radio stations to listen to music and catch up on the news. After the coup, radio stations frequently featured rock and pop music from Spanish- and English-speaking countries, Nueva Ola songs, military marches, and folk pieces from *música típica* ensembles such as Los Huasos Quincheros. Except for military marches, this repertoire often appeared on Chilean radio stations before the coup. As expected, radio stations stopped broadcasting music from Nueva Canción artists once the military took power.

On a radio device circulating in the dressing rooms of the Estadio Nacional, Cifuentes listened to a song recorded by the English singer-songwriter Cat Stevens (known as Yusuf Islam since 1978) to build up courage for imminent torture sessions: "I had an obsession for 'Morning has broken,' and when a supportive comrade lent me a radio receiver, I would look for that song because it was reassuring."[8] One may suggest that the song's idyllic verses referring to the book of Genesis—"Morning has broken, like the first morning / blackbird has spoken, like the first bird"—provided an imaginary scene that contrasted with the gloomy cells in which Cifuentes and other prisoners were confined. When existence was so uncertain, the song's dealings with the passing of time and its simple and regular harmonies would have probably provided hope and a sense of continuity and agency.

Parra listened to music on the radio before and after being tortured at the Estadio Nacional. For him, the two essential songs were "Without You" by Pete Ham and Tom Evans of the Welsh rock band Badfinger, and "Alone Again (Naturally)" by the Irish singer-songwriter Gilbert O'Sullivan. Both songs emphasize suffering and loss. While the former deals with a relationship break-up, the latter explores the emotions of a person in a full-blown existential crisis, hinting at suicide. Another song that helped Parra transcend torture was "Clair," also by O'Sullivan, which recounts the quasi-incestuous feelings of a man toward his young niece. One could imagine that Parra's emotional attachment to these three songs was not owing to the dubiously comforting lyrics—whose meaning may have been lost in translation—but because of the simplicity and lightness of their melodies.

Cifuentes and Parra shared that the songs they used to build the courage to face and recover from torture were significant for them before the coup. As I will argue in Chapter 4 regarding the repertoire sung at Tres Álamos camp, besides any deliberate reason for choosing this song or that, each prisoner brought with them sound worlds that formed part of their identities, which extended beyond their political activism. A particular song may have been important during someone's childhood or adolescence, or it may have just been an enjoyable or feel-good piece, regardless of politics.

Disclosing Harmful Experiences of Music

Through the interviews discussed here and testimonies available on the *Cantos Cautivos* platform (discussed in Chapter 5), it has been possible to expand the evidence base of experiences interlaced with torture and other mistreatment. The prevalence by which survivors refer to these experiences of music is, however, relatively low, with other themes appearing more frequently in testimonies about music in imprisonment facilities. The more frequent themes include interactions with other prisoners and agents, descriptions of prison life, general mistreatment and torture (not involving music), reflections on remembering, music shows, music during visits, music in celebrations and farewells, musical instruments, music and resilience, music and solidarity, music as protest, and music and humor.

My probing of these interview excerpts finds some overlaps between how music was viewed by these three people and their captors (or rather, the perceptions that prisoners assumed their captors had). First, the linking of musical taste to political activism (seen in Cifuentes's and Parra's memories). Second, the perception that certain music genres and the songs of some musicians are apolitical (seen in Parra's and Jiménez's memories). And third, the repurpose of songs via elements of song lyrics (seen in Jiménez's and Cifuentes's memories). Although these connections are subtle and may appear non-central to overall experiences of political imprisonment, my findings challenge the established belief that the worldviews of political prisoners and those of state agents have nothing in common whatsoever.

In the Introduction of this book, I outlined the complexities, methodological and ethical challenges of working with memories dealing with traumatic events, and the biases toward positive events in autobiographical accounts. Furthermore, the decision whether to share these difficult memories is likely influenced by legal typology and survivors' involvement with other entities requiring testimonies—courts, truth commissions, and human rights advocacy agencies, among others.

Regarding typology, torture was technically not a crime in Chile until recently, despite Chile had signed in 1987 and ratified in 1988 the UN Convention against Torture (United Nations 1984) and the Inter-American Convention to Prevent and Punish Torture (1985). In 2016, almost three decades later, the Chilean Parliament passed a law typifying and criminalizing torture and other cruel, inhuman, and degrading treatment; this law was subsequently incorporated into the Penal Code. Before the change of law, Chile's Penal Code did not mention torture at all; instead, it referred to torments and unlawful harassment. Although torture and other forms of cruel, inhuman, and degrading treatment have been punishable crimes since 2016, cases dealing with human rights violations during the dictatorship are still judged by the offenses stipulated in the Penal Code in force in 1973–1990.[9]

For decades, providing testimony on human rights violations had no legal or political consequences. For example, between 1978 and 1989, the Vicaría de la Solidaridad (Vicariate of Solidarity), an agency of the Catholic Church that played a central role in defending human rights, filed more than 1,300 cases of torture without ever obtaining any satisfactory results. Using this legal remedy became meaningless, even more so if the decision to reveal experiences of torture put survivors' own lives at risk (CNPPT 2004: 188). After the return to democracy, progress regarding legal cases has been slow—as of 2025, only the courts have made 414 judgments only, and many are still waiting to be resolved.[10]

Disclosures of harmful musical experiences occurring in political imprisonment centers, like any experiences of torture, are challenging to make and are inevitably interlaced with previous histories of revealing torture, the various understandings of torture, and the changing need to talk about torture. The horrific violations of human rights committed during the Pinochet dictatorship are facts that speak for themselves. Denouncements have already been made by survivors, relatives of victims, governmental and non-governmental organizations, truth commissions, the press, documentaries, and so on. Is there, then, a need to address case studies exclusively focused on music as torture practices?

While music has the capacity to sensitize broad audiences to human rights issues and allows survivors to address extreme experiences that extend beyond spoken or written language, we should never forget that torture is a life-altering experience. Focusing exclusively on, and going public about, misuses of music may or may not be welcomed by those affected by political violence, and researchers should prioritize the needs of research participants and communities over research agendas.

The emphasis on music used for harmful purposes only has the potential to produce unintended negative consequences.[11] For instance, as Papaeti (2020) noted, readers of a *Mother Jones* article titled "The Torture Playlist," listing the musical choices of U.S. prison guards and interrogators in Iraq, joked in public fora that music's torturous quality related to the genre, singer, or composer of the piece, and discussed which music was better for torture.

Additionally, as various chapters included in Stone et al. (2018) and Wilson et al. (2017) testify, music has been used in exhibitions and as merchandise at sites of so-called dark tourism (defined as travel to sites relating to death or complex heritage) and prison tourism around the world, often commodifying suffering. Wilson et al. (2017: 5) warn that prison museums' capacity to conduct educational work "is often more dependent on questions of what is thought most likely to entertain, titillate, amuse or 'frighten' the average member of the public," and query whether the histories of those imprisoned can be represented with integrity and fidelity by these institutions.

Consequently, researchers working on the topic of music in prison and torture contexts should be wary of the risks of disseminating research that emphasizes angles that could lead to the fetishization of mistreatment. In my case, I have turned down requests from media outlets when the requirement has been to speak exclusively about harmful uses of music, yet I have been keen to contribute when the approach has been balanced and non-sensationalist. Uncovering stories of mistreatment is also at the root of investigative journalism, and much can be learned from the ways in which some journalists communicate their findings to wider audiences. Investigative journalist Mauricio Weibel Barahona (2019: 14), who has worked extensively on topics relating to Pinochet's regime, queries if it is necessary and ethical to detail all the horrors and humiliations that someone may have been subjected to impact audiences. He reminds us that silences speak, arguing that these are preferable over excessive description to encourage reflection.

Some of the questions I have raised above resonate with those posed by Clelia Rodríguez (2017) in relation to the acquisition of knowledge from vulnerable populations and subsequent use for career advancement. At the heart of my concerns is to create horizontal relationships with research participants and balance their and my personal wishes to make these stories public with the duty of acting ethically above and beyond individual and institutional research agendas.

2

The Memories and Songs of a Convicted Perpetrator

In 2012, I conducted two interviews with a former Non-Commissioned Officer and a founding member of the DINA secret police, whom I call by the pseudonym of González. At the time of our interviews, González was free yet under prosecution for his role in Operation Colombo, a DINA operation that resulted in at least 119 people being abducted and assassinated in 1975. He received a criminal sentence in March 2023.[1] As a DINA agent, he operated at the torture centers of Tejas Verdes, Villa Grimaldi, and Londres 38, and the Chacabuco concentration camp.

In the lead-up to our first meeting, I experienced an emotional rollercoaster of anxiety and sleepless nights. For personal safety reasons, I decided we would meet at a semi-public space, but let González choose the location. A couple of days before the interview, he emailed me to suggest that we meet at a café located in the financial quarter of central Santiago. I agreed with his choice, unaware that the meeting place he chose was a *café con piernas* (a slang term meaning "café with legs" or "coffee with legs"), where coffee is served by women wearing very little clothing.[2]

When I arrived at the café on the day of our meeting, I was shocked when I realized what type of place my interviewee had chosen. I asked myself how much I wanted the interview and was concerned that a *café con piernas* would not be an appropriate setting to conduct an interview. As a woman, I felt uncomfortable, to say the least, about being in such a place. I considered canceling the interview, but in the end, I decided to go ahead anyway. González, however, appeared very at ease in the environment of a *café con piernas*, and our conversation went smoothly. At the end of that meeting, he extended the offer to accompany me to the former torture center Villa Grimaldi, which I accepted. In contrast with the first interview, at Villa Grimaldi he seemed tense and introspective, and his replies were noticeably more succinct and carefully thought.

Music and Political Imprisonment in Pinochet's Chile. Katia Chornik, Oxford University Press.
 DOI: 10.1093/9780190052294.003.0003

Throughout both interviews, which lasted about two hours each, I experienced raw, intense fear. I purposely did not directly tackle torture, assassination, and disappearance of political prisoners, yet González referred to these, nonetheless. I let him speak freely, and from time to time, I would prompt questions about music. I noted a deliberate effort to present himself as a mere witness to human rights violations. He insisted he was just a guard, using the pronouns *he* or *they* when referring to crimes that occurred at the centers where he worked. Yet sometimes, when narrating these episodes, *he* or *they* got mixed up with *I* or *we*, suggesting that he had at least a degree of responsibility.[3]

Over a year or so after these interviews, I gradually realized that I could take on the challenge of interviewing another former agent. I began toying with the idea of meeting Álvaro Corbalán Castilla, a retired Army Major and a culprit of manifold human rights violations who played a crucial role in the machinery of the dictatorship (see Figure 2.1). A committed *pinochetista*, Corbalán was Head of Operations of the CNI secret police, where he was nicknamed *el faraón* (the pharaoh).

Corbalán currently serves sentences at Punta Peuco prison for disappearances and murders of scores of political opponents, mostly

FIGURE 2.1 Álvaro Corbalán. Chile. Diario La Nación. Unknown date. Fondo Diario La Nación, Cenfoto UDP.

from the Movimiento de Izquierda Revolucionaria (MIR) and the Frente Patriótico Manuel Rodríguez (FPMR), and for assassinating people without known political involvement to cover up crimes against political opponents.[4] As I learned from a guard at Punta Peuco, Corbalán is known as *el Mozart* by the guards due to his passion for writing music. He has given guitar lessons to over twenty students, all human rights offenders serving prison sentences. Outside the prison, Corbalán's support base is significant; for example, the Facebook group "Amigos de Álvaro Corbalán Castilla" has hundreds of members.

Circumstances converged, and through a chain of contacts, I could get in touch with Corbalán's wife, who facilitated communication. Corbalán claimed to me that he had not accepted an interview for fifteen years.[5] I believe that his immediate agreement to be interviewed by me was facilitated by my music credentials. He may have assumed that I would focus on music and not discuss human rights matters. Our meetings took place in April and December 2014 in Punta Peuco prison, located in the surroundings of Tiltil, a small sleepy town north of Santiago.[6]

Since prison rules do not allow visitors to bring any recording devices into Punta Peuco, I had to rely mostly on my memory and that of my companions to reconstruct what Corbalán said, sang, and played during our meetings. I wrote down as much as I could remember immediately after the meetings and asked my companions to share their notes and check mine for accuracy and any missing details. It was possible to recall a great deal of what Corbalán said, and my memories of watching him singing remain vivid. It was challenging to experience not only the physical proximity and intense gaze of a man so heavily implicated in human rights violations but also the evidence of performative qualities that, in a different context, one may have perceived as strong or even charismatic. Confronted with the possibility of moral abhorrence sitting alongside aesthetic curiosity, the mind boggles. Are these attitudes completely irreconcilable? This question disturbed me then and still disturbs me.

Engaging with Perpetrators

Unquestionably, giving the floor to and engaging with perpetrators is contentious. Some critics of Hannah Arendt's 1963 *Eichmann in Jerusalem: A Report on the Banality of Evil*, on the trial of Adolf Eichmann, accused her of offending the dead and exculpating murderers; these critics asserted not only that she was wrong in being interested in the personality of Eichmann, but that he should not have been allowed to speak at all (Arendt 2006: 285). Arendt had portrayed Eichmann as a banal and efficient bureaucrat, rather than a psychopath monster, who by not questioning orders and his own actions, participated in evil acts. She was interested in understanding Eichmann's mind and the moral collapse caused by the Nazis; she felt that reporting on the trial was an obligation to her past as a displaced person, witness, and survivor of the Holocaust (Elon 2006: xi–xii).[7]

Referring to Argentina's last dictatorship (1976–1983), Claudia Feld and Valentina Salvi (2019: 12–13) note that paying attention to perpetrators' testimonies has generally not been accepted by society unless it directly helps the identification, denunciation, or judicialization of culprits. Yet perpetrators have rarely collaborated in clarifying human rights cases, often justifying and denying the crimes committed, or disqualifying and denigrating their victims and their families. These phenomena have occurred in Chile too. A notable example was the late convicted perpetrator Manuel Contreras (founder and Director General of the DINA), who in a television interview denied the torture, execution, and disappearance of political opponents, brushed off any responsibility for these acts, and dismissed the suffering of victims and their families (Contreras 2013).

Álvaro Corbalán has expressed himself extensively in the public sphere through his music and writings. In 2013, recordings of his own compositions "Canción por el reencuentro" (Song for the Reunion) and "Himno de Punta Peuco" (Anthem of Punta Peuco) as well as his cover of "My Way" were widely disseminated by *The Clinic* outlet. These recordings were allegedly leaked to the press. Subsequently, the "Música y política" program of the Universidad de Santiago's radio station broadcasted an hour-long episode based on the recordings disseminated by *The Clinic*.[8] For over a decade, Corbalán's supporters have also posted on YouTube some of his music recordings, including "Canción por el reencuentro," "My Way," "Himno de Punta Peuco," "¡Hola! ¡Qué tal!" (Hello! How Is It Going?), and "Vieja casona" (Old House).

Corbalán has written open letters defending the Pinochet regime and complaining about the imprisonment of former state agents convicted of human rights crimes. His letters have been further disseminated by mainstream media outlets such as *Televisión Nacional de Chile* and the newspaper *La Tercera*.[9] He has published four books: *La verdad está enferma* (1998),

Anécdotas de mi general: las que viví y—las que me contaron (2008), *Las respuestas de Corbalán* (2018), and *Belleza y sentimiento de los poemas de mi madre* (2019). The launch of *Las respuestas de Corbalán* took place in a high-profile hotel in Santiago and attracted not only supporters but also protesters staging a *funa* (a public denunciation and vilification of those implicated in human rights violations), generating further media coverage.

In contrast with studies by Feld and Salvi (2019), Michael Lazzara (2014), Nelly Richard (2001), and Nancy Guzmán (2000), my approach to ex-agents has sought to focus not on their public interventions but on their memories of music in centers where they operated during the dictatorship. In the case of Corbalán, I also wanted to explore how his role as a CNI agent had connected with his musical side and influenced his own experience as a prisoner. Music-making, music listening, and discussions of songs were central to my meetings with Corbalán.

As Eleonora Natale (2022) shows in her anthropological investigation of military families' narratives of everyday life in Argentina during the last dictatorship, the media and social scientists view the military almost exclusively as perpetrators. Natale argues that while the unquestioned perpetrator category is grounded in the moral and judicial universe of human rights violations, it neglects other elements of military identity such as kinship, gender, class, and educational background.

As this chapter shows, in the case of Corbalán, additional identities come into play: musician, writer, and politician. I posit that engaging with individuals like him does not imply the justification, relativization, or validation of human rights violations, or stain the memory of the victims. Yet paying attention to these other identities complicates the ways in which these individuals are seen, and it may even risk diluting their prevalent identification as perpetrators of human rights violations, showing how this work might generate memory cacophonies.

Furthermore, for those who associate art with good moral values, characters like Corbalán can be deeply problematic, as music may make them be perceived as less monstrous and more human. I argue against the idea that music and other art forms imply good moral values. Morally flawed individuals capable of appreciating and playing music abound in history—Hitler and Stalin (both enthusiastic music lovers), Benito Mussolini (a keen violin player), and Hans Frank (a keen piano player), to name a few. Corbalán held powerful positions in Pinochet's repressive state apparatus and was directly responsible for horrific crimes. He is a convicted perpetrator who can write, play, and discuss music, yet music does not lessen the severity of his crimes.[10]

Much of the knowledge about the music behaviors of members of the repressive bodies comes from survivors, who have extensively commented on how the former used music in imprisonment centers and the effects of these practices on inmates. Yet survivors speak from their own position, at times speculating about their captors' music knowledge and abilities. Take, for instance, a testimony from Eduardo Ojeda, a survivor of Isla Dawson concentration camp in Patagonia, who claimed that the marines "were really ignorant about music" and had "no idea what they were listening to" when a fellow prisoner sang Víctor Jara's song "Te recuerdo Amanda." Similarly, Sergio Vesely, a survivor of Melinka-Puchuncaví camp, recalled that when the prisoners dressed up for a musicalized play to entertain children who visited their imprisoned parents, the soldiers "watched us from a distance not understanding what was going on."[11] Although we do not have the views of the agents referred to by these survivors, the testimony of González, the ex-DINA agent and non-commissioned officer, contradicts survivors' beliefs: while watching prisoners, González was well aware that the songs they were singing were by Víctor Jara, Violeta Parra, and other musicians associated with the left (Chornik 2014: 119, 121). Engaging with former members of the dictatorship thus allows the possibility of discussing questions that only they could answer because of their roles and actions.

In contrast with González, Corbalán was reluctant to discuss music in Pinochet's political imprisonment centers. Remarkably, he used music to block and divert some of my questions, picking up his guitar and singing. However, he was very keen to talk about his musical activities in the 1980s bohemian scene and during his own imprisonment in the last three decades.

Music or Intelligence?

Álvaro Corbalán was born in Santiago, Chile, in 1951.[12] He was exposed to music from an early age through his mother, who was a pianist. He joined the Military Academy as a cadet, aged fourteen. Around that time, he developed a passion for music writing and singing. He formed a vocal quartet called Voces de Manquehue with fellow cadets, performing at school festivals in Santiago. He told me that the repertoire was mainly original songs composed by him and that the Army viewed his music activities with reticence.

In 1971, Corbalán attended a CIA training course at the School of the Americas at Fort Gulick, a U.S. Army base in Panama. When I asked him what he learned and how he applied it in Chile, he said he studied various manuals on counterintelligence, anti-subversive warfare, and anti-sabotage. Although he did not mention it by name, it seems likely that he studied the CIA's *Kubark Counterintelligence Interrogation Manual* (1963). This text describes the use of techniques such as electric shocks, threats, fear, isolation, and the so-called no-touch torture, involving a mixture of sensory overload and deprivation of factors like heat and cold, light and dark, and noise and silence. Regarding practical training, Corbalán only shared that he had to ride a zip line. He claimed he did not apply any practical learning back in Chile, yet he took away the ideological viewpoint of the course.

Apart from Corbalán, other top officers of Pinochet's regime who trained in U.S. military bases were General Manuel Contreras and Brigadier Miguel Krassnoff. A major channel for disseminating torture techniques was the School of the Americas at Fort Benning in the U.S., attended by thousands of Latin American officials to receive training on anti-subversive operations, intelligence, and counterintelligence, among other topics. Between 1950 and 1970, the School of the Americas trained 4,374 Chilean officers—a significantly higher number compared with the 2,808 officers from larger Argentina (McSherry 2015: 38).[13]

After the CIA course, Corbalán was assigned to the Pudeto Regiment in Punta Arenas, at the southernmost tip of Chile. According to Lagos (2014), Corbalán may have started his intelligence work in the Army between 1971 and 1972. In 1973, after graduating from the Military Academy, Corbalán was allegedly offered a contract to make music recordings for Odeon Records. During our first interview, he told me he had to give up that contract due to pressure from his boss, who had warned him: "You must choose: either music or intelligence." Corbalán told me, in a regretful tone: "I don't know if I did the right thing." In 1975, after returning to Santiago to work for the Tacna Regiment, he joined the Army's intelligence body, reaching a senior position the following year.

In 1981, Corbalán began commanding the Cuartel Borgoño in Santiago, also known as La Casa de la Risa (The House of Laughter). The heavy use of torture at Cuartel Borgoño was first publicly denounced in 1983 by the Movimiento contra la Tortura (see Figure 2.2). Survivor Ignacio Vidaurrázaga Manríquez, who was imprisoned in this facility between

FIGURE 2.2 Protest of the Movimiento contra la Tortura in 1983 outside Cuartel Borgoño. Fundación de Documentación y Archivo de la Vicaría de la Solidaridad.

August and September 1984, gives a vivid account of the horrific treatment that political prisoners endured:

> [At Borgoño] torture becomes scientific, regulated, and dosed with the help of doctors. There, torture follows planned intelligence work and screening of clandestine structures. There, torture is administered fast because time is pressing. [. . .] Cells with permanent lighting and thick metal doors with surveillance windows. And the brown color below and pale yellow from the middle to the sky. A bed of concrete is the only piece of furniture. [. . .] The bath of wet towels and boiling shower. The aluminum jars. The "confessions and self-incrimination" film room. Torture is muffled by the volume of Radio Cooperativa or a television program. Those Sábado Gigante shows [a long-running Saturday TV program] extended for hours to drown out screams and bellowing. And that potential fear of hearing footsteps and the door opening, to return to torture again. And that electric torture that dulls and dumbs down, makes the body jump and contort from the tied limbs.[14]

Corbalán claimed to me that during his time at Cuartel Borgoño, he had no time to make music; however, at night, he frequented clubs such as Rodizio and Bar Oliver (both located in affluent neighborhoods of Santiago), where well-known musicians performed. For twelve years, he also commanded the security team of the Festival de Viña del Mar, which granted him further possibilities to mingle and establish collaborations with famous artists aligned with the regime.

In the early 1980s, the Festival de Viña del Mar awarded Corbalán a Silver Seagull, an accolade given to some of the winning musicians. However, the award was not granted to Corbalán for his musical talents but "for his services provided in defense of the homeland," as reported by the media.[15] During my first interview with Corbalán in Punta Peuco prison, I spotted a Silver Seagull with a different dedication and a more recent date: "To Lieutenant Colonel Álvaro Corbalán, First Prize for having defeated Marxist terrorism in Chile. February 2010." When I asked him to tell me how this award came about, he declined to answer.

In 1988, shortly before the referendum that would put an end to the dictatorship, Corbalán was called to retire. He joined Avanzada Nacional, a right-wing nationalist party seeking to provide a political support base for Pinochet. Corbalán became Avanzada Nacional's President in 1989. Near the end of the dictatorship, he plotted a plan to assassinate the incoming President Patricio Alwyn to prevent Pinochet's exit, according to a declassified CIA document written in December 1989.[16]

Since 1991, Corbalán has been incarcerated in various prisons of the Chilean Army and Gendarmerie. The number of sentences and the total length Corbalán serves are unclear. Media outlets often claim that his sentences total over 150 years yet provide no source. The *Justicia* database of Chile's Museum of Memory of lawsuits brought by the Chilean state (excluding private and reserved lawsuits) lists thirty-five court convictions involving Corbalán. Yet a response to a freedom of information request submitted by me in 2019 to Chile's Ministry of Justice and Human Rights stated twenty-three criminal court cases against Corbalán, of which eleven were sentenced then.[17]

Between 2004 and 2015 and since 2017, Corbalán has been imprisoned at Punta Peuco Prison, a special facility for agents of the state convicted of human rights crimes, built in the mid-1990s during the government of President Eduardo Frei Ruiz-Tagle. Although Corbalán and other residents of Punta Peuco fashion themselves as political prisoners, it would be inaccurate to use such a term for these individuals. (There is no universally accepted definition, yet a political prisoner is generally defined as a person imprisoned for their political activities, particularly those who oppose or criticize the government of their country.) At Punta Peuco, inmates have kept their military grades and pensions and have privileges that are absent in all other jails in Chile, including tennis courts, private bedrooms with flat-screen monitors, satellite television, and minibars.[18]

Chilean media outlets have published countless reports on developments of the criminal cases Corbalán is involved in, his attempts to be granted conditional freedom, and his misconduct in prison. Notable transgressions committed by Corbalán at Punta Peuco that have made headlines include orchestrating an intelligence operation in 2012 and using laptops and cellphones in 2015. In 2020, a female social worker based at Punta Peuco filed a legal complaint for sexual harassment after Corbalán sent her various WhatsApp messages, songs, and a short story. As reported by the media, the messages said: "it's me, Álvaro Corbalán, who has sent you some things. Register me in your life, even if it's for a few minutes [. . .] it is the only way we currently have for getting tied together."[19]

Corbalán has had ten children, the last three with an Argentine model he met while in prison. With a cheeky smile, he tells me that giraffes are not the only animals that reproduce in captivity. When I asked if music has helped him in love, he confided that "music helps to consolidate conquests."

Interviewing Corbalán

In the run-up to meeting Corbalán, the prospect of facing him is exceedingly daunting and stressful. I am conscious that I might be prone to manipulation, abusive language, and inappropriate behavior. My concerns are, no doubt, exacerbated by some of my preparatory readings, which include the books on the CNI by Manuel Salazar (2012) and Andrea Insunza and Javier Ortega (2017) as well as assorted media pieces, several of which account for Corbalán's manipulative and abusive behavior toward female interviewers.

I read about journalist Zayda Cataldo of *Cosas* magazine, who confided that when she interviewed Corbalán in 1989, "he tried to play nice, but he was rude, he resorted to double meanings. He made his power felt, he threatened." Furthermore, Corbalán told Cataldo: "I have already undressed you" (Lagos 2014). Even the noted journalist Raquel Correa, who had a track record of interviewing very powerful men—Henry Kissinger, Augusto Pinochet, and Manuel Contreras, among others—recalled that her interview with Corbalán in 2000 was "terrible" and "very difficult." She added that Corbalán said: "You frighten me," to which Correa replied: "Imagine how frightened I am of you" (Correa 2011).

I reach out to a journalist acquaintance who has previously interviewed other agents of the dictatorship. I ask for his advice on what I should wear for the interview. He recommends me to wear a miniskirt so that I can get more information out of Corbalán. I am shocked and disgusted by the advice at first. On reflection, I take it as a warning about Corbalán's susceptibility to women's physical appearance and decide to follow the journalist's advice but in the opposite direction. Aiming to avoid drawing his attention to my physique, I choose to wear very plain, long, loose clothes, and no make-up or accessories. I reject the idea of wearing revealing clothes, not just because it feels unethical as an interview tactic but also because that is not how I normally dress. Yet ironically, the way I dress for the interview will show me as a different persona from my usual self.

I feel I need someone to accompany me to Punta Peuco, as I am too scared to be with Corbalán on my own. Given his attitudes toward women, I put aside my firm belief that women should stand on their own without the need to be protected by men and decided that my companions should be male. I ask musicologists Juan Pablo González Rodríguez and Daniel Party, both experts in popular music, to accompany me, provide practical and moral support, and join in the conversations—González Rodríguez for the first interview and Party for the second one. I have known both for over twenty years, from my time as an undergraduate student in Chile. Before the interviews, I share my planned topics for discussion, methodology, and ethics with my companions, and debrief extensively after the meetings.

It is not easy to find Punta Peuco. The first time, we take the wrong road and end up at a nearby facility of Sename, the National Children's Service. We do not realize we are at the wrong place until a guard informs us that there is no child called Álvaro Corbalán living there. Our mistake only increases my nervousness. We arrive at Punta Peuco half an hour later than the agreed time. Corbalán greets us in an effusive way, as if we were long-term friends. He invites us to his bedroom. Easy-listening music is in the background, played from a large plasma television set that dominates the room. I spot books by linguist Noam Chomsky and by historian Gonzalo Vial (former Education minister of Pinochet). Several drawings made by his youngest daughters hang on a wall—one says "Papito, eres el mejor papá del mundo" (Daddy, you're the best dad in the world). Despite my precautions, I receive unwelcome comments from Corbalán when I ask him where I should sit. Smiling, he instructs me to sit on his bed so that I can later tell people that I have been "in the bed of Corbalán."[20]

For the second meeting, I consider the idea of making music with him, inspired by Mantle Hood, a U.S. ethnomusicologist specializing in gamelan music from Indonesia. Working at UCLA, Hood coined the concept of bi-musicality (1960) and proposed that researchers should learn to play the music of the culture they study, arguing that they might properly understand that music only by immersing themselves in it.

Corbalán's music, his musical taste, and the cultural spaces he inhabits are all alien to me. Hood's method has the potential to deepen my understanding of my interviewee's relationships with music, and it might even make our conversations smoother. I am inclined to try it as an experiment, yet I am not fully convinced that I can genuinely comprehend the music and the world-view of Corbalán. Before finding out if he is keen to play music together and before requesting permission from the prison authorities, I run my idea by Daniel Party and suggest that we take his guitar and my violin to Punta Peuco. He agrees with the idea, and we discuss possible songs that we could learn beforehand. We consider "My Way" (one of Corbalán's favorites) and perhaps one of Corbalán's own songs. Yet days later, we abandon the plan, as it seems too big an emotional challenge for us to make music with a convicted criminal. My companion also fears that if we play "My Way" with Corbalán, he will dislike the song forever.[21]

At Punta Peuco, shortly after greeting him, Corbalán tells us that he has invited some friends and that they are all waiting for us in the kitchen. This announcement comes as a worrying surprise. It is possible that his decision to have supportive company is motivated by fear of the interview, mirroring my own anxiety about being alone with him. Among the friends of Corbalán we meet are a former General, a journalist, and others who do not disclose their occupation. As part of a conversation about supporters and critics, Corbalán tells his friends: "my detractors are always people who don't know me. The people who know me, like Katia, are not my enemies." I am mystified to hear my name invoked in this way—I have only met him once before and have kept my political views strictly private in our conversations, yet Corbalán has likely conducted searches on my work and personal links to the topic, none of which align with his politics and that of his supporters. I say nothing.

The group then turns its attention to Daniel Party, firing questions aimed at finding out his political viewpoints. When one of Corbalán's friends asks,

"What is your position regarding the military government?," he responds: "I was too little—I was born a month before Pinochet took power." (Party later told me that he said so as an attempt to evade disclosing his political views.) Corbalán bursts into laughter and proudly says: "We didn't have enough time to torture you." Party seems utterly horrified.

When questions turn to music and Party discloses that he is a guitarist, Corbalán gives him his own instrument and asks that he play something. As I discovered during my previous visit to Punta Peuco, my interviewee's instrument has a loaded history: he told me that the guitar was a personal gift from Lieutenant General Jorge Rafael Videla, who at the time headed the military junta of the last dictatorship in Argentina. Corbalán explained that he received the gift during a work trip he made to Buenos Aires. The link with the infamous Argentine dictator suggests that Corbalán may have had a role in Operation Condor.

Party agrees to Corbalán's request and sings and plays the *bolero* "El reloj" (The Clock), receiving a warm reaction from the Punta Peuco audience. I am surprised that my companion concurs, given his previous reservations about making music at the prison. Later, Party told me that he agreed to sing and play out of fear and that the pressure of being surrounded by Corbalán's allies had been overwhelming. He also recalled that his fear was exacerbated by having seen, on entering the kitchen, a corpulent man holding a large butcher knife. Party told me: "I remember being impressed by how he grabbed the knife to let us pass (backwards, with the handle in his hand and the edge stuck to his forearm), because it looked like a movie, like someone who is used to hiding a knife. I remember thinking, 'Can you have such a knife in a prison?'"

During the meetings, Corbalán handed me three gifts: a dedicated copy of his 2008 book *Anécdotas de mi General: las que viví y... las que me contaron* (Anecdotes of my General: those I lived and ... those I was told), a DVD of a documentary film titled *Pinochet* (2011) directed by Ignacio Zegers, and the typescript of his 2014 essay "Saludo del Teniente Coronel (R) Álvaro Corbalán Castilla, en el aniversario de la gesta heroica del 11 de Septiembre de 1973" (Greetings from Lieutenant Colonel (R) Álvaro Corbalán Castilla, on the anniversary of the heroic deed of September 11, 1973).[22] As their titles suggest, the book, the documentary, and the essay are all tributes to Pinochet. The documentary, which includes Corbalán's song "Canción por el reencuentro" (Song for the Reunion), was premiered at Miami's Grand Hispanic American International Film Festival in 2012 and won the Hispania de Oro prize. According to Corbalán, the documentary cost U.S. $1.5 million and was financed by his friends. The former CNI agent also provided me with the lyrics of some of his songs and anthems, which I will briefly discuss below. I have made the deliberate decision to avoid including direct quotations of his lyrics for reasons I shall debate at the end of the chapter.

I feel very uneasy about looking at these presents, particularly the book, as it includes a personal dedication: "For Katia Chornik, with the great pleasure of meeting you and sharing the most beautiful thing that unites us: Music." Months pass until I dare to inspect them properly. I convince myself that I must do so to be able to comprehend Corbalán's worldview better. The experience is not particularly illuminating and becomes rather unpleasant. The book, the essay, and the song from the documentary are consistent in conveying devotion to Pinochet as the savior of a country in ruins, asserting religious commitment, justifying the coup and actions of the Armed Forces during the dictatorship, and proposing that the violence from the left was comparable to that of the state. This enemy narrative glosses the fact that most victims of state terrorism did not have weapons, and it bears some resemblance to the so-called Theory of the Two Demons, referring to the political violence during the last dictatorship in Argentina.[23]

Anécdotas de mi General is a collection of petty stories about Pinochet and other military officials, politicians, journalists, bankers, the Pope, and comedians, containing a plethora of dull word games and drab mischief. In his preface to this book, Corbalán expresses his pride of having been part of "the most successful Chilean Government of the twentieth century"; he presents Pinochet as a liberator who "saved Chile from becoming Cuba" and made the country "harmonious, whole, strong, secure, free, deep, without foreign mediatization, or colonial treatment, protectionisms, [and] economic dependencies" (Corbalán Castilla 2008: 13–15).

For Corbalán, the coup was "glorious" and marked a "Second National Independence." Not surprisingly, he plays down human rights violations committed by state agents and justifies these as necessary actions to prevent "an imminent civil war." He laments that the human rights discourse relating to the Pinochet period is unilateral, claiming that human rights legal cases are "a political and economic business that is very profitable for many." Despite being imprisoned since 1991 for what he considers a profound injustice, he is "grateful to God and to life" (Corbalán Castilla 2008: 13, 15).

Corbalán's "Canción por el reencuentro," featured in the *Pinochet* documentary, addresses the much-debated matter of political reconciliation. As stated by my interviewee, it was the former Archbishop Cristián Precht who asked him to write the song. Precht, known for his work for the Vicariate of Solidarity in defense of human rights during the dictatorship, was suspended from ministry between 2012 and 2017, and ultimately laicized by Pope Francis in 2018 after being found guilty of pedophilia; currently, Precht is being investigated by Chilean criminal courts in relation to the aforementioned matters.[24] The media reported that Corbalán's song was performed in 2011 at an ecumenical ceremony led by Precht and the Anglican minister Pablo Álvarez, in which around 500 people prayed for former military officers imprisoned for their role in human rights violations.[25]

The lyrics of "Canción por el reencuentro" describe what needs to be done to achieve reconciliation and assert that time helps to forgive. Although the lyrics do not explicitly say what needs to be forgotten and forgiven, it seems apparent that it is about human rights violations and that it addresses those seeking truth and justice, who are told to leave grudges behind. Listeners are advised that good is better than evil if reconciliation is sought. Patriotism and allegiance to the Virgin Mary provide a crowning touch to the song. After Corbalán finished singing "Canción por el reencuentro" during our second meeting, I asked him whom he had forgiven. "I have forgiven everybody," he answered without giving details, and asserted that "music and friendship allow you to reach peaks beyond politics."

In "Saludo del Teniente Coronel (R) Álvaro Corbalán Castilla," he makes an impassioned plea to current commanders of the Armed Forces to be aware of the "evasive truth" around the context and reasons for the coup (referred to as "the military pronouncement"), as well as the "national reconstruction" carried out by the dictatorship. The crux of the text is his answers to a series of questions on the matter of torture and disappearance of political prisoners that, he writes, he is always asked (Corbalán Castilla 2014: 1, 3). (During our second interview, Corbalán claimed that these are his answers to the hardest among hundreds of questions that journalists have sent him after he has rejected their interview requests.)

In his essay, Corbalán does admit that he tortured and, unsurprisingly, he justifies his actions by invoking Chile's greater good and claiming that he followed orders. Regarding the disappearance of detainees, he sustains that some have been found alive, have died a natural death abroad, or have died in combat and not been reclaimed by relatives. As expected, Corbalán is not cooperative regarding trials relating to human rights violations: "I am available to be summoned to the Courts, but not to testify. I became absolutely weary of Justice; I forgot everything and what I did not forget . . . just as well." (Corbalán Castilla 2014: 3–5). In the last section of the text, "Mi sentir personal" (My personal feeling), he looks at his past and present, and shares how he spends his days:

> I was a good student, a bad husband and a worse father, a good professional and a good son, and on my personal balance to present, in this uncertain, fickle, difficult, deceptive life, in which time flies, I think I did not come into the world to be a number in the flock. I find myself in a busy solitude, I don't have freedom, but I imagine it and remember it. Most of the day, I'm alone, I play my keyboard and my guitar, I listen to music, I read texts that don't bore me in the first thirty pages. (Corbalán Castilla 2014: 5)

The lines above bear resemblance to the spirit of the lyrics of "My Way," which are the words of a virile man who looks back on his life and finds plenty to question. The character of "My Way" admits to having remorse ("Regrets, I've had a few") but attempts to justify past actions by putting them down to the circumstances ("I did what I had to do") and preempts criticism with the ultimate disclaimer in the chorus: "I did it my way."

Corbalán's Songs and Memories

Corbalán told me that he likes music of all types, including folk music, provided it has content and is not repetitive. As reported in the media in the 1980s, Corbalán also likes listening to European composers of the Classic and Romantic periods (Mozart, Liszt, and Chopin) and musicians of his time, from Chile (Mario "Huaso" González) and abroad (Paco de Lucía and Frank Sinatra). The list of Corbalán's favorites suggests that his music taste is inconsistently linked to his political ideology—while Mario "Huaso" González is a pro-Pinochet *folklorista*, Paco de Lucía publicly expressed himself in favor of the left. When the Chilean folk musician Tito Fernández (also known as El Temucano) died in February 2023, Corbalán wrote an obituary for *El Mercurio* newspaper, in which he referred to Fernández as "an outstanding folklorist and friend." That piece confirmed the long-standing rumor that the deceased musician, who in the early 1970s was closely associated with the Nueva Canción movement, maintained a close friendship with Corbalán and allied with the dictatorship.[26]

When I asked Corbalán why he likes "My Way" so much, he told me that he does because the song conveys "the idea of being the way one is, and that is not easy." Corbalán's recording of "My Way" closely emulates the arrangement, orchestration, and performance style of Sinatra's rendering. Yet it is substantially slower and uses only the first verse of the English language version, after which it switches to the Spanish language version ("A mi manera").

Corbalán's songs composed in prison are highly autobiographical. Mostly ballads, they appear strongly influenced by Spanish ballads of the 1970s. They tend to be written in major keys and in verse-chorus form, with some harmonic elaboration and often a kitsch sound, especially those with keyboard accompaniment. He has also composed several anthems: "Himno de Punta Peuco," "Himno de la Inteligencia," and "Himno del Regimiento Soberanía." Only "Himno de Punta Peuco" is available on YouTube.

Corbalán explained to me that he first composes the melody, sometimes on his guitar and on occasions on his keyboard, and then writes the lyrics. For him, his music reflects his lived experiences, but he admitted that his life has not changed for a long time. He quickly dismissed that his own music is political. When asked if he had composed songs in honor of Pinochet, he replied: "No, never. But I evoke him in several songs. I don't rule out that I'll do it in the future because the bravery of my General will be recognized." Corbalán's crooner singing style recalls Frank Sinatra, Julio Iglesias, and Raphael. He has a baritone voice effortlessly covering two octaves and uses a range of dynamics, voice tones, vibrato, and rubato to enhance expressiveness.

In "Somos tres" (We Are Three), the imprisoned musician expresses nostalgia for having a family life and dreams about his release. It is a highly personal and intimate song in which he flaunts his competence as a composer, singer, and acoustic guitarist. The music combines vocal lines of fast and sustained notes in steps and long intervals with plucked and strummed chords in ostinato and harmonic progressions. Corbalán composed this song in honor of his newborn daughter, one of his three children born since he became a convict. The lyrics convey the pride of a father coming home after work. He rejoices at the sight of his beautiful daughter, who resembles her mom, her granny, and, of course, her dad.

"Cree en mí" (Believe in Me), with accompaniment of acoustic guitar, addresses Corbalán's partner. In the song, he dismisses her doubts about his past and instructs her about what she needs to do and not do. Although there is an admission of a mistake made by him, that mistake, which is also her responsibility, needs to be forgotten. Forgetting is a condition for happiness and comes with an imperative to leave his past behind. The lurking possibility of repeating mistakes invalidates remorse and threatens a break-up that is dependent on the truth in question.

Regret for lost time features in "¡Hola! ¡Qué tal!" (Hello! How Is It Going?), a song he wrote for his friends. Corbalán explained to me that he has set it aside for when he is released from prison. However, he had already shared this song with friends and supporters in 2008 at the launch of his book *Anécdotas de mi General* (held at the Hotel Crown Plaza in Santiago and hosted by his wife) via a recording made by him.[27] In the song, he tells his friends he has needed them and missed them during his long wait, justified as a painful consequence of being a military man and devoting himself to Chile and Pinochet, as witnessed by God. He resisted hard times and resurrected. Now, reunited with his friends, he is happy again.

During our first interview, Corbalán sang "En la plenitud de mis heridas" (At the Height of My Anguish) to avoid answering my question about how agents used music at Cuartel Borgoño and other centers where he operated. In this song, he laments his solitude and pain and emphasizes a will to keep to military values. After that, Corbalán sang "Siempre he sido libre" (I've Always Been Free), a song full of optimism and patriotism, in which he affirms his desire to transcend his confinement.

When I queried again, during our second meeting, about agents' uses of music at Cuartel Borgoño and other facilities, Corbalán skirted my question once more. He clearly did not want to talk about this matter. When I asked if he had any memories of prisoners' music-making at Cuartel Borgoño, he said there was no music as inmates "were not in the mood." Corbalán also ignored my question about whether he had composed any songs during the time he oversaw that center. However, earlier during that interview, he sang a song he said he composed in the 1980s, entitled "Qué bonito es vivir" (How Beautiful Is to Live). Given Corbalán's responsibility in cases of kidnappings, torture, homicides, and disappearances during those years, one wonders how he could write a song celebrating life.

While several testimonies from survivors of Cuartel Borgoño exist, there is scarce available evidence that deals explicitly with music at this center. One testimony collected through the *Cantos Cautivos* project shows that agents did make use of music at Cuartel Borgoño. Gabriela Durand, a teenager at the time of detention, shares that agents at Borgoño used music played on the radio to irritate inmates and recalls an experience of having to listen to and sing an iconic song by Violeta Parra:

> I was 18, and already I had been tortured on the *parrilla* [a metal frame bed used to torture prisoners with electricity] several times. One day I was with some other comrade prisoners, and as sometimes happened, the guards put some music on. The guys used to put the radio on, playing popular tunes of the time. For us young people, the songs were a bit corny, but still, we enjoyed them, they were a relief. [. . .] There was one who specialized in bugging you by turning the volume up high, then down, then up again, and he also sang. It made us laugh, but we also knew it was his way of showing his power over us. I was sitting down, handcuffed, and at some point, the song "Volver a los diecisiete" ("To Be Seventeen Again") came on; I don't know if it was the radio or a record being played. A guard came up to me, pulled me up and said: "Look, girl, listen to this song, it's yours, you revolutionaries; let's see, sing it!" I told him I couldn't sing, and he said, "Yes you can—sing to your comrades, they're all feeling screwed." I didn't want to sing, I was embarrassed. I'd always been told that I couldn't sing, that I was out of tune. I was standing up, feeling a mix of fear and shame, totally intimidated.[28]

For Durand, the agents' choice of "Volver a los diecisiete" was not coincidental but "was like going back to the time of the Unidad Popular. They did it to traumatize you." She recognized another prisoner after peering under the blindfold, and made him the reason for singing:

> That's when I started to sing. It was as if I just surrendered to the music, feeling, at the same time, rage that they were making me do that. It was humiliating but it was also comforting. That was my take on that situation, and I sang. [. . .] I told myself that I was singing it for him [for the fellow prisoner], and that I would forget everything that was going on.[29]

Further to Durand's experience, the CNPPT (2004: 535–36) mentions that at Borgoño, there was a soundproofed room containing sound and video equipment and that detainees were taken there to be filmed and photographed. The room setup and practices point to the use of so-called no-touch torture.

Given the strongly hierarchical nature of the Armed Forces, it is difficult to imagine that Corbalán, as the commander of Borgoño, did not order, instruct, or at least tolerate the actions of his subordinates. His skirting tactics and avoidance of questions about his past do not surprise. Perhaps his disclaimer, "I forgot everything and what I did not forget . . . just as well" (Corbalán Castilla 2014: 5), explains why some of his memories may be so elusive.

Navigating Ethics, Aesthetics, and Regulations

Corbalán's music invites the question of how we might judge it. As Cobussen and Nielsen (2012: 6) note regarding Leni Riefenstahl's 1935 Nazi propaganda film *The Triumph of the Will*, "our judgement is challenged because we need to decide not only whether our response is still appropriate in ethical terms, but also whether our moral response must necessarily have an impact on our aesthetic interpretation." In the case of Corbalán, our knowledge of his ethical character certainly has an impact on our aesthetic understanding.

Yet in my view, unlike the films of Riefenstahl, the music of the ex-CNI agent is not groundbreaking and does not sustain itself on aesthetic qualities: it is his biography that drives our judgment, and I suggest that this is applicable to both supporters and non-supporters of Corbalán. In the speculative circumstance that we were able to detach his songs from his biography, his songs would probably have gone unnoticed. The substantial airtime and exposure that media outlets have granted to his songs may be explained by the quirkiness of these pieces being written and recorded by a renowned convicted perpetrator.

The life of Corbalán's songs on YouTube deserves discussion. While these pieces can be deeply offensive to some listeners, their actual musical and lyrical song content does not appear to show tangible, explicit, and demonstrable breaches to YouTube's Community Guidelines. Furthermore, it could be argued that through these songs, Corbalán is exerting his right to freedom of expression, given that prisoners generally retain all their basic rights except freedom of movement. However, the fact that these songs were recorded in prison puts a question mark over compliance with Chile's prison regulations, which state that it is serious misconduct to introduce or possess recording and filming equipment, cameras, long-sight lenses, intercoms, cell phones, and the like.[30]

During the first meeting with Corbalán, I asked him how he recorded his songs. He told me that recording equipment was smuggled into the prison, as well as a computer, with the help of a gendarme. Corbalán stated that he recorded most songs a cappella and that a musician friend of his subsequently added an arrangement. "After so many years, people get to know you," he said. During both interviews, Corbalán disclosed that he received a commission from a regiment to write an anthem ("Himno del Regimiento Soberanía"). When a professional recording session was arranged in Punta Peuco to record the anthem, he took the opportunity to record another twenty songs with guitar accompaniment. One wonders about the ethics of using public money to pay a convicted perpetrator to write an anthem and of regiment personnel singing and listening to it.

Beyond and above the regulations of social media and Chilean prisons, facilitating the recording and wide dissemination of this music risks wounding sensibilities, as it cannot truly be decontextualized from its author's biography. Inevitably, we are faced with the ethical question of whether Corbalán's music should be publicly available. In my view, it should not.

3

Beyond Canonic Narratives of Resistance

Jorgelino Vergara, aka "el mocito" (the little waiter), was an unknown character until 2010, when he suddenly became the center of public attention through a documentary, a book, and a television program widely disseminated in Chile and abroad. As a teenager, Vergara was a house servant of Manuel Contreras, Director General of the DINA. Among other tasks, he did errands, served coffee to torturers, cleaned the blood from the floors of torture rooms, and prepared the bodies of prisoners to be thrown into the sea. Referring to characters like "el mocito," Michael Lazzara (2014: 89) has noted that the memory archive of the Pinochet dictatorship is constantly evolving. Sometimes, it admits new voices and stories that break into the public scene. The invisible may turn visible as a novelty, and the *obscene*—or what has been left outside the stage and is known but has been overshadowed—may become present (Lazzara 2014: 89).

Following discussions on characters such as "el mocito" and on the memories and songs of Corbalán, this chapter looks beyond narratives of resistance. I highlight the notion of memory cacophony by focusing on music stories about or voiced by characters that are unconventional in political imprisonment testimonies and on music stories, music pieces, and music happenings that may be loose ends and counterintuitive, have no particular purpose, or are funny and witty, deviating from canonic stories that are so often tragic. I explore the implications of spotlighting these expressions and ultimately ask: Whose voices and stories should we listen to?

Except for an episode around a song sung by a guard at Colonia Dignidad, all stories I explore here are expressions of dissent. I view these stories as situations of "paradoxical happiness," a term coined by the cultural critic and writer Jorge Montealegre Iturra (2018), himself a former political prisoner. Montealegre Iturra explains that through music, writing, reading, drawing, crafts, and other activities initiated by inmates, some individuals triggered a process of psychological flight, even in the worst moments such as torture or solitary confinement, displacing to an imaginary elsewhere (Montealegre Iturra 2018: 406).[1] Yet, as Rebecca Waxman (2021: 19) suggests in relation

Music and Political Imprisonment in Pinochet's Chile. Katia Chornik, Oxford University Press.
 DOI: 10.1093/9780190052294.003.0004

to female political prisoners, their participation in musical activities was as real as everything else they dealt with; music was not merely something they did or took part in, but an experience that defined their time under captivity.

Stories of paradoxical happiness have not been generally welcomed as society has predominantly considered memories of aspects of everyday life of political prisoners as inadequate, inappropriate, and inconsistent with the tragic discourse around the dictatorship. In Montealegre Iturra's words:

> The magnitude of the crimes and the urgency to clarify them as a legal, ethical, and political priority have played down the need for more reflection about aspects of daily life in a mourning situation; mainly about those experiences that, without being extraordinary, are perceived as dissonant in a testimony of political imprisonment, altering a certain *duty of being* heroic in that situation, moving away from an expected behavior that should represent *the role* of the political prisoner. (Montealegre Iturra 2018: 412–13)

But it is not just society at large that has silenced the personal experiences and cultural memories of those suffering political violence: survivors' self-censorship has played a significant role in the concealment of these experiences. Ex-political detainee Rosalía Martínez, in a 2015 testimony on *Cantos Cautivos*, asks: "How could a person who had survived worry about what he or she had lived through, if this meant nothing compared to the fate of the missing and the executed?"[2]

The Julio Iglesias Stories

When I interviewed the poet and musician Mauricio Redolés in September 2013, he recounted an intriguing story involving the famous Spanish singer and former footballer Julio Iglesias. In February 1975, Iglesias had a gig in the Cárcel de Valparaíso, a men's prison in the historic port of Valparaíso (see Figure 3.1). The event did not go according to plan and had an unfortunate outcome due to the words that the artist pronounced before his audience, which was composed mostly of inmates, both regular and political. Redolés and other former prisoners I later interviewed say that the singer insulted them. Iglesias sometimes remembers the episode and sometimes does not.

The Cárcel de Valparaíso was, to say the least, an unusual choice for a singer accustomed to performing in prominent arenas. Throughout

FIGURE 3.1 Iglesias at the Cárcel de Valparaíso, 1975. Unknown photographer.

his career, Iglesias would sing to over sixty million people, sell more than 300 million albums in fourteen languages, and receive many awards, including Sony's Most Successful Latin Artist of All Time in 2014 and the American Recording Academy's Lifetime Achievement Award in 2018. The singer's appeal remains an unexplained phenomenon, even to him. "You cannot understand the reason why people follow you," Iglesias once said. "If success had some logic, we would all have it."[3]

The Cárcel de Valparaíso was a brutal and bleak place. Political prisoners were held on the top floor of the jail and included workers, artists, students, teachers, journalists, and lawyers (see Figure 3.2). The two floors below housed common prisoners, usually separated according to crimes—the ground floor was for those charged with financial crimes, and the first floor was for those sentenced for violent offenses.

Despite the harsh conditions, inmates were able to make music. "It was difficult because it was banned, but we still tried," says Redolés, who came to the Cárcel de Valparaíso in April 1974 in a precarious state, weighing a mere twenty-five kilograms because of torture and illness while imprisoned in various centers of the Valparaíso region—the Academia de Guerra Naval, Buque Lebu, Cuartel Silva Palma, and Campamento de Prisioneros Melinka-Puchuncaví. Redolés served a total of two years as a political

FIGURE 3.2 Cárcel de Valparaíso, 2000. Third floor, where political prisoners were held. Photograph by Mario Patricio Cordero.

prisoner. At the time of his arrest, he was a law student, but in prison, he turned to music and poetry. He spent ten years in exile in England, where he started experimenting with rock and poetry. A well-known artist since the 1990s, Redolés has released nine albums, published four poetry books, and received numerous awards for his works.[4]

Redolés told me that at the Cárcel of Valparaíso, he communicated with other inmates by singing tangos through the windows of his cell. A fellow inmate called Álvaro Vidal—a musician who played jazz, rock, and folk—lent him his guitar and taught him some tricks. For his first recital, Redolés sang popular songs from Chile and Mexico. But there were pieces from the so-called classical music tradition, too: Vidal remembered playing Vivaldi's Concerto for Guitar in D major, which he and another political prisoner who was a distinguished classical musician played to the whole jail population. "I had a hard time learning it, but it was very well received," said Vidal.

How did Iglesias end up in such a harsh, gloomy, and volatile place like the Cárcel de Valparaíso? In 1975, the singer was in Chile to perform at the Festival de Viña del Mar. According to Vidal, a prisoner convicted of fraud who was a huge fan of Iglesias came up with the idea of inviting him. The details of how the agreement was reached are uncertain. Iglesias's visit was announced two days in advance. The regular inmates were excited, the political prisoners not so much. "We couldn't have cared less about Iglesias, we were worried about our situation, our health, and politics," Redolés told me. They assumed Iglesias was pro-Pinochet, to some extent, because the government was so heavily involved in the Festival de Viña del Mar. For Mario Patricio Cordero, a constitutionalist sailor opposed to the military coup who was also imprisoned in the jail, Iglesias was part of "the dictatorial showbiz."[5]

The common prisoners built the stage the night before the event, keeping the rest of the prison awake with the noise. Vidal told me he was surprised when he saw the completed stage: instead of it being in an open space like the courtyard, it had been placed on an extremely narrow area on the first floor. The stage was three meters by two meters at most and had a single microphone of poor quality. Vidal said to himself: "Iglesias will not sing there." The show was scheduled for 10 am. The prison authorities eased off: roll call took place only once instead of three times.

Such a change of routine had never occurred before, not even for the visit of General Sergio Arellano Stark, leader of the Caravan of Death, an Army squad that executed seventy-five political opponents. The prison guards attempted to make all the prisoners gather at the front of the stage. The regular inmates agreed, but all the political prisoners rebelled, remaining on the upper floor but observing every detail. Cordero explained that acting as a human block gave them strength. Over time, they could demand improvements in living conditions and increase the pressure on the military to allow inspections by human rights commissions.

Iglesias arrived at the prison six hours later than the scheduled time, accompanied by an entourage of about twenty people. There was an uproar, as the regular prisoners demanded songs and autographs. When order was restored, Iglesias addressed his audience. According to Vidal and Redolés, he declared: "Apparently, I'm a free man, but actually, I'm a prisoner of my commitments, of singing here and there, of hotels and planes. My fans do not leave me in peace. I understand you very well. I bring you a fraternal hug and hope you recover your freedom as soon as possible." The singer's words did not go down well. The political prisoners were offended. "He was laughing at us," Vidal claims. "We began yelling in unison, 'You son of a bitch!' And we called him worse things than that. There was a surprised expression on Iglesias's face. He looked this way and that, clearly disconcerted."

Redolés adds: "Iglesias asked, 'You up there, why are you so angry?' Someone explained to him that his rowdy detractors were political prisoners.

Then the manager announced that Iglesias was leaving. And he left without singing a single song." For Vidal, it was the most ridiculous event he had ever seen in his life. "Iglesias was very cheeky: he left without saying goodbye or anything. Political prisoners feared there would be retaliations, but none occurred. The regular prisoners didn't even react badly to our booing, they felt offended too," says Vidal.

Why had Iglesias agreed to sing in this men's prison? Had he been motivated by curiosity, a charitable impulse, or a desire for publicity? Did he have in mind the U.S. singer Johnny Cash, whose recordings in two California prisons, Folsom and San Quentin, earned him the top spot in the Billboard charts in the late 1960s, and album sales higher than those of The Beatles? And why did he leave without singing a single note? Maybe it was learning about the presence of political prisoners. Perhaps it was just the response his words had received. Or it could have been the makeshift stage.

In 2014, when I learned that Iglesias would give two concerts at the Royal Albert Hall in London, I wrote a journalistic piece narrating the episode at the Cárcel de Valparaíso, which, until then, was practically unknown outside the circle of witnesses. I attempted several times to get an interview with Iglesias to ask him about his memories of the incident. My request was never granted, yet his representative explained to me that the artist did not remember the episode. My piece was published in English by *The Guardian* (U.K.) and in Spanish by *El Mostrador* (Chile). One reader of *El Mostrador* commented online that he was related to the presenter of the event in the prison, Mario Herrera, formerly a well-known radio host. Thanks to that reader, who offered to make introductions, I could interview Herrera and publish a new piece in the Spanish media outlet *Diagonal*.

"The story isn't simple," Herrera warned me at the start of our conversation. He told me that before the event featuring Iglesias, he had hosted other events in that prison with a friend who worked in television. Some of these events featured cabaret dancers and magicians. Herrera considered himself "a friend of the prisoners, of those convicted of common crimes and scams. They were the good prisoners, the prisoners that one can trust. The gallery above was full of bad little children [the political prisoners], they were the dangerous ones."

Herrera confirmed that the regular prisoners orchestrated the Iglesias event. One of the reasons for holding the event was to give Iglesias a guitar made especially for him by the common inmates. Herrera recalled that

Iglesias came very late, straight from a party, and that after being introduced, a common prisoner took the stage and gave him the guitar; the inmate shared that in prison, "they listened to his songs a lot, and that's why they had dedicated a guitar to him." Herrera remembered that the guitar that common prisoners made was "perfect" and that Iglesias expressed: "I really appreciate the guitar, but I cannot sing now because I'm sick." Herrera explained that Iglesias was sick "because of that little party he went to," and believed that the Spaniard must still have the prisoners' guitar hanging in his wardrobe.

When I mentioned the insults that the artist received from inmates, Herrera jumped on the defensive: "No, no, it's the first time that I've heard that the prisoners shouted political slogans at him." I clarified that they were not political slogans but insults. Herrera insisted there were no insults and rephrased these as slogans again: "I am not aware that they shouted slogans. I did not hear anything." I asked Herrera if he did not find it curious that Iglesias went to that prison. "Not in any way," he said, highlighting the Spaniard's altruism, for he did not charge for attending the event. Herrera added: "Iglesias said words that showed a good upbringing, those things that artists say. Prisoners did not boo him, no: they applauded him." According to Herrera, Iglesias said: "I'm glad to be here because I know you listen to my songs, and songs have life. I feel imprisoned by my situation, a prisoner of my audience, a prisoner of commitments. Have hope of freedom."

In 2015, journalist José Vásquez of *El Mercurio* newspaper interviewed Iglesias on the occasion of the release of his album *México* that year. When the journalist addressed the event at the jail, the artist commented:

> I remember perfectly well [. . .], I do not know who invited me and brought me there. I sang, they shouted at me, they probably would have called me "bastard, fagot," and I left. [. . .] I do not remember the nonsense I said, which means it was very banal, because there have been moments in my life when I have climbed a cloud and waited until the heavy rain came to climb down. And when the rain came, it was probably too late, and I would have said some nonsense and those who were there would have reasoned soundly. These people probably have already forgiven me and I, of course, am regretful.[6]

Iglesias remembers having sung, in contrast with the memories of the ex-prisoners and the event host. There is also inconsistency between the booing and insults that Iglesias and some ex-prisoners remember, uttered by the latter, and the memories of former prisoner Luis Madariaga, who was at the scene too. Madariaga recalled there was "total silence" after Iglesias spoke; he explained that "the word had spread asking that no one should applaud whatever Iglesias had to say. This led Iglesias to later ask the man who had brought him to this place who those guys were up in the prison's third gallery, who never once applauded him and kept quiet."[7] The inconsistencies above evidence some of the complexities of working with memories as source materials, as outlined in the Introduction.

The story of the political prisoners' rebellion against Julio Iglesias is a heroic narrative of the oppressed triumphing over the powerful through collective action. Two other testimonies concerning Julio Iglesias—this time his 1974 song "A flor de piel" (Under my skin)—present a less straightforward story. The testimonies are from a couple, Carmen Espinoza and César Montiel (see Figure 3.3), who were detained at the torture and extermination center Colonia Dignidad in April 1975 and had "A flor de piel" sung to them by a man they identified as a guard.[8]

Espinoza and Montiel started dating in the early 1970s after meeting at the Communist Youth of the southern city of Talca. They would attend demonstrations and do volunteer work together. "Our day-to-day lives revolved around that, and our love revolved around that, and it continues.

FIGURE 3.3 Screenshot from Cantos Cautivos (@cantoscautivos). "Colonia Dignidad | Testimonio de Carmen Espinoza y César Montiel," YouTube. December 14, 2022. https://www.youtube.com/watch?v=h4veS_fWsbY.

And there is a very special song that defined us as a couple, as girlfriend and boyfriend: 'A flor de piel' by Julio Iglesias," says Montiel. This song is a love declaration from someone imbued with happiness and devotion toward their loved one: "For that love that you give me / for being like that, just like that / because your love is faithful to my love / because always I've got you under my skin."

Montiel recalled that after being tortured, "the DINA guard used to whisper things to us—your girlfriend is here [and sang] 'A flor de piel.' He arrived and he sang to me and afterwards he went to sing to her." Espinoza, in turn, shared that "the song really proved to me that César was there, that I was not alone, that is how I felt. Because who else would know? No one. So, when he came to sing to me, it was like César would send me a message. That's how I received it, as a message that he was alive. Because between so many voices and moans, sometimes I could not tell if it was him or someone else that they were torturing. So, when he [the guard] arrived to sing me the song, I would say, 'César is alive.' That was it. That brought me a little peace knowing that he was there. That's how I felt."

To the present day, Espinoza and Montiel continue to love Julio Iglesias's song "A flor de piel" because it reminds them of their youth and their difficult days. When sung by the Colonia Dignidad guard, the song gave them "strength" and the certainty that they "were always together." To me, however, the redeeming meaning that the couple makes of this story leaves an uncomfortable feeling, as there are indications of psychological manipulation through the guard's singing of Iglesias's song. Montiel himself noted: "He [the guard] knew it was our song and that way they could do whatever they wanted with us. The person we least expected reminded us of our song. I still ask myself how they managed to perfect their ability to cause us psychological distress. That's the curious thing, to this day we wonder how they knew that that song was our song, the song of our love."

When I asked if any staff at Colonia Dignidad had queried them about their musical taste, Montiel firmly denied it, arguing that interrogators were not interested in that information. (However, as seen in Chapter 1, former prisoner Luis Cifuentes recalled being asked about his musical taste during torture sessions to discover his political militancy.) Montiel then wondered if one of his cellmates knew that the song was so special to them. Although it is uncertain how this information reached the guard (and possibly the DINA and Colonia Dignidad interrogators too), his repeated singing to the couple does not suggest that the knowledge of the song's importance was irrelevant or that that action was fortuitous or unintentional. As in other testimonies of political imprisonment and torture, there is every chance that survivors have shaped their narratives to suit their emotional needs at the time of their arrest and thereafter, accommodating and forgetting certain details, possibly because of the trauma itself.[9]

The story is also complex because it highlights prisoners' development of positive feelings through listening to the guard's singing, despite their explicit reference to psychological distress caused by jailers knowing about their emotional bond with the song. Espinoza stated: "I felt protected. It was a relief to hear this song; I felt that César was sending me a message that he was alive." Montiel, in turn, noted that he "became more receptive and began to enjoy listening to the guard coming to sing to us. I don't remember him singing with arrogance or violence. He arrived friendly and stealthily, and left singing or humming." This portrayal of the guard as someone friendly goes against the canon of much testimony production of the dictatorship and post-dictatorship, which has generally presented guards as agents of the repression who committed or were complicit in violent acts.[10]

Festive Occasions

In February 1975, as the Festival de Viña del Mar was taking place, inmates at Ritoque camp decided to have their own song contest (see Figure 3.4). While winners of the Viña del Mar contest received trophies in the shape of seagulls, winners of the Ritoque competition obtained medals made of coins that were defaced and engraved with seagulls.

From a testimony by Ignacio Puelma, member of the Bellatrix group and co-author of the song "Se escucha muy lejos" (You Hear It from Far Away), we learn that this piece was deemed unsuitable by a political leader, despite attracting the first prize in the contest and a standing ovation from the audience. The political leader solemnly expressed his criticism a few days after the contest, during a conversation with Puelma in the camp's bathroom: "Comrade Puelma, with that music you can't put up resistance."[11] Although the lyrics contain explicit references to imprisonment, repression, and pain, the song is not a call for action, drawing on past, present, and imagined sensorial experience to express wishes for a better future.

FIGURE 3.4 Posters made by political prisoner Miguel Lawner at the time of the Ritoque song festival. The posters show the lyrics and performances of the winning songs of the festival's three categories. Miguel Lawner collection.

Se escucha muy lejos
Voy a cantarle al aire,
pero está en una burbuja
de gruesas paredes, alambres y rejas.
Quisiera cantarle a los niños
que corren y duermen
que botan riendo castillos de arena.

Siempre hay un quisiera
que intenta volar
siempre una burbuja para encadenarlo.
Dos voces quisieran cantarle a la vida
es sólo quisieran,
no pueden poder.
Se escucha a lo lejos
el rumor de un niño
el clamor de un sueño,
se escucha a lo lejos.

Queda la esperanza, un beso caliente
en medio de abismos, dolor y sudor
quedan los recuerdos, pálida sonrisa
en medio de voces que mandan callar
son muchos quisieran,
tanta la esperanza
tantos los temores, los besos al aire
que un grito muy ronco
de muchas gargantas
rompe las burbujas,
surca los espacios.

Se escucha a lo lejos,
el grito y los niños
se escucha muy lejos
el ruido del sueño,
se escucha muy lejos.

You hear it from far away
I want to sing to the air,
but it is in a bubble
of thick walls, wires, and bars.
I wish I could sing to the children
that run and sleep
who laughing kick over sandcastles.

There is always an "I wish I could"
trying to fly
always a bubble to chain it.
Two voices wish they could sing to life
it's only they wish they could,
they can't be able to.
From a distance, you can hear
the sound of a child
the cry of a dream,
you can hear from a distance.

You are left with hope, a hot kiss
in the midst of abysses, pain, and sweat
you are left with memories, pale smile
amid voices that command silence
there are many who wish they could,
so much hope
so many fears, kisses in the air
that a very hoarse cry
from many throats
breaks the bubbles,
soars through the spaces.

From a distance, you can hear
the cry and the children
you can hear very far away
the sound of the dreams,
you can hear it very far away.

In his testimony, Puelma reminisces about the sound of the sea he heard from the camp ("the daily music given to us as a gift by the ocean"). The torture centers seemed something of the past to him and his companions, and that perception helped them recover through activities like crafts, sports, debates, chess, theater, literature, and songs ("life was throbbing after we'd lived through the worst nightmares").

Before Ritoque camp, Puelma, then a university student, had been detained at the Academia de Guerra Aérea (the Air Force Academy) and Tres Álamos camp in Santiago, spending a total of nine months imprisoned. When his family sent him a guitar, Puelma began to put together the initial chords and melody of the song. Little by little, the other band members added jazzy guitar chords, a recorder melody, a bongo rhythm, and the lyrics. The only recording of "Se escucha muy lejos" that exists, made in 2015 by Puelma and relatives, also includes a piano part played by Puelma himself.

As Puelma explains in his testimony, the music and lyrics of "Se escucha muy lejos" departed from the music of the Chilean left (dominated by Nueva Canción) and drew inspiration from vanguard rock and fusion bands such as Los Jaivas and Los Blops. Puelma tells us that when the day of the Ritoque contest arrived, the song sounded innovative. It is possible that its musical style and the festive occasion for which it was written and performed convinced the political leader that "Se escucha muy lejos" was not functional for high-level political needs. Puelma was immune to the criticism and took it with humor—he shared that he felt that the song "may be captive, but the fact that it aroused suspicion revealed it was also captivating."

Humor and deliberate dissent are central to a light-hearted song titled "El rey Ñaca Ñaca" (King Ñaca Ñaca), performed in July 1975 at the Campamento de Prisioneros Melinka-Puchuncaví. Poking fun at Pinochet himself, the song was written by Sergio Vesely, a prolific singer-songwriter and visual artist who composed twenty-five songs for voice and guitar while imprisoned for twenty-two months in seven different centers. He subsequently went into exile in Germany, where he still resides. All of Vesely's songs written in captivity and his accompanying testimonies are found on the *Cantos Cautivos* platform.

In his testimony on "El rey Ñaca Ñaca," Vesely explains that "Ñaca-Ñaca" was first an interjection used by political prisoners whenever they wanted to signal and poke fun at any dark thought that might cross their minds.[12] "Ñaca-Ñaca" then became the name of a papier mâché puppet representing a perfidious medieval king, made and used by inmates in Friday evening shows to entertain the children who would visit their captive parents.

Vesely's song was performed at the opening of a play of the same title created by a collective of prisoners. The play narrated the gory tale of King Ñaca-Ñaca, who mistreats his prisoners Woolen Belt, Metal Ring, Little Bone, and Seahorse, all puppets named after handicraft objects made by real-life political prisoners. The song's first four stanzas are a character assassination of the monarch, and the last two describe the fall of his regime and the emancipation of his subjects—note that the King's regime is explicitly called "this brutal dictatorship." Each stanza ends with a warning: "Watch out, King Ñaca Ñaca."

El rey Ñaca Ñaca
El rey Ñaca Ñaca era un rey muy malvado
amo y señor de su reino privado.
De plata su cetro y su alcoba real
de oro su trono y su globo imperial.
Cuidado, el rey Ñaca Ñaca.

Nunca en la historia hubo
un rey más avaro
más cruel, más avieso, más feo y ufano.
Y cuando andaba de mal talante
la gente decía de su semblante...
Cuidado, el rey Ñaca Ñaca.

Como era un tirano muy endemoniado
gustaba de ser un déspota odiado.
Mil enemigos tenía el monarca
y ningún amigo en su comarca.
Cuidado, el rey Ñaca Ñaca.

El rey Ñaca Ñaca era un rey opulento
que a todo vasallo negaba el sústento.
En montes y valles de aquel territorio
las fiestas del pueblo eran como un velorio.
Cuidado, el rey Ñaca Ñaca.

Hasta que un día la suerte cambió
y una noche en silencio el pueblo emigró.
El rey dormía
y no supo de nada
la guardia en palacio roncaba, roncaba.
Cuidado, el rey Ñaca Ñaca.

Y así se acabó esta brutal dictadura
pues sin servidumbre el poder no perdura.
El triste tirano murió acongojado
sin pena ni gloria
y sin nadie a su lado.
Cuidado, el rey Ñaca Ñaca.

King Ñaca Ñaca
King Ñaca Ñaca was an evil king
master and lord of his private kingdom.
His scepter and royal chambers
were made of silver
his throne and orb were made of gold.
Watch out, King Ñaca Ñaca.

Never has History known
a more miserly king
nor one as cruel, sinister, ugly, and vain
And when he was in a bad mood
people would say of his demeanor...
Watch out, King Ñaca Ñaca.

Since he was a devilish tyrant
he enjoyed being a hated despot.
The monarch had a thousand enemies
and not a single friend in the district.
Watch out, King Ñaca Ñaca.

King Ñaca Ñaca was an opulent king
who refused his vassals' sustenance.
In the hills and valleys of that territory
the people's feasts were more like wakes.
Watch out, King Ñaca Ñaca.

Until one day his luck changed
and one night, in silence, all the people left.
The king was sleeping
and didn't suspect a thing
the palace guards snored and snored.
Watch out, King Ñaca Ñaca.

So this brutal dictatorship came to an end
Since, without servants, power cannot last.
The sad tyrant died broken-hearted
without fuss or ado
and with no one by his side.
Watch out, King Ñaca Ñaca.

For Vesely, the production of the play was "a staged and metaphorical enactment of our own story. And we did it with a good measure of optimism, as shown in the fact that at the end Ñaca-Ñaca loses his voice—that is, his power—and he loses his mind. Thus, the captives become free." The single performance of the play took place in the dining area of the camp on July 26, 1975, coinciding with the anniversary of a significant date of the Cuban Revolution, the 1953 attack on the Moncada Barracks.

Renato Alvarado was in the audience and remembered that the play was very well received. In his testimony, he recalled that the authorities were confused about Ñaca Ñaca's story, even though its allegories of the dictatorship were evident, including the names of the tyrant's supporters, *unifernos*, a play on the words *uniforme* (uniform) and *infierno* (hell). Alvarado recalls hearing a sergeant sitting in the audience say, "What a beautiful thing, things like this should always be shown."[13]

Toying with Anthems

Chile's National Anthem forms part of various stories of challenges to authority. During the dictatorship, the military imposed the Anthem inside and outside political imprisonment centers by constantly making people sing or listen to it on record, radio, or television. The continuous repetition of the Anthem was problematic for many, as was the "brave soldiers" stanza glorifying the Army, made mandatory by Pinochet.[14] In places such as theaters or cinemas, a common form of dissent was to stop singing or sit down at the point of that stanza, which came from the Anthem's 1847 version but had been in disuse for fifty years. For Robert Neustadt (2011), the stanza represented the regime's views of the 1973 coup as a struggle between good Chileans and bad leftists, and of the deposed socialist president Salvador Allende as a tyrant.[15]

In prison facilities throughout Chile, it was mandatory to sing the National Anthem daily. In Melinka-Puchuncaví camp, it had to be sung at dawn and nightfall during a ceremony of raising and taking down the Chilean flag on the flagpole. Before the singing of the Anthem, political prisoners were first assembled, and roll call was taken; they were then marched to the camp entrance while singing songs from the Chilean Army repertoire, like "Lili Marlene."

For Sergio Vesely, this ritual was unpleasant and made him associate the National Anthem with the military: "no prisoner would have wanted to have anthems in common with those people." The inmates found a way of turning unpleasant feelings around. They amused themselves by singing at the top of their lungs one recurring line from the Anthem's lyrics, which clearly connected with the oppressive situation they were living in: "May you be the grave of the free or the refuge from oppression." Vesely commented: "We greatly enjoyed placing great emphasis on that part of the song. It must have been the only act of open subversion that the military could never punish us for, even though surely many must have wanted to. It would have been hard for a rank-and-file soldier to justify mistreating political prisoners to his boss for an enthusiastic rendition of the National Anthem."[16]

Mauricio Redolés remembers that at Melinka-Puchuncaví, the singing of the National Anthem was always preceded by a speech delivered by the camp's commander every day with minor variations. The speech used a racial discourse centered on national unity, devoid of social classes and cultural diversity, and aligned with the regime's ideology of *chilenidad*.[17] Redolés recalls the commander's words: "The messing about is over now. You are in prison for some nonsense that came to nothing in the end. Because in Chile, there are no social classes: there is one nation, a single country. The Peruvians can have their revolution because they have Blacks, Mulattos, Sambos, Whites, and Chinese. But not us, we are a single race, so there can be no revolution. Let's sing the National Anthem."

Redolés recounted that inmates were obliged to shout "Viva Chile!" at the end of the Anthem. On one occasion, some sabotaged the order, yelling "Viva China!" instead. The commander responded to their affront by ordering all prisoners to sing the Anthem again so that he could reassure himself that tribute was being paid to the correct country. As remembered by Redolés, one fellow prisoner was also ordered to shout "Viva Chile!" on his own, after the commander learned why he had been arrested.

On the coup's day, that prisoner had shouted one word—*revolución*—after the final verse "and a refuge from oppression," when hearing Pinochet supporters singing the Anthem in the street, drawing on a tradition originating in left-wing political meetings and rallies.[18] Redolés recalled the commander's harangue: "Now, how you gonna go and do some stupid shit like that? Yelling *revolución* and tarnishing and degrading our National Anthem. This time, when we sing the Anthem, you're going to yell 'Viva Chile!' all by yourself. And standing behind you, there will be a corporal with a revolver in his hand to put three bullets in your head if you yell *revolución* instead."

In the northern city of La Serena, Lucía Chirinos sang the National Anthem during her imprisonment at the Cárcel de Mujeres Buen Pastor in 1973–1974, run by nuns (see Figure 3.5). She did so on her own initiative to cover up other pieces that would surely get her and other prisoners in trouble.[19]

Chirinos, a piano player, borrowed an accordion from the jail's priest. Discreetly, while other prisoners watched a soap opera on television, she learned the chords of two iconic anthems of the left, "Venceremos" (We Shall Prevail) and "L'Internationale," and those of Chile's National Anthem and the "Himno de Carabineros de Chile" (the Anthem of the Police).[20]

FIGURE 3.5 Political prisoners and nuns at the Cárcel del Buen Pastor. Unknown photographer. La Serena, December 20, 1973. Lucía Chirinos collection.

When the soap opera finished and the other prisoners ran where Chirinos had positioned herself, she started playing "Venceremos" on the accordion. She recalls their reaction: "They all turned around, and their jaws dropped. Then they closed their fists, lifted their left arm and we sang at full blast, crying, raising our voices so they resonated in the corridor. It was glorious."

When the police came, Chirinos thought they had indeed decided to reprimand them or something worse. She then cleverly transformed "Venceremos" into the National Anthem, making use of their musical similarity regarding harmony, meter, and tempo. In her words: "We were singing loudly 'How pure, Chile, is your blue sky.' We sang with force and courage. When they heard the National Anthem, the police officers stopped, stood to attention, and stayed still in the middle of the court. They had to wait until we finished the anthem. We sang with rage: 'and a refuge from oppression.' We then sang the Anthem of the Police: 'Order and Fatherland is our motto . . .' The police officers looked at each other and burst out laughing."

Hidden Mockeries

At Chacabuco camp in the Atacama Desert, a prisoner's performance of the *ranchera* "Volver, volver" (Return, Return) concealed dissent. The song, written by Fernando Z. Maldonado y popularized by Vicente Fernández, voices a man's tormented wish to come back to a lost romantic relationship: "And return, return, return to your arms again / I'll go wherever you are / I know how to lose, I know how to lose / I want to return, return, return." As recalled by Jorge Montealegre Iturra, "Volver, volver" was sung by an inmate nicknamed Pollito (Little Chicken) during a show in 1974 and again for a reunion of survivors for the coup's fortieth anniversary in 2013.[21] While the song, performed at the camp, evoked the possibility of returning to prison, the mischief, dark humor, and gestures of the performance, particularly the verse "I'm on the path to madness and still everything tortures me," provided comic relief. Montealegre remembers that "the entire captive audience would laugh at a verse that was not just funny but also bold: the word 'torture' was accusatory and symbolized our story prior to being taken to Chacabuco." There were no known repercussions against the captive performer and audience at Chacabuco for singing and laughing about "Volver, volver." However, prisoners shared a complicit and mischievous concern about retaliation from the authorities.[22]

Prisoners' shows at Chacabuco also featured various examples of *cueca* (a folkloric music genre and partner dance found in Chile, Argentina, and Bolivia) to convey mockery of the military and the living conditions of those imprisoned. "El suertúo" (Lucky Devil), with original lyrics by Víctor Canto and Luis Cifuentes written over the pre-existing music of "El chute Alberto" by Roberto Parra, chronicles a political prisoner's arrival and daily life in the camp. "El puntúo" (A Cocky Fellow), with new lyrics co-written by the same men over the same pre-existing music by Roberto Parra, contains similar themes, coded language, and humor.[23] Using scathing irony, the character of "El suertúo" makes fun of the harsh treatment at Chacabuco, extreme weather conditions, water shortage, and the bodily effects of a diet based on beans. He entertains the possibility of escaping the camp after discovering that its electric fence has not been properly electrified. Yet, after noticing a mine exploding, he realizes he better stay in the camp and rejoices at his good luck.

El suertúo
Llegamos desde el Estadio
volando y sin mucho atraso
nos recibieron con banda
caramba, y su buen charchazo
llegamos desde el Estadio.

Mucho frío en la noche,
caliente el día
seguían en Chacabuco
las penas mías.

Las penas mías, sí
no veo una
casi me voy cortao
con la vacuna.

Con la vacuna, ay sí
flor de patagua
cada vez que me baño
se corta el agua.

Se corta el agua, ay sí
pónete el gorro
porque a puro poroto
ya vuelo a chorro.

Ya vuelo a chorro, ay sí
sobre la reja
no tiene na' 'e corriente
cayó la teja.

Cayó la teja, ay sí
allá en la esquina
ya me iba echando el pollo
voló una mina.

Voló una mina, ay sí
dijo un canario
más mejor que me quede
en el balneario.

Puchas, que soy suertúo
dijo un puntúo.

Lucky devil
From the Stadium we arrived
flying and without delay
a band greeted us
damn, and a good beating
from the Stadium we arrived.

Freezing at night,
hot during the day
my sorrows
would go on at Chacabuco.

My sorrows, oh yes
I don't see one
I nearly passed out
from the vaccination.

From the vaccination, oh yes
lily of the valley tree
every time I bathe
the water cuts off.

The water cuts off, oh yes
put on your cap
because eating just beans
I will rocket away.

I will rocket away, oh yes
over the fence
it ain't got no electricity
the penny dropped.

The penny dropped, oh yes
there on the corner
I was about to take off
a mine exploded.

A mine exploded, oh yes
said a canary
but I best stay here
at the spring resort.

Gosh, I sure am a lucky devil
said a plucky fellow.

The multiple mockeries in the lyrics were so well hidden that there were no repercussions for the captive musicians or the captive audience when "El suertúo" was sung. As can be heard in the recordings secretly made inside the camp during an event to bid farewell to Ángel Parra, the audience laughed and clapped throughout the performance and gave the musicians an ovation.

Whose Voices and Stories Should We Listen to?

The memories presented here show how multi-faceted dissent was in Pinochet's political imprisonment centers. Employing the typification of Hislop and Hockenhull (2018), we find stories of getting away with dissent (such as singing the militant anthem "Venceremos" and blending it into the National Anthem), dissent hidden in plain sight (like the performance of the *ranchera* "Volver, volver," containing the accusatory word "torture"), and the art of dissent (like the creation of "El rey Ñaca Ñaca," about a dictatorial king who loses his power). These acts involved high risks of being discovered, and prisoners found ingenious ways of circumventing these. Humor is central to these stories and, as Hislop and Hockenhull (2018: 20) assert, it can be "a stick with which to beat the powerful, with far more vigour and venom than would ever be permitted through sober critical commentary". The presence of dissent in political prisoners' musical endeavors is not surprising. For a start, dissent against the dictatorship was, in the great majority of cases, the very reason why tens of thousands of people ended up behind bars.

Reconstructing the story about the revolt against Julio Iglesias at the Cárcel de Valparaíso has involved bringing to the fore the voices of fortuitous visitors—Iglesias himself and Herrera, the presenter of the show. These types of voices are not typically present in narratives about political imprisonment under Pinochet. The views of Iglesias, who equated political imprisonment with artistic commitments and pressure from fans, and Herrera, who called political prisoners "bad little children," are disruptive in debates about the dictatorship's legacy; so is the redeeming story around Iglesias's "A flor de piel" sung by a guard at Colonia Dignidad to people suffering horrific torture. While it may be argued that tangential voices such as Iglesias and Herrera are inappropriate as sources of commentary on political imprisonment and that spotlighting these may overshadow more fundamental matters, ignoring them risks reducing the memory archive to validated voices only. I contend that the archive of the dictatorship admits more stories than those about exertion and defiance of power.

How should memories about funny episodes, music shows, and songs that are humorous, witty, or purportedly unsuitable for building up resistance be handled nowadays, half a century after the onset of the dictatorship? Vinicius de Carvalho (2020) has asked related questions about music from the Holocaust period, reflecting on his experience of directing the *Brundibár* children's opera at a school in Brazil in 2007. *Brundibár* was written in 1938 by Jewish Czech composer Hans Krása, with a libretto by Adolf Hoffmeister. Shortly after *Brundibár*'s premiere in 1942 by children living in Prague's

Jewish orphanage, Krása and most of those youngsters were transported to Terezín ghetto, where the opera was staged fifty-five times. Tragically, most of the performers, the composer, and the director of the opera died from hunger and illness in Terezín or from being gassed in Auschwitz.[24] For de Carvalho (2020: 7), *Brundibár* strangely subverts the logic of the concentration camp by enabling the audience and participants to experience a sense of uplift, despite the violence, intolerance, and death surrounding them. Context is therefore key: students need to be provided with a broad understanding of the history of *Brundibár* and the Holocaust, as well as the significance of the opera's restaging.

The need for historical contextualization of music and memories relating to the Pinochet regime is essential too, as knowledge about that period cannot be taken for granted, particularly among generations born after the dictatorship. Education has a key role in this respect. Chile's school curriculum recognizes human rights violations during the dictatorship, yet the unjustifiability of those violations is hardly discussed (Instituto Nacional de Derechos Humanos 2015: 31–32). Furthermore, human rights topics are not tackled from historical and memory perspectives at all education levels (Defensoría de la Niñez 2022: 135–36).

Given these gaps, it is not surprising that mixed levels of knowledge about the dictatorship were found in the latest survey of a longitudinal study conducted since 1987 by Barómetro Político CERC-MORI. Of all respondents aged between eighteen and thirty-five, 36% had little or no knowledge of the dictatorship, 53% had much or some knowledge, and 11% did not respond. The survey also found that in 2023, across age groups, 34% were in favor of Pinochet's coup, significantly more than the support that respondents' own mothers (25%) and fathers (28%) had for the coup (Barómetro Político CERC-MORI 2023: 23).

When sharing materials such as the stories and pieces explored in this chapter in seminars or presentations, on occasions, I have been questioned if the treatment received by political prisoners was really *so bad*, given that they were able to make music and even enjoy themselves. It appears, then, that music has the potential to be viewed as something that relativizes or negates human rights violations. Even if we address gaps in knowledge or attitudes of denial through contextualization, there are still potential risks of these materials being trivialized.

Why, then, present and discuss music and stories about music from places where human rights were systematically violated, particularly those conveying happiness and enjoyment? Montealegre Iturra's (2018: 20) words are a helpful reminder: "Before emerging, we were sunk; before resilience there was crushing. After maximum loneliness, surviving with companions of misfortune is the sum of countless everyday details, apparently banal." Music's ability to generate and elicit feelings can facilitate debates and sensitization to human rights issues and contribute to the collective memory of the dictatorship. It is my view that the more diverse the voices and stories we preserve and create space for, the richer the cultural legacy for present and future generations.

4

Grassroots Commemoration and Revival

This chapter focuses on the choir Voces de la Rebeldía (Voices of Rebellion), based in Santiago and constituted primarily by ex-political prisoners of the Pinochet regime. Voces de la Rebeldía emerged in 2013 in the context of the commemorations of the fortieth anniversary of the Pinochet coup (see Figures 4.1 and 4.2). A decade on, the choir is still active.

In 2013, unlike previous anniversaries of the coup, public discussions of the dictatorship's human rights violations involved very broad sectors of society. There was extensive media coverage, including special reports and interviews with survivors and perpetrators of human rights violations. The body representing Chilean judges made an unprecedented apology for the actions of its members under military rule, admitting that they had abandoned their role as protectors of fundamental rights. Even the right-wing President Sebastián Piñera (serving from 2010 to 2014 and from 2018 to 2022) spoke about the need to condemn human rights violations during the dictatorship in a firm, clear, and permanent way. However, at the time, public expressions of dissatisfaction with truth and justice processes, such as demands for information about the fate of the dictatorship-era disappeared, were censored.[1]

Voces de la Rebeldía is a sequel to a nameless ensemble that Ana María Jiménez (see Chapter 1) founded and directed in 1976 while she was a political prisoner in Tres Álamos camp.[2] Voces de la Rebeldía is an amateur choir, as was its predecessor at Tres Álamos camp. I trace the development of both choirs, drawing on interviews with directors and members. I shall discuss the choice and resignification of repertoire, and the drivers and issues around membership, participation, and motivation.

Voces de la Rebeldía and its predecessor tie in with the main features of community choirs. As outlined by Caroline Bithell (2014: 222), generally, community choirs do not require music reading skills; they are open to all (including those without previous musical experience) and tend to sing non-Western classical music repertoire. In contrast, amateur choral societies

Music and Political Imprisonment in Pinochet's Chile. Katia Chornik, Oxford University Press.
 DOI: 10.1093/9780190052294.003.0005

FIGURE 4.1 Choir of former political prisoners performing at Parque por la Paz Villa Grimaldi. September 2013. Corporación Parque por la Paz Villa Grimaldi.

FIGURE 4.2 Ana María Jiménez leading the choir at Parque por la Paz Villa Grimaldi in September 2013. Corporación Parque por la Paz Villa Grimaldi.

often hold auditions, expect music reading skills, and perform repertoire mainly from the Western classical canon.[3] As Gregory Barz (2006: 25–26) indicates, community choirs are groups of people who gather for a *reason*: to remember and recall, to share or create new experiences; they typically connect the cultural past to the present. Voces de la Rebeldía has come together for commemorative reasons, using music as a vehicle for memory activism. I follow Yifat Gutman and Jenny Wüstenberg's (2023: 5–6) definition of memory activism as "the strategic commemoration of a contested past to achieve mnemonic or political change by working outside state channels [. . .] [and] intervening in the process of societal change from below."

I view Voces de la Rebeldía as a revival initiative that engages with all the main processes and issues identified by Caroline Bithell and Juniper Hill (2014: 3–4) as typical of revivals. These are activism and the desire for change, the valuation and reinterpretation of history, recontextualization and transformation, legitimacy and authenticity, transmission and dissemination, and post-revival outgrowths and ramifications. Revival in Voces de la Rebeldía does not center on bringing back old or endangered music—most of the repertoire the choir performs is well known in Chile and other Spanish-speaking countries to the present day. Instead, its pursuits are focused on bringing back a bygone age evoked by the memory of communal singing in a political imprisonment center several decades ago, departing from understandings of music revival as "an effort to perform and promote music that is valued as old or historical and is usually perceived to be threatened or moribund" (Bithell and Hill 2014: 3).

The Choir at Tres Álamos

Ana María Jiménez and I meet for the first time in late August 2013 at her home in south Santiago. She is beaming with enthusiasm and joy: it is only a couple of weeks before the first performance of the new choir. She tells me that in 1973, before the coup, she was in her final year of a degree in music pedagogy at the University of Chile. She also ran a weekly music workshop at an industrial school in San Miguel (south Santiago). In that workshop, she taught music theory, solfege, and music history. The repertoire included pieces by Handel, Tchaikovsky, and Schoenberg, alongside The Beatles, Víctor Jara, and Patricio Manns. With the coup, she had to give up her studies and teaching and went underground. She was detained in 1975 and spent eighteen months imprisoned in Santiago, first in the Villa Grimaldi complex and then in Tres Álamos camp.

Jiménez reflected on Pinochet's treatment of musicians and the assassination of Víctor Jara:

> From the first days after the coup, the dictatorship raged against musicians. The torture and assassination of Víctor Jara were not only the work of some crazy guards: it corresponded to a political decision of the new government. Víctor's work was a much more dangerous weapon than rifles. Music has always been a tool of struggle and resistance among those fighting the dictatorship, and thanks to its universality, it could denounce the horrors that were happening.

When Jiménez arrived in Tres Álamos camp, she was pleased to find that fellow prisoners regularly sang. She remembered that the most common song was "Palabras para Julia" (Words for Julia), a setting of José Agustín Goytisolo's 1965 homonymous poem made by Spanish singer-songwriter Paco Ibáñez. Jiménez also remembered that inmates sang popular songs by Violeta Parra (Chile), Chabela Vargas (Costa Rica/Mexico), Daniel Viglietti (Uruguay), and Joan Manuel Serrat (Spain).

Soon after arriving at Tres Álamos, Jiménez started a music workshop for fellow prisoners. Once or twice a week, she would teach guitar, recorder, and singing, using the repertoire that circulated among prisoners already. Political prisoners ran various other workshops, including creative writing, history, foreign languages, dance, embroidery, carpentry, chess, and sciences. Jiménez recalled that when the Inter-American Commission on Human Rights of the Organization of American States (OAS) announced an inspection, the camp's authorities suddenly banned all workshops and intensified the repression against detainees.[4]

Following the workshop ban, Jiménez devised a plan to form a large choir, which, she thought, would allow inmates to spend time in the courtyard and communicate with others. She presented her idea to the authorities, arguing that a choir would improve the camp's image during the expected OAS visit. She told me that she did not truly wish to sing for the OAS, yet she proposed the idea to the authorities, hoping to get their go-ahead for her choir project. She ensured that she phrased her proposal in a way that would appear apolitical and suggested that the choir sing some of the songs that were regularly sung in the camp, such as "Palabras para Julia" or "Vagabundear" (To Loiter) by Serrat. The authorities did not approve of the proposal that prisoners sing for the OAS commission and ordered them to stay in their cells. Jiménez believes the decision was motivated by fear that OAS inspectors would learn inconvenient information from inmates. However, officials authorized the running of the choir on the condition that Jiménez provide all song lyrics beforehand and that only those approved would be sung.

When the choir of Tres Álamos camp was formed, it had approximately eighty members, among whom only three people regularly sang before the coup. Rehearsing twice a week, the choir helped inmates develop communal resilience. In Jiménez's words:

> Many participants did not know how to sing or sang really badly. I asked comrades who sang very badly to sing quietly. Of course, there were people who had no singing aptitude at all. But it didn't matter: the important thing was not to sing well. It was a form of resistance and defiance, a way of reasserting solidarity. It was joy amid so much pain. Singing had a therapeutic role after living episodes that were so terrible and traumatic. It was healing to prepare and participate in an activity, for instance for Christmas, New Year, birthdays, or when someone arrived or was released. It was notorious how resilience increased, as well as empathy, faith, self-esteem, confidence, and reconciliation with oneself. Everybody integrated, even those who were in separate factions. We were happy singing; it was a breath of life.[5]

The Tres Álamos choir lasted five months, until September 1976, when most prisoners were freed or exiled. Sara De Witt, who was not chosen to be released then, remembers that moment:

> Those of us who were to stay behind tried to help, which in my particular case, was not very productive. We had mixed feelings: disbelief, sadness, and also joy for the friends who were leaving. But I also felt disappointed and frustrated, since I and twelve other women were staying behind in prison. [. . .] We stood in the barracks yard and began to sing in unison. We sang the "Ode to Joy" [by Beethoven] and another song of which I remember just one verse: "se va, se va, se va hacia la libertad" (going away, going away, going away towards freedom) ["El barco de papel" by Julio Numhauser]. The departing comrades were moved to tears, but they had

to go. We kept singing to accompany them with our voices as they regained their freedom.[6]

Voces de la Rebeldía

Jiménez began to plan a revival of the choir of Tres Álamos in early 2013, drawing inspiration from the choir Coro Quiero Retruco, formed in Buenos Aires by survivors and relatives of the disappeared of the last dictatorship in Argentina. Her idea was supported by a committee at the Villa Grimaldi Park for Peace, tasked with commemorations of the fortieth anniversary of Pinochet's coup. Jiménez contacted many survivors who sang at Tres Álamos, but only five responded positively. She told me: "There were people who could not be bothered, others smoked too much and lost their voices. Forty years have passed: those who are eighty now aren't able to stand and sing. They are tired, or ill."

Lucrecia Brito, a former member of the Tres Álamos choir, was also involved in recruiting members for the revival. She said that many members of the original choir ridiculed the project, calling it "pathetic." For her, this kind of reaction was "an attack to our self-esteem." Despite these criticisms, Jiménez and Brito managed to convince five members of the old choir to join the new one and recruited three additional members from friendship groups, who, although they were not ex-political prisoners, had good musical skills.

Further members were selected via auditions. Jiménez clarified to me that the choir "is not for anyone who just wants to sing." Although, according to her, no one who applied was left out, it is possible that some potential members were discouraged by the idea of having an audition and decided not to try it out. As a non-professional choir, and given the challenges to recruit members, the decision to hold auditions seems counterintuitive. Moreover, some ex-prisoners I talked to, who were admitted to the new choir but were unable to attend all the rehearsals, told me that they were not allowed to perform in the event commemorating the coup's fortieth anniversary at Villa Grimaldi. In contrast, the Tres Álamos choir was wholly inclusive, not only of people who had poor or no musical skills but also of members of political parties that were in tension with each other.

The new choir began rehearsing in July 2013. Two weeks before their first performance, three musician friends of the director—a flutist, a guitarist, and a percussionist—were invited to join for the final rehearsals and performance. I attended a rehearsal of the choir on a Saturday morning, four days before their debut at Villa Grimaldi Park for Peace. Members beamed with enthusiasm and happiness, laughing and chatting between songs. They told me they really looked forward to the performance. For Lucrecia Brito, the event's significance was to remember the past, "commemorating life despite torture, a homage to all those who went through Villa Grimaldi and other imprisonment and torture centers." For others, like Carena Pérez, it was about the future: she would sing for those who did not live through the events "because there are still people who do not know what happened, and singing is our way of denouncing it."

The new choir's debut was part of Villa Grimaldi Park for Peace's annual memorial held on September 11. It took place in a large, open round tent where events are usually held. Several hundred people of all ages were in the audience. Jiménez and fifteen singers made their way to the stage, accompanied by the guest instrumentalists. They were introduced as the Coro de Ex Prisioneras de Tres Álamos (Choir of Ex-Prisoners of Tres Álamos).

Jiménez gave a short speech that honored those tortured and murdered in Villa Grimaldi, the disappeared, and two former political prisoners who had died the week before the performance. She stated: "Let us sing then to remember our comrades, to put life and its sacredness at the center of our interest, to reaffirm the values of solidarity and affectivity, to continue fighting for justice and truth, [and] to keep shouting, always at the top of the lungs: Never Again." The performance was powerful and phenomenally emotive. When the choir started singing "Candombe para José" (Candombe for José), the audience stood up and clapped the beat throughout the song, building up to an exalted ovation and demanding an encore.

A couple of months after the new choir's debut, members decided to rename themselves. Among all the names proposed and voted on, Voces de la Rebeldía (Voices of Rebellion) won unanimously. The word *rebeldía* in the name appears to be a nod to the ethos of the Movimiento de Izquierda Revolucionaria—which had substantial representation in the original Tres Álamos choir—and other radical leftist movements in Latin America that emerged after the Cuban Revolution. Furthermore, the outfit worn by Voces de la Rebeldía members (black tops and bottoms, a red scarf around the neck or wrist, and a red flower brooch) and the design and color scheme of their logo (white letters over a horizontally split red-and-black background) suggest references to the MIR's colors and logo.

In 2018, due to health reasons, Ana María Jiménez could not continue directing the choir. She and members of the choir began looking for a new director. Ignacio Ugarte, a member of Napalé and Barroco Andino (two groups originating in the Canto Nuevo movement) who had played the guitar with Voces de la Rebeldía in a few gigs, agreed to take up the role. In an interview in March 2022, Ugarte told me that before accepting the position, he thought about it carefully "because it's not easy to lead a choir of former political prisoners." Ugarte is from a younger generation than the members of the Tres Álamos choir. He has a history of political activism that began in the 1980s when he was a secondary student and was involved in pro-democracy movements. At university, while studying music pedagogy, he was one of the leaders of a movement campaigning for educational reform. Ugarte recognizes that Voces de la Rebeldía is a space of testimony. He acknowledges his political kinship with members yet stresses that his contribution focuses on artistic matters. As director of the choir, he has made a requirement to work on short-, medium-, and long-term projects.

Under Ugarte, the choir no longer rehearses at Villa Grimaldi and instead uses members' and Ugarte's homes, union branches, and parks as rehearsal spaces. They have prioritized singing in schools and public parks because they want to reach out to new audiences. Performances in former imprisonment centers and the Museum of Memory are reparatory for ex-prisoners, but the public is always the same, he says. Voces de la Rebeldía have also sung in demonstrations during the social uprising of 2019, on International Women's Day and International Human Rights Day, in events marking anniversaries of the coup, and in funerals of left-wing militants. They have sung in significant memory sites and high-visibility spaces like the Estadio Nacional, sharing the stage with high-profile musicians such as Quilapayún, Isabel Aldunate, Elizabeth Morris, and Magdalena Matthey (the last two named are prize winners at the Festival de Viña del Mar). Other activities have included recording an album (with funds from the Chilean government) and working on a documentary (self-funded and self-directed), both focused on the repertoire and experiences of political imprisonment.

The launch of the choir's album in December 2022 received an Instagram video of support from the Chilean feminist performance collective LasTesis, most famous for their anthem against sexual violence, "Un violador en tu camino" (A Rapist in Your Path), which became viral around the world in 2019.[7] As can be seen, Voces de la Rebeldía has been driven to transmit and disseminate its work broadly. Establishing affinity with young artists born in the post-dictatorship, such as LasTesis, not only updates and legitimizes their work but also signals emerging outgrowths and ramifications. As we will explore later, these outgrowths and ramifications are also appearing in the membership of the choir.

Repertoire Choice and Resignification

The repertoire of Voces de la Rebeldía builds on and expands the repertoire of the Tres Álamos choir. Both consist exclusively of songs in the Spanish language. In Tres Álamos, detainees made use of recorders and guitars circulating in the camp to accompany themselves, as well as bottles and spoons as percussion instruments. Since 2013, Voces de la Rebeldía has often performed with accompaniment of guitars, flutes, cello, and percussions. The vocal arrangements are simple, with generally no more than two parts. Songs were and still are taught by ear.

The initial repertoire of the Tres Álamos choir was selected by Jiménez and consisted of four core pieces: Paco Ibáñez's setting of the "Palabras para Julia" poem by José Agustín Goytisolo; a three-part canon titled "Ya te vas" (You're Leaving Now) of unknown authorship and provenance; "Candombe para José" by the Argentine singer-songwriter Roberto Ternán, popularized in Chile through a cover of the Nueva Canción group Illapu; and the *ranchera* song "No volveré" (I Won't Come Back), written by Manuel Esperón and Ernesto Cortázar for the 1956 Mexican comedy film *El inocente* (dir. Luis Alcoriza), starred by Pedro Infante. Occasionally, prisoners would sing the tango "Volver" (To Return) written by Carlos Gardel and Alfredo Le Pera for the 1935 film *El día que me quieras* (dir. John Reinhardt), starred by Gardel himself. Inmates also learned "Valparaíso" by Osvaldo "Gitano" Rodríguez, a well-known Nueva Canción artist.

All the above songs were written outside imprisonment spaces, and in some cases several decades before the onset of the Pinochet regime. The lyrics of songs like "Valparaíso" (a homage to the port city of Valparaíso, invoking poverty, hunger, and death) and "Candombe para José" (dealing with a Black man who enjoys the *candombe* dance, originating in Uruguay among enslaved people) connect with left-wing ethos directly via the social content of the lyrics or indirectly via the association of the musicians who wrote or recorded the song with the Nueva Canción movement.

The presence of the above songs suggests that censorship at Tres Álamos was not strict or tightly enforced, or that these songs circulated as coded messages.

Other songs in the Tres Álamos repertoire were written or adapted by artists who were activists, yet the songs themselves do not tackle socio-political matters. It may have been the political persona of the authors, rather than the lyrics' themes, which influenced the choice of certain pieces at Tres Álamos. Such is the case of the poem "Palabras para Julia," set to music by Paco Ibáñez, who was a vocal critic of the Franco regime; the song's words, devoid of socio-political content, revolve around a father conveying to his daughter his wisdom on the challenges of life.

Songs like "No volveré," dating from the Golden Age of Mexican cinema and dealing with unrequited romantic love, show no ideological links with Chilean prisoners' socio-political worldviews. The statement "no volveré" (I won't come back) in the title and several verses of the song are the singer's bitter promises to a former lover never to return. Yet the phrase can acquire other meanings in the context of imprisonment—an obvious one would be the wish to not return to prison. Modifying the lyrics of pre-existing songs to make them more meaningful was a common practice at Tres Álamos—for example, the verse "friend Negro José" of the "Candombe para José" song was changed to "courage Negro José," to show solidarity with those being punished. In a similar line, male inmates tweaked Numhauser's song "El barco de papel," changing the verse "going away, going away, going away and will come back" to "going away, going away, going away, never to come back."[8]

Whether the chosen repertoire had some level of concordance with the ethos, political views, experiences, and wishes of Tres Álamos prisoners or not, what is central here is the new meanings these songs acquired in the context of political incarceration. Songs were re-signified, and because they were collectively sung in out-of-the-ordinary circumstances, they became prisoners' shared heritage. Besides any deliberate reason for choosing this song or that, each prisoner brought with them sound worlds that formed part of their identities, which extended much beyond their political militancy. A particular song may have been important during someone's childhood or adolescence, or it may have just been an enjoyable or feel-good piece, regardless of politics. I would suggest that whichever songs were chosen, they would have become meaningful for the prisoners; thus, the repertoire selection was less important than the act of communal singing in that situation.

Since 2013, the repertoire of the Tres Álamos choir has undergone a second process of resignification when adopted by Voces de la Rebeldía, who has re-signified what the old choir had re-signified decades earlier. The authors, background, or the purpose for which the songs were initially written has little, if any, relevance. Voces de la Rebeldía embodies these songs, *their* songs, and Tres Álamos has become the mythical point of origin. As Owe Ronström (2014: 44) puts it, in revivals, "By means of decontextualization, recoding, and transvaluation, things, actions, or ideas are transformed into examples or exhibits of themselves."

To their core repertoire of Tres Álamos, Voces de la Rebeldía, under Jiménez, added titles from the folk, folk-inspired, Nueva Canción and Canto Nuevo repertoire of Chile: "El chilote marino" (The Sailor from Chiloé) and "Qué pena siente el alma" (How Sad the Soul Feels) by Violeta Parra, "El cautivo de Til" (The Captive of Til Till) by Patricio Manns, "El cigarrito" (The Little Cigarette) by Víctor Jara, and "A mi ciudad" (To My City) by Santiago del Nuevo Extremo. They also added two songs by singer-songwriters of the Nuevo Cancionero (Argentina) and Nueva Trova (Cuba) movements: Víctor Heredia's "Todavía cantamos" (We Still Sing) and Augusto Blanca's "El regalo" (The Gift).

Since 2018, under Ugarte's direction, the choir has incorporated further socially conscious Latin American songs of the 1960s and 70s: "Arauco tiene una pena" (Arauco Has a Sorrow) and "Qué dirá el Santo Padre" (What Will the Holy Father Say) by Violeta Parra, "Solo digo compañero" (I Just Say *compañero*) by Daniel Viglietti, "Como la cigarra" (Like the Cicada) by María Elena Walsh, and "El barco de papel" (The Paper Boat) by Julio Numhauser. More recently, they started singing the feminist song "Canción sin miedo" (Song Without Fear) by Mexican singer-songwriter Vivir Quintana (born in 1985). This last piece, written in 2020 and performed in protests against gender-based violence in various Latin American countries, is so far the only song in the choir's repertoire that is from the current decade, in contrast with the rest of the repertoire, which is mainly from the 1960s through the 1980s. The inclusion of "Canción sin miedo" signals a wish to engage with current socio-political struggles of broader remit, and it may be influenced by the process of generational replacement in the choir's membership. As time passes, one may predict that the choir's repertoire will incorporate further pieces from recent times.

Participation and Motivation

Voces de la Rebeldía has a core group of about fifteen or sixteen people who attend regular rehearsals, usually on a weekly basis. There is also a peripheral group that does not attend all rehearsals but still participates in activities. Men are a minority (two or three members in the core group) and, according to Ugarte, they have no right to speak or vote. Around fifty additional women joined the choir specifically to make a recording at the Museum of Memory in October 2021. Ugarte says that male members became inhibited and did not participate in the recording. He adds that his own leadership has limits: "The choir doesn't depend on me. The women are powerful and leading enough."

Most Voces de la Rebeldía members are former MIR militants, yet Ugarte clarifies that it is not a requirement to have had a connection with the MIR to join the choir—some have had no militancy or have been associated with other left or center-left organizations. Voces de la Rebeldía have also diversified by including members from generations that are younger than those who partook in the Tres Álamos choir, namely persons who were imprisoned in the late years of the dictatorship, the descendants of victims and survivors, as well as people with no lived experience of political imprisonment or blood connection with the former groups.

Despite this heterogeneity, Voces de la Rebeldía emphasizes the centrality of survivors on their website and social media, and in spoken interventions in performances, thus affirming their legitimacy and authenticity as a choir of former political prisoners. The participation of younger people in the choir allows older members the possibility to bequeath their memories. The memories transmitted to, and subsequently embodied by younger choir members, bearing to the personal, collective, and cultural trauma of others, may be viewed as postmemories, borrowing Marianne Hirsch's notion.[9]

Under Ugarte's direction, there have been no auditions. He asks: "What would the criteria be if you auditioned? Musical? It is not a professional choir. Auditions would leave people out. The idea is that the choir is as numerous as possible and that members have a connection with its political and social ethos." Ugarte outlines challenges to participation in the choir: "Many arguments arise. There are people who leave the choir because it hurts them to be in it. There are people who join and are not welcomed by other members. Sometimes, they are very harsh with each other. We have had some difficulties, for example, when the choir sets a rule that ends up weakening rather than strengthening the group. But there is mystique in the choir, we support and love each other very much."

Ugarte attributes the turnover to illness and the damage and personal shocks that former political prisoners have suffered. "It is very difficult in terms of human relationships, which have nothing to do with politics. I do not take a position. Because I am external and they like me, they respect me." Ugarte's words point to physical and mental health issues as underlying barriers to survivors' participation in the choir. As outlined in the Introduction of this book, health data, and clinical and sociological research show that the populations directly affected by the human rights violations and violence under Pinochet display substantial levels of polytraumatization, with prevalent anxiety and depressive syndromes, interpersonal conflicts, psychosomatic symptoms relating to re-traumatization, and a range of physical health issues. In this respect, like the Tres Álamos choir, Voces de la Rebeldía has the capacity to play a therapeutic function.

Beyond the effects of imprisonment and torture experienced by former political prisoners, old age, the aging process, loss, grief, and the reality of approaching death may be additional factors affecting their participation in the choir. Not specific to torture survivors, research on older adults and the arts sheds light on barriers. Emily Keaney and Anni Oskala (2007) show that artistic participation decreases as people age, with poor health acting as a barrier. On the other hand, unwanted experiences such as illness may facilitate participation, promoting the search for meaningful leisure occupations and influencing the creative process, as shown by Frances Reynolds (2004) and others. Karima Chacur et al.'s (2022) systematic review of older adults' participation in artistic activities (examining 129 peer-reviewed articles published between 1960 and 2020) found that studies tend to focus on outcomes, particularly benefits. Regarding participation in choirs, the review highlighted benefits around higher physical quality of life and enhanced cognitive aspects, including verbal working memory, executive processes, learning and attention, and visual-spatial abilities (Chacur et al. 2022).[10]

While the above considerations may play a part in the participation of the older members of Voces de la Rebeldía, memory activism and the desire for change appear central to their motivation to sing, as are the valuation and reinterpretation of history, as shown in the choir's self-description on their website and in oral interventions during performances:

> We are living proof of what happened. We are the stubborn memory of our detained comrades who are still disappeared. We sing to them and for them. And we sing because we trust in our people and their strength, because the future is ours. We do not want justice to the extent possible; we do not want the cloak of oblivion to cover our disappeared and executed under torture and false confrontations, we do not want genocides stepping on our streets. And we also sing to our heroic young people on the front line, our secondary school boys and girls who leaped to freedom and the cry of rebellion in October 2019, to our new political prisoners imprisoned with lies, false and crude montages, as well as the Mapuche prisoners of the forever untamed Araucanía. We want the whole truth, we want justice now, we want freedom for all those unjustly imprisoned. Nothing more but nothing less![11]

The choir makes direct criticisms of official dealings with truth and justice, asserting community agency. It assumes the symbolic role of singing for the dictatorship-era disappeared and those imprisoned for their participation in the social revolt of 2019 and the long-lasting so-called *conflicto mapuche* involving indigenous people, the state, forestry companies, and landowners.[12] Weaved in are allusions to two well-known phrases from historical figures: "*el futuro es nuestro*" (the future is ours), found in speeches by Che Guevara and Salvador Allende, and "*justicia en la medida de lo posible*" (justice to the extent possible), from a 1990 speech given by Patricio Aylwin, Chile's first President after the return of democracy. All in all, music performance allows members to revisit and reinterpret history and connect their political experiences from imprisonment periods with broader sociopolitical issues of relevance today.

Revival as Self-reparation

Voces de la Rebeldía highlights how significant a role music can play concerning memory activism and commemoration. The choir is a grassroots initiative that reveals the main processes and issues identified by Bithell and Hill (2014: 3–4) as typical of revivals. First, it engages in activism by using music performances to draw attention to human rights violations in Chile, voice discontent with truth and justice processes, and demand sentences for perpetrators of dictatorship-era crimes. Second, it values and reinterprets historical struggles and figures of the past, highlighting their relevance in current settings. Third, it recontextualizes and transforms preexisting music repertoire, first in prison, and again in freedom decades later. Fourth, it establishes legitimacy and authenticity by stressing the centrality of survivors in performances and its presence on the web and social media. Fifth, it transmits and disseminates their pursuits by seeking a broad audience not restricted to those affected by the repression and by sharing performance stages with famous musicians. Finally, post-revival outgrowths and ramifications include an ongoing process of generational replacement, the expansion of its membership to include people beyond circles of survivors and victims, and the establishment of affinity groups with well-known artists concerned with related social causes.

Voces de la Rebeldía's ten years of existence is a testament to the centrality of political imprisonment to survivors' lives. Five decades after the dictatorship's onset, many survivors are still affected by the physical and psychological effects of imprisonment and torture, and the grief of having lost relatives and friends. As substantial dictatorship-era human rights crimes remain unresolved and unpunished, there is a general feeling of justice and reparative measures not being sufficient, timely, or meaningful. I claim that Voces de la Rebeldía is an instance of self-reparation, achieved through singing. Public performances are essential, as they allow the revelation of human rights violations and the commemoration of survival.[13]

Caroline Bithell's (2014: 45) words remind us of the agency and profound meanings that voices can bear: "The voice is a musical instrument we are all born with. We carry it with us, unseen, wherever we go. It may be suppressed or temporarily silenced, but it cannot be mislaid. Unlike our material possessions, it cannot be confiscated or stolen. We may be stripped of all that we own, but our voice, like our memories, remains. And when it is heard, it says something vital about the deepest layers of our identity, our commitment, our intentions, and our aspirations."

5

Archiving Memories: The *Cantos Cautivos* Digital Project

Héctor Fernández L'Hoeste and Juan Carlos Rodríguez (2020: 11) note that Latin American digital humanities projects generally function within a digital preservation and toolmaking paradigm that sometimes "does not allow for the problematization of digital disparities whose impact includes institutional practices of cultural preservation, but is also linked to broader questions of power, inequality, participation, and access as they relate to other digital practices." The authors suggest a dichotomy between Latin American digital humanities projects preserving cultural patrimony and those promoting human rights through the combination of academic work and civic interventions, citing the *Cantos Cautivos* project as an example of the latter type of projects (Fernández L'Hoeste and Rodríguez 2020: 11).

As it will become clear in this chapter, *Cantos Cautivos* does not just focus on promoting human rights but also preserves cultural patrimony, collecting and disseminating it in Latin America and other corners of the world. The project operates within a digital preservation and tool-making framework, and also acknowledges and addresses questions of power, inclusion, participation, and ethics. *Cantos Cautivos* may be classed as "archival activism," for it has embraced "an *active* social engagement in the processes of records creation, capture, description and dissemination" (Vukliš and Gilliland 2022: 2). Through its platform (www.cantoscautivos.org) and social media accounts (Facebook, X, Instagram, and YouTube, all @cantoscautivos), the project has publicly recognized and amplified the voices and stories of people who experienced human rights violations, adding to the collective memory of the dictatorship.

In this chapter, I first provide an overview of the *Cantos Cautivos* archival content, looking at general trends and particularities of contributors, testimonies, and repertoire. Needless to say, there are many possible readings of this archive, and I hope that my overview is only a starting point for readers to explore it in whichever ways they wish. I then recount the history of the

Music and Political Imprisonment in Pinochet's Chile. Katia Chornik, Oxford University Press.
 DOI: 10.1093/9780190052294.003.0006

project, the different methods used, and how the team operated, reflecting on challenges and opportunities encountered. I discuss the structure and technicalities of the current platform, the project's various collaborations, where it has been featured, and approaches to social media to drive public engagement. Finally, I outline the relevance of *Cantos Cautivos* beyond research and its societal contributions.[1]

Archival Content

From December 2014 to June 2025, the project collected a total of 168 testimonies accounting for music activities in forty-one political incarceration centers. Of these, thirty-nine testimonies refer to music pieces composed in detention (most have original lyrics too), and twelve refer to pre-existing songs with new lyrics created or modified by prisoners. The majority of testimonies narrate experiences of singing or playing music, and around a third of all entries refer to listening experiences. The facilities where these experiences took place were of various types, from clandestine torture houses to officially recognized prisons located in all sixteen current regions of Chile. The regions with the most significant number of testimonies are Metropolitana de Santiago, Valparaíso, and Antofagasta.

Many *Cantos Cautivos* testimonies have come from ex-prisoners living in the diaspora. As Maxim Karagodin (2022: 43) shows in his study of Chilean memoryscapes, communities in the diaspora actively preserve mnemonic legacy online, using digital archives as one of the few primordial mechanisms to perform restorative truth-telling and mourning rituals. A long-standing example of a project created and run by Chileans abroad is the digital archive *Memoria Viva* (www.memoriaviva.com), which since 1996 has compiled information on victims, perpetrators, and imprisonment centers.

Testimonies from former agents of the dictatorship's repressive bodies were deliberately excluded from the *Cantos Cautivos* platform. As I argue in Chapter 2, while engaging with these individuals does not stain the memory of the victims or entail the justification, relativization, or validation of human rights violations, displaying their voices on a public, well-visited platform could trigger distress among some users of *Cantos Cautivos*, particularly survivors and the bereaved.

The two most prolific contributors to the *Cantos Cautivos* project are Luis Cifuentes and Sergio Vesely (featured in Chapters 1 and 3). Their combined number of testimonies accounts for nearly a third of the total number in the archive. Whereas Vesely has contributed with twenty-nine testimonies mainly referring to experiences in Melinka-Puchuncaví camp and to twenty-seven songs composed in prison, Cifuentes has shared twenty-three testimonies, of which eighteen refer to his ensemble Los de Chacabuco, formed in Chacabuco camp. Cifuentes is the co-author of the lyrics of two *cuecas* written in Chacabuco over pre-existing music by Roberto Parra.

Vesely's testimonies include digital copies of audio recordings of his original songs. Vesely recorded these songs in Germany for his album *Documento*, released in 1986 by Dolphin Records. Many of Cifuentes's testimonies have digital copies of audio recordings of music shows in Chacabuco camp. These recordings were clandestinely made by prisoners on cassettes, using a basic non-professional recording device. One of the cassettes was smuggled out of the camp by Ángel Parra and released as an LP the following year. A second cassette recorded in Chacabuco in 1974 was kept by Ernesto Parra (featured in Chapter 1) and was restored and digitized in 2015 for the *Cantos Cautivos* project.

Cifuentes's testimonies include recordings of six music pieces from the first cassette ("Amalia Rosa," "Alma de Chacabuco," "Caliche," "El puntúo," "El suertúo," and "Tonada del viejo amor") and recordings of seven music pieces from the second cassette ("Ojos azules," "Oratorio de Navidad según San Lucas," "Pasión según San Juan," "Barlovento," "La salamanca," "La Adelita," and "Misa chacabucana"). *Cantos Cautivos* also features a speech given by Marcelo Concha Bascuñán, a member of Los de Chacabuco ensemble who was later transferred to Villa Grimaldi and made to disappear by the DINA police.

Jesse Freedman (2022) views Vesely's and Cifuentes's contributions as distinct sets that show different, albeit related, musical responses to political imprisonment and as two similarly distinct models of memorializing and narrativizing surrounding these musical activities. Freedman notes that Cifuentes's testimonies are typically short and direct, but taken as a whole, they chronicle a profound history of music-making and resistance under harsh conditions. Among various topics, Cifuentes's testimonies commemorate the disappearance and torture of fellow prisoners, as well as the songs themselves as dynamic and living artifacts of creative activity. In Cifuentes's texts, there is a general absence of a first-person pronoun (unless framed as a collective "we"), highlighting music as part of communal activities and celebrating his compatriots' achievements and the joint effort involved in bringing this musical history to life.

As Freedman observes, Vesely's songs and testimonies are characterized by wit, tongue-in-cheek criticism, and storytelling. Each text is a kind of vignette, but taken as a corpus, they articulate the life of a man deliberately searching for and creating meaning and identity under dehumanizing conditions. Freedman posits that Vesely's corpus negotiates its relationship to a broader political movement on the periphery and from an observational stance. Although Vesely was previously a political militant, he distances himself and his music from the political or propagandistic, centering instead around a kind of "human condition." In songs such as "Cueca punteada de un solidario" (A Finger-Picked Cueca from a Solidary Companion) and "Reflexiones" (Reflections), Vesely acknowledges and ponders over his political past and conflicts within leftist ideologies.

Vesely had a solid musical foundation as a boy in a familial and social context, yet he truly became a composer during his imprisonment as a means to document, mentally escape from, and make sense of that experience. His compositions deal with wide-ranging subjects, from love and tributes to historical and political figures, to miners' slang and stray dogs in the camps. Like the case of "Se escucha muy lejos" by Ignacio Puelma and others (discussed in Chapter 3), Vesely's compositions depart from conceptions and uses of music to exert resistance against repression, galvanize political sentiments, and support political and social change, as epitomized in leftist anthems such as "L'Internationale," "Venceremos" (We Shall Prevail), and the "Himno guerrillero" (Partisan Anthem). All of these iconic anthems were sung by political detainees in Pinochet's Chile—even in torture centers like Villa Grimaldi.[2]

The platform has digitized copies of a small number of music manuscripts. Among these is an unfinished ten-bar melody written by Jorge Peña Hen (featured in the Introduction) while in solitary confinement at the Cárcel of La Serena shortly before his execution (see Figure 5.1). Peña Hen wrote the melody on a scrap of paper, using burned matchsticks—presumably, he did not have access to pencils or pens. The score contains no instrumentation or performance instructions.

The platform holds several music manuscripts from Alfonso Padilla, who learned how to read and write music during his imprisonment at the Campamento Prisioneros Estadio Regional in the southern city of Concepción. To learn music notation, Padilla transcribed a recording of

FIGURE 5.1 Unfinished melody written by Peña Hen with burned matchsticks. Cárcel de La Serena, October 1973. Peña Camarca collection.

the iconic *Cantata Santa María de Iquique*, composed by Luis Advis and recorded by Quilapayún in 1970. At first, Padilla was only able to annotate the letters of the accompaniment chords. After borrowing a music theory book from a fellow inmate, he gradually learned how to write on the stave (see Figure 5.2).

Padilla's transcription of the *Cantata Santa María de Iquique* was part of his larger project of collecting the lyrics of hundreds of songs, which he sourced from fellow inmates' memories, popular music magazines, and vinyl LPs. The LPs were smuggled into jail, as were the record players that inmates used in the cells.[3] As Vesely, Padilla discovered his vocation in music during his imprisonment and would later make it his profession. Exiled in Finland, he became a composer and musicologist, holding positions at the University of Helsinki and the Sibelius Academy.

Except for contributors like Vesely and Padilla, and Ángel Parra (not a contributor but mentioned in others' testimonies), most stories in the archive concern ordinary musicians and people with limited or no musical skills who, due to circumstances, had musical experiences in prison.[4] Narrated musical experiences are often interlaced with other experiences, most commonly interactions with other prisoners and agents, descriptions of prison

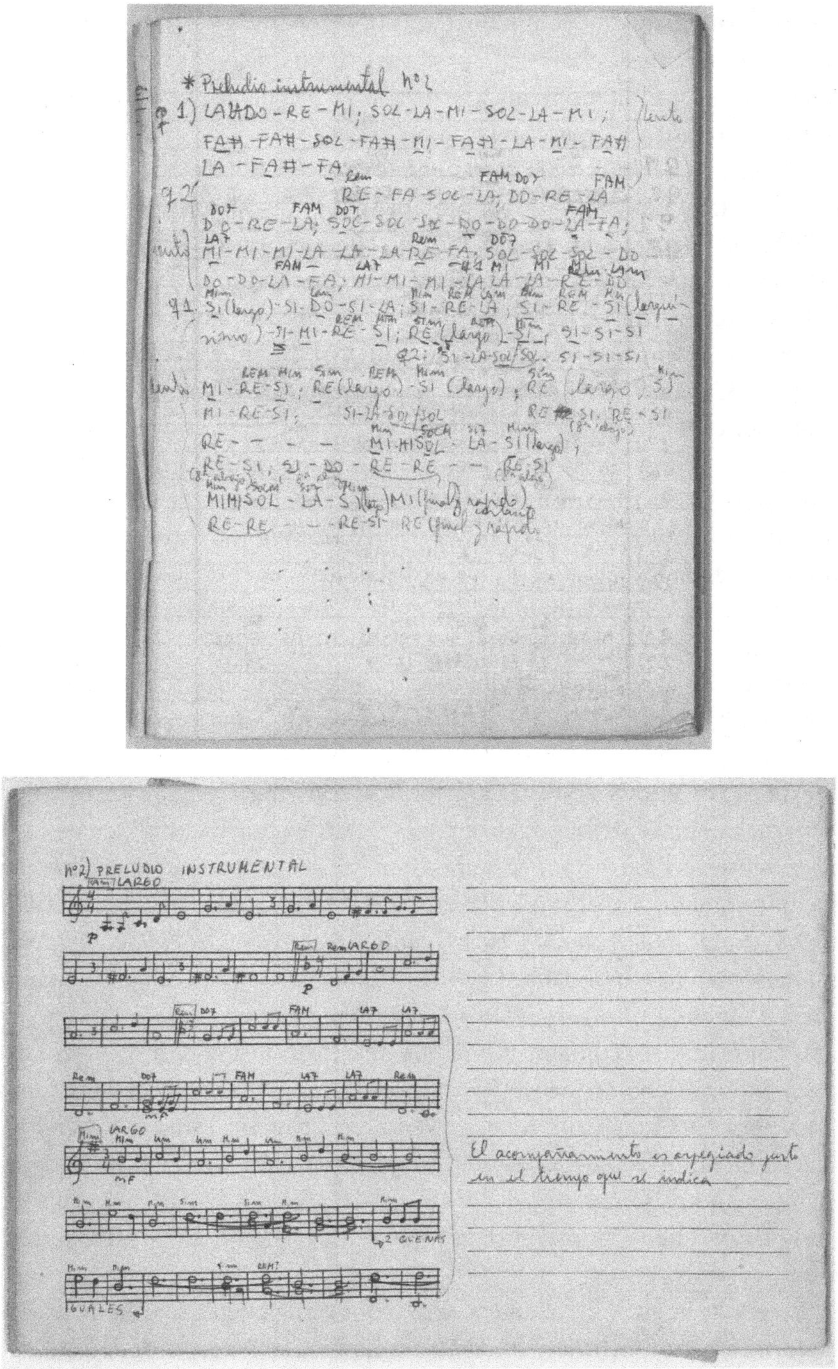

FIGURE 5.2 Adolfo Padilla's transcription of Luis Advis's *Cantata Santa María de Iquique*. Cárcel de Concepción, March–April 1975. Adolfo Padilla collection.

life, general mistreatment and torture (not involving music), reflections on remembering, music shows, music during visits, music in celebrations and farewells, musical instruments, music and resilience, music and solidarity, music as protest, and music and humor.

Twenty-five entries refer to experiences of music linked to torture and other mistreatment against political prisoners in thirteen centers of the DINA, the CNI, and the Armed Forces.[5] These experiences mention forced listening to music played on record players or the radio, always at deafening volume; repertoire included Beethoven's Fifth Symphony, Tchaikovsky's *Swan Lake*, and some of the popular songs of the time—"Gigi l'amoroso," "El bimbó," "Libre" (Free), "Un millón de amigos" (A Million Friends), "Hoy canto por cantar" (Today I Sing for the Sake of Singing), and "A flor de piel" (Under my Skin). These testimonies indicate that music would announce the torture, mask screams, or put pressure to collaborate. The platform also includes testimonies of survivors being forced to sing and being punished for not singing songs such as "Volver a los diecisiete," marches like "Lili Marlene" and "Brazas a ceñir" (Trim the Sails), and Chile's National Anthem.

Group singing of pre-existing music was the most common activity. *Cantos Cautivos* testimonies allude to an eclectic repertoire originating in nineteen countries in South, Central and North America, and Europe—Argentina, Bolivia, Brazil, Chile, Cuba, Ecuador, France, Germany, Italy, Mexico, Peru, Russia, Serbia, Spain, the U.K., Ukraine, Uruguay, the U.S., and Venezuela. This repertoire spans a period of five centuries, from Renaissance vocal music to 1980s pop. Types and genres of pieces featured in testimonies include anthems, ballet music, *bolero*, *candombe*, carnival music, children's songs, choral music, *corrido*, *cueca*, *cumbia*, easy listening, *huayno*, *joropo*, military marches, musicalized poems, *pasillo*, *polka*, pop, religious chants, rock, symphonies, *tango*, *tonada*, *villancico*, and *zamba*.

Cantos Cautivos contains numerous references to music pieces with explicit political content, many of which were composed or recorded by Nueva Canción artists from Chile and elsewhere. Yet browsing through the archive reveals many examples of non-political repertoire. Censorship in some facilities and prisoners' avoidance of certain pieces may partly explain the presence of songs on topics such as romantic love, home, and nature, or religious music works.

As we saw in previous chapters, some songs circulated as coded messages, and the repertoire chosen by detainees had variable levels of consistency with their political ethos and views. Songs in fashion at the time and those meaningful to people's sound identities beyond political militancy were sung deliberately or by chance, on occasions, causing ideological discomfort. As a member of a choir of political prisoners at the Cárcel de Santiago, Roberto Navarrete sang "O salutaris Hostia" (Oh Saving Victim), a religious composition by Lorenzo Perosi (1872–1956) based on a thirteenth-century hymn by Saint Thomas Aquinas. Navarrete had mixed feelings about singing this piece: "I'd never sung a song of this kind before. I was a complete atheist. I also felt an inner reluctance: how were we going to sing religious songs if what we normally sang were revolutionary songs?" Yet Navarrete recalls having "a good time" while rehearsing "O salutaris Hostia" and that the choir sounded "nice." Perosi's piece was featured in various events organized by the political detainees, and they even sang it to the ordinary prisoners. "We felt we had done a good deed," says Navarrete.[6]

More than 90% of the testimonies refer to prison experiences in the 1970s (mainly during the 1973–1975 period), with the remaining relating to the 1980s. It is a relevant fact that *Cantos Cautivos* contributors have shared their stories between four and five decades after the events recalled and in very different socio-political contexts and life stages. Yet only a few refer to developments from recent decades. An example is Eduardo Andrés Arancibia Ortiz's story around Los Prisoneros' song "El baile de los que sobran" (The Dance of Those Left Behind), which became significant to him as he listened to it on the radio while imprisoned at the Cárcel de Santiago in 1986. In his testimony, Arancibia Ortiz links the barking dog of "El baile de los que sobran" to a stray dog nicknamed Negro Matapacos (Black Cop-Killer), which participated in student protests in Santiago in the 2010s and became a symbol of the 2019 social revolt.[7]

As expected, more than one person recalls certain pieces. The most remembered pieces are Chile's National Anthem, the "Himno a la alegría" (a 1969 free version of Beethoven's "Ode to Joy" by Amado Regueiro Rodríguez and Waldo de los Ríos, recorded by the Spanish rock pioneer Miguel Ríos), and "Libre" (Free, by José Luis Armenteros and Pablo Herrero, popularized in 1972 by the Spanish singer Nino Bravo). Each of these two pieces is the subject of four different stories from four different people. The following most remembered piece, with three testimonies, is "Candombe para José" (Candombe for José, by Roberto Ternán, known in Chile through Illapu's 1976 rendering). Popular music and music of folk traditions vastly surpass the number of pieces by canonical European composers. Among the latter are Mozart's "Dona nobis pacem," Piotr Ilich Tchaikovski's *Swan Lake*,

Beethoven's *Fifth Symphony*, and "Ode to Joy" (in Rodríguez and de los Ríos's free version mentioned above).

Only two contributors acknowledge their Indigenous heritage in their testimonies. Both recalled being poorly treated because of their roots. Paicavi Painemal, a Mapuche man imprisoned in the southern city of Temuco, shares that he was in jail for five years and could not go into exile "because the politicians said that I was a *Mapuchito*. They pulled the chair from under me." Painemal recalls having to listen to a recording of "Libre" while he was experiencing electric shocks and mock executions. Pedro Humire Loredo, an Aymara man, recalls receiving harsh treatment and being singled out by the authorities at a police station in Santiago. His "Tonada San Gregorio" was born out of that experience. In his song and testimony, he expresses nostalgia for his mother, his native land, and the traditions of northern Chile.[8]

Various testimonies refer to foreign political prisoners in Chile, some of whom could be Operation Condor victims. Luis Muñoz González, for instance, mentions an Argentine woman and a priest of Belgian or Dutch origin in his testimony, centered on "Casida de las palomas oscuras" (Casida of the Dark Pigeons, a poem by García Lorca musicalized by Paco Ibañez) at Cuatro Álamos camp.[9] Just as in Chile, there is evidence that music was used at Condor sites in other countries, for instance, in the secret center Orletti Motors in Buenos Aires (Chornik and McSherry 2017).

In addition to testimonies from former prisoners, the archive contains a set of three texts from three daughters of detainees. These women were young children when their fathers were imprisoned. María Fedora Peña (Jorge Peña Hen's daughter) recounts how the aforementioned melody written by her father in solitary confinement reached her ten years after his death, as well as the sensory feelings and memories that the manuscript activated in her. María Soledad Ruiz Ovando and Mónica García Cuadra share memories of the journeys they made with their mothers and siblings to visit their fathers imprisoned at, respectively, the camps of Isla Dawson (Patagonia) and Chacabuco. While Ruiz Ovando mentions various songs that she and her siblings sang in the car while traveling to the camp, García Cuadra refers to a metaphorical "tacit song" that sealed the bond between prisoners and relatives at the time of farewells. Ruiz Ovando's testimony also recounts how her father, once out of prison, taught her and her siblings a song composed by a fellow detainee on Isla Dawson and how that piece has been passed on to the second and third generations of descendants, showing the importance of intergenerational music memory.[10] The testimonies of these three women describe with great warmth the loving bonds with their fathers and the centerpiece roles of music in their recalling and construction of memories of the repression, as experienced by them in their childhoods.

Being a collaborative project that welcomes any source dealing with music in Pinochet's political imprisonment facilities (except those from ex-state agents), *Cantos Cautivos* presents an expansive and heterogeneous collection of memories and music repertoire, embracing discordances between these. As Karagodin (2022: 49) asserts in reference to projects like *Cantos Cautivos*, these "are able to unfold individual memories along with their conflictive potential, arranging a mosaic of a diverse memoryscape that transcends preconceived and historiographically polarizing notions."

Project Origins and Methods

The origins of the *Cantos Cautivos* project date back to the early 2010s. At the time, I became increasingly concerned about the rapidly diminishing number of survivors and the practicalities of reaching as many people as possible in the quickest time. I was conducting most of my research work in situ, and then, video communication platforms were less commonly used than they are nowadays. Furthermore, given Chile's geography and the fact that many survivors live worldwide, it was not feasible to travel extensively to collect their stories.

In late 2013, on request of Chile's Museum of Memory, I tested and contributed to their first online crowdsourcing project, titled *Memorias de Exilio* (Memories of Exile, www.memoriasdeexilio.cl), which would soon be launched. This experience prompted me to think that digital media could be a suitable method for speeding up the process of collecting materials for my own research. I shared with museum staff my idea of starting an online crowdsourcing project around music and political imprisonment and proposed to work on it jointly. After a positive response from the museum, I began working with various teams, especially Collections and Research, IT, and Communications.

The first version of the *Cantos Cautivos* platform was developed by the museum on WordPress, closely following the structure and design of their *Memorias de Exilio* project. Some survivors who contributed to the planning of the platform design and a handful of others we contacted by word of mouth shared the first testimonies. Shortly before the launch event, we initiated a press campaign that resulted in substantial national and international media coverage of *Cantos Cautivos*, as well as many contributions from survivors who learned about the project through media outlets. The platform was launched in Santiago in January 2015 at the Museum of Memory's auditorium. Luis Cifuentes, who was present in the audience, commented on the significance of the event and the project:

> It was an unforgettable evening that, unlike other activities commemorating the consequences of the 1973 coup d'état, went beyond the suffering of the victims, emphasizing their creativity and their tenacity to turn to music and other forms of vernacular culture to forge their ability to survive. And the musical theme was there, waiting to be presented thoughtfully and systematically for wide dissemination. I emphasize that several interventions highlighted the fact that a new generation is taking the preservation of our historical memory into its own hands. May it not stop. May it grow and spread across the planet. We owe it to our dead, but more urgently, we owe it to our living.[11]

Cantos Cautivos's partnership with the Museum of Memory lasted until 2016. The project continued independently for nine years, run by a multigenerational team formed by Hernán Theiler (software engineer), Núria Bonet and Jesse Freeman (subeditors), Lisandro Concatti (social media coordinator), Roberto Riveros (documentary maker), and I (general editor).[12]

During the early phases of the project in 2015, it became clear to me that there was a need to address various challenges around online crowdsourcing that hindered participation. Although we made the platform as simple and user-friendly as possible and tested it extensively with volunteers, some potential contributors had basic IT competence gaps that prevented them from sending their contributions online. Furthermore, not everyone interested in contributing to *Cantos Cautivos* had access to computers and a good internet connection. Communication and psychological barriers relating to the crowdsourcing methodology became evident too: as contributors were encouraged to send their experiences in written form, they were solely able to employ propositional language, meaning that prosody and nonverbal communication could not be conveyed, and subjectivity diminished or disappeared.

At first, I offered those wanting to contribute to my research but not keen on the online crowdsourcing method the possibility of being interviewed.

While they agreed to be interviewed, they made it clear that they wanted their stories published on the platform. Their wishes posed a dilemma: Should we combine different methods for collecting materials? Or should we use only online crowdsourcing for *Cantos Cautivos* and other methods for the broader research? It was eventually decided that the project should be open to using different methods to meet contributors' wishes and access needs. To online crowdsourcing, we added edited interviews and oral testimonies as well as music performances from public events, when explicit consent to record and use these materials online was given. Prior to publication, we always emailed drafts to contributors to check that they approved of our edits. We also allowed them to change or add anything they wished to, provided that it complied with the project's terms and conditions.

Structure and Technicalities

The software for the current version of the *Cantos Cautivos* platform was developed in 2016–2017 by the software engineer Hernán Theiler, evolving from the initial version developed by the Museum of Memory. Based on our analysis and user feedback, we made three main decisions. First, we redesigned the web interface, focusing on its ease of use, coherency, and dynamicity. Second, we changed the blog-oriented structure of WordPress to a category-based relational data model, taking inspiration from the Omeka content management system and using various internet technologies, including dynamic HTML, PHP, JavaScript, GitHub, Google Maps, and YouTube. Third, we made the project bilingual in Spanish and English languages, with easy switching between each language version through buttons in the top-right corner of each page. Translating all testimonies, song lyrics, and sections of the platform into English was one of the most time- and effort-consuming yet useful tasks: it grew and diversified the project's audience and attracted media coverage from non-Spanish-speaking countries, which in turn helped increase the participation of survivors based abroad.

Archive entries, available from the "Testimonies" section (https://www.cantoscautivos.org/en/testimonies.php), can be sorted by witness, alphabetically, or by publication date. All entries are named after the main music piece referred to in the testimony, which can be listened to through embedded videos. Under the testimony title, the author of the music piece and the author of the testimony are shown, and the place and date of the experience that is narrated. A hyperlink allows users to view a page containing a map with the geolocation of the imprisonment center, a link to a page of the Museum of Memory's *Recintos* platform (https://interactivos.museodelamemoria.cl/recintos/) with further information about that center, and a preview of other *Cantos Cautivos* testimonies relating to that place. Where a piece of music has lyrics, these are provided underneath the video.

We created and embedded hundreds of brief descriptions of slang expressions and references to historical events, musicians, music terms, political figures, and organizations mentioned in testimonies and lyrics, which our international and multigenerational audience may be unfamiliar with. These are visible when hovering the mouse over or clicking on words underlined in black. Tags at the bottom of each testimony allow users to find other testimonies relating to the same person, imprisonment center and region, and title and author of the music piece. When testimonies mention victims by name, we included these at the bottom and hyperlinked them to the Museum of Memory's *Víctimas* site (https://interactivos.museodelamemoria.cl/victimas/). An example is a testimony by Rosalía Martínez titled "Oración para que no me olvides" (Prayer So You Don't Forget Me). As this testimony mentions two victims, Cecilia Bojanic and Flavio Oyarzún, hyperlinks to pages from the *Víctimas* site with information about them are included.

The "Victims" section (https://www.cantoscautivos.org/en/victims.php) contains the photographs and names of twenty-eight people who were executed or disappeared. The total number of victims is several thousand, yet those featured on the website are only those mentioned in *Cantos Cautivos* testimonies. When users click on a photograph or name, a page containing a preview of testimonies relating to that victim and a hyperlink to that victim's page on the *Víctimas* site appears. The "Imprisonment Centres" section (https://www.cantoscautivos.org/en/centres.php) shows a list of the facilities relating to testimonies in the collection, along with their location on a map of Chile. Users can click on a location icon on the map or the name or region of an imprisonment center to navigate to a page containing a preview of testimonies relating to that facility.

Until June 2025, when the project stopped collecting materials, users could send texts, audio, videos, and images relating to music experiences under imprisonment through the "Share your Memories" page (https://www.cantoscautivos.org/en/collaboration.php). Materials sent through this page did not automatically appear on the platform. The team first needed to ensure that materials fitted with the project's remit and policies. We also edited and translated testimonies and lyrics, added tags, explanatory notes, images, audio, or videos, and if necessary, partially or fully anonymized the names of third persons mentioned in testimonies. As mentioned earlier, prior to publication, we always shared drafts with contributors to check that they approved our edits and allowed them to change or add anything they wished to.

Users can search testimony entries not only in the "Testimonies" section and via hyperlinks in the "Victims" and "Imprisonment Centres" sections but also through a search box found on each page of the website. The platform incorporates contextual searching, inspired by current standards of web-based search systems that increase result precision based on relevance to users. All search types return results in the form of previews, which contextualize the searched term via a brief excerpt of the testimony, the name and author of the music piece, the name of the person sharing the testimony, the place and date of the experience, and tags, capitalizing on the internet's capacity to link various types of information and create dynamic narratives.

The search system is built upon a database that uses a dictionary linking different categories of information to contexts, where a context could be the name of a victim, a testimony, a song, the name of an imprisonment center, the author, or a musical piece, or any text handled by the system. Each dictionary element, or token, is part of more complex elements that are categorized at different levels: a word is part of a testimony or song lyrics, a testimony is related to an imprisonment center or a victim, a victim is linked to other testimonies or centers, and so on.

This flexible structure allows the system to connect information in multiple and complex ways. The concept of context is enhanced with weights based on the accuracy of searches or assigned values (e.g., testimonies are shown before imprisonment centers). We opted for this approach because getting results in context is more appealing and useful than a mere list of links. Furthermore, as discussed in Chapter 3, the need for contextualizing information is vital, given the potential for audiences to have gaps in knowledge and attitudes of denial about the dictatorship.

Collaborations and Dissemination

From 2015 to 2025, the *Cantos Cautivos* project collaborated with culture and memory institutions and grassroots movements, including networks of ex-political detainees, memory sites, the Museum of Memory and Human Rights, UNESCO Santiago, the Ministry of Education, the Ministry of Cultures, Arts and Heritage, and the International Coalition of Sites of Conscience. Survivors were involved in various aspects beyond the production of archival content, from contributing to the planning of the platform design and sitting on the Advisory Board, to advising on partnerships and participating in public events and media interviews. This involvement sought enduring and equitable outcomes for all those involved in the project and ensured that the ways in which survivors' stories are presented are suitable.[13]

Most of the contributions during *Cantos Cautivos*'s first year were from ex-prisoners living in Chile's capital, who learned about the project through national media coverage. This showed that the information about the project did not effectively reach other areas of the country, where regional media outlets are often preferred. We subsequently engaged and organized events with communities outside Santiago (in the regions of Coquimbo, Valparaíso, O'Higgins, Maule, Biobío, Araucanía, Los Ríos, Los Lagos, and Magallanes) and in the diaspora (particularly in France, Sweden, and the U.K., where significant numbers of former political prisoners of the Pinochet regime still live).

Through time, the *Cantos Cautivos* project reached audiences beyond communities of people directly affected by human rights violations during the dictatorship. There was broad media coverage of the project coinciding with the launch of the first and second versions of the platform, anniversaries of the coup and Pinochet's death, the social revolt of 2019, the reconstruction of a piece composed at Chacabuco camp, and the featuring of *Cantos Cautivos* in a British Museum exhibition.[14] We are aware that the project has been used as pedagogical material in music, history, and education programs in universities and secondary schools in Chile and elsewhere in the Americas and Europe. As of mid-2025, a UNESCO project to create pedagogical guidance and classroom resources for human rights education, based on *Cantos Cautivos* materials, is being developed as part of UNESCO's Global Citizenship Education strategic area.

Social media channels were instrumental for expanding audiences. We generally published the same content on Facebook, Instagram, and X (in Spanish and English), adapting the format to each network's features. We used YouTube to store original audio and short-form (reel) video content produced or collected by the project team. For testimonies referring to pre-existing music pieces, we used videos found on various external YouTube channels. The primary website users and social media followers are based in the Americas (primarily Chile, Argentina, Colombia, Peru, Mexico, Brazil, and the U.S.) and Europe (mainly the U.K., Spain, Germany, and France). Except for the Facebook audience, approximately 70% of followers are under forty-five years of age, indicating that most of the project's audience was born after the Pinochet regime ended.

We focused social media activity on promoting materials from our platform. The main complexity was to convey the essence of the original testimony and music piece in a few images or short videos and brief copytext. In most publications, we sought not only to disseminate testimonies but also to provide contextualization. We used historical and recent images to make former political imprisonment centers known, aiming to promote testimonies from different regions of Chile. Examples are the posts below (see Figure 5.3), which highlight music activities on Christmas Day in Chacabuco camp in the Atacama Desert and in the Estadio Nacional in the southern city of Concepción.

Sometimes, we posted on dates marking significant Chilean and international anniversaries and have connected these dates with materials from our archive. The example below (see Figure 5.4), posted on International Women's Day, brings to light historical images of women protesting the repression, and four different stories of women who survived political imprisonment and torture.

We sought to use a visually striking and accessible style for our posts, combining our own aesthetic with formats that have trended on social media networks. For instance, using an existing format mimicking WhatsApp, available as a template on Jitter and made viral through various external accounts, we created two reels titled "Messages from Memory" (see Figure 5.5). In these, selected sentences from testimonies gradually appear as if they were WhatsApp messages, with the audio of the referred songs played in the background.[15]

Due to the high sensitivity about political repression, human rights, and memory matters, as well as the unpredictability of the social media environment, we defined parameters for the content, language, and style of our posts. We could express factual commentary and professional judgments on controversial political issues currently subject to political debate but avoided expressing personal opinions. As the project has a specific focus on music, the content we generated and shared on social media typically

FIGURE 5.3 Social media posts on prisoners' performances of the "Christmas Oratorio According to St. Luke" and Víctor Jara's "El cigarrito." Cantos Cautivos (@cantoscautivos), Facebook, December 25, 2021.

FIGURE 5.4 First two cards of carousel commemorating Women's International Day. Cantos Cautivos (@cantoscautivos). "Día Internacional de la Mujer Trabajadora," Instagram, March 8, 2023.

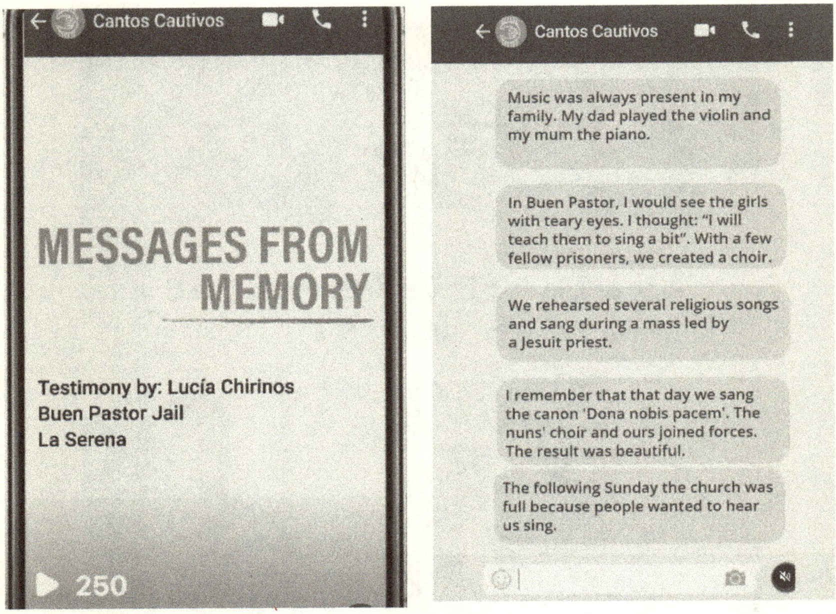

FIGURE 5.5 Cantos Cautivos (@cantoscautivos). "Messages from Memory," Instagram, September 10, 2021.

referred to or linked to music or musicians and may be related to contemporary developments in Chile and abroad. Having a structured approach to social media prevented crises and trolls—a significant possibility, given the recurrent social media commentary denying human rights violations under Pinochet and attacking memory initiatives.[16]

Beyond Research

The *Cantos Cautivos* project, as I conceived it, was in its beginnings a method to speed up the process of collecting research materials. Yet it soon became apparent that it also had civic and public roles, disseminating information and educating through the platform itself and its social media channels, media coverage, an exhibition and public events, and in classrooms. I would posit that *Cantos Cautivos* has contributed to addressing some shortcomings of knowledge about the Pinochet dictatorship and denials of human rights violations (as noted in Chapter 3).

As Christoph Bareither (2021) shows, sites of remembrance have emotional affordances, that is, the capacity to enable, prompt, and restrict particular emotional experiences. Through music and stories about music located in remembrance sites, the *Cantos Cautivos* project allows audiences the opportunity to sensitize to and comprehend a complex heritage, engaging with and interpreting the big Histories (with a capital "H") like the coup and human rights violations, as well as small, sometimes micro histories (with a small "h") of daily-life experiences. Given that many former political imprisonment centers of the dictatorship have been dismantled, destroyed, or repurposed, and are not open to the public, digital projects such as *Cantos Cautivos* have an important role in making these places known.

Like the choir Voces de la Rebeldía's self-reparation through singing, the efforts and materials of the *Cantos Cautivos* project are meaningful to those who directly suffered the consequences of the dictatorship. Relatives of victims have learned new aspects of their loved ones' lives. For example, Lilia Concha Carreño (daughter of Marcelo Concha Bascuñán) shared that it was reparatory to listen on the *Cantos Cautivos* platform to a recording of a speech her father gave during a performance of Los de Chacabuco. She was eight years of age when she last saw him as he was made to disappear forever. Her response below illustrates the power of sound and music in evoking memories and the contribution to moral reparation that archives can make:

> I had not heard this recording. You can't imagine how much it has shaken me. I am infinitely grateful for this work. This is an invaluable contribution to memory, to the role that culture must fulfill, but listening to the voice of my father is also a powerful contribution to reparation, even more so in those circumstances, it's the closest thing to bringing him back to me, it's the closest thing to trying to repair, if this could be repaired at all. Listening to this recording is the possibility of building memory.[17]

Coda

I see this book playing various roles. First, by using the framework of memory cacophony, it has exposed a discordant kaleidoscope of testimonial voices, emblematic and non-emblematic memories of musical happenings, music repertoire, and commemorative music initiatives relating to political imprisonment. This framework, which is both theoretical and methodological, has extended and contrasted dominant memory discourses of political imprisonment that focus on music as a tool for resistance against oppression and are commonly voiced by direct victims of the repression. Among other contributions, it has highlighted the richness of non-emblematic memories about music, music pieces, and musical happenings that may not have a particular purpose or use, are funny and witty, and come from divergent and purportedly unsuitable voices. Examining subtleties in memories of music experiences in prison challenges the notion that the worldviews of political prisoners and state agents have nothing in common, as does the knowledge that both have used music as a pastime and source of hope. Evidently, by no means am I overlooking that some state agents performed horrific abuses and violations against political adversaries. Music was part of that violence, and agents' ability to appreciate, write, and play music does not lessen the severity of their actions.

This book adds to ongoing debates about representation, inclusivity, extractivism, and co-production of research and public and community engagement. There is a tension between the growing scholarly interest in music in contexts of imprisonment, torture, and trauma, and, on the other hand, the risks of conducting and disseminating work on such topics. It is necessary to reflect on why we are conducting this type of research and to whom we hope to bequeath this work, ensuring that we create horizontal relationships with those who have had these experiences and that we, as researchers, act above and beyond individual and institutional research agendas.

I hope this book encourages reflections on what it may mean for researchers, on a personal level, to work on these topics, particularly concerning perpetrators of human rights crimes. When interviewing these

Music and Political Imprisonment in Pinochet's Chile. Katia Chornik, Oxford University Press.
 DOI: 10.1093/9780190052294.003.0007

individuals, I have endured fear, stress, disgust, and unwelcome comments, and some of those emotions have also been felt by the colleagues who supported me with this work. I shall not put myself through this experience again. Figures like Corbalán mean horror for society, and their crimes are facts that speak for themselves. Denunciations have been made by survivors, relatives of victims, and human rights organizations, and these crimes have been ratified by the courts and truth commissions. Other condemnations are those of silence, erasing these figures from history.

By publishing about these individuals, I am not employing the condemnation of silence, and as a result, I might be prone to criticism. Furthermore, by discussing Corbalán's music, the murderer's "human" side surfaces, a controversial matter appearing in various films and other cultural objects. A noted example is Miguel Littin's 1969 film *El chacal de Nahueltoro* (The Jackal of Nahueltoro), based on the real story of an illiterate farmer named Jorge del Carmen Valenzuela Torres, who murdered his partner and five of her children in Nahueltoro (southern Chile) in 1960. In prison, *El chacal* repented, and while waiting for his death sentence, he composed a song, made guitars, learned to read and write, and converted to Catholicism. After his radical transformation, public opinion of the time began viewing *El chacal* as a human being who deserved redemption before society and pardon by the authorities.[1] Regarding Corbalán and other perpetrators of human rights violations, I firmly oppose any suggestion that their "human" side should invite redemption or pardon, and I shall remind readers that my central reason for interviewing the ex-CNI agent was to elicit his memories of music in the imprisonment centers where he operated during the dictatorship. I did not achieve this aim, as he skirted my questions.

In revealing my conundrums, feelings, and unachieved objectives, as well as the topics Corbalán did want to talk about, this book contributes to the growing trend of publishing about research projects that did not go according to plan. Even in STEM disciplines, where the publication of null or negative results is not usually encouraged, there is an emerging movement geared at publishing research that did not yield expected results, which recognizes its intrinsic value for scientific progress.[2]

Finally, my work collecting testimonies, particularly through the *Cantos Cautivos* project, adds to the material legacy of the dictatorship. *Cantos Cautivos*'s long-term preservation will be key to ensuring access to future generations. More research is needed around the project's capacity to generate intergenerational dialogues and links between the past and present, and its effectiveness in tackling memory and human rights topics in educational settings. Another future avenue is to expand the project to research music in political imprisonment centers in other Latin American countries. Recent developments, like Javier Milei's rise to power in Argentina and his government's denials of consensuses on the legacy of the dictatorship, might suggest it is a timely moment for *Cantos Cautivos* to take on an international dimension.

Acknowledgments

First and foremost, I would like to thank everyone who participated in my research. Without people's generosity in sharing their experiences and music, this book would not exist. I hope I have done justice to their stories. My special gratitude goes to Luis Cifuentes Seves for galvanizing others to share valuable historical materials.

To Michelle Bachelet Jeria, endless thanks for her generous addition to this book. Her groundbreaking contributions to gender equality and commitment to human rights have been truly inspiring. I also wish to thank Diego Zurita and Claudia Farías for their crucial support.

I am grateful to Alejandro Madrid for encouraging me to write this book for OUP. His advice at various stages was most insightful, as were the comments of the anonymous reviewers. Former OUP editor Suzanne Ryan-Melamed played a crucial role in getting the ball rolling, and I thank her for being an early supporter of this project. I appreciate the diligence of Norman Hirschy, Anna-Lise Santella, Egle Zigaite, Alexandra Rouch, Loga Veera Puviyarasi and Swarna John, at the OUP and Newgen editorial teams, who took great care of my work.

I am indebted to colleagues, friends, and family for their expertise, thoughtfulness, and practical support. Huge thanks to the wonderful people behind the *Cantos Cautivos* project, who generously gave their time and dedication and made invaluable contributions. From the bottom of my heart, I thank Hernán Theiler for his work developing and updating the current platform; Jesse Freedman and Núria Bonet, for editorial and translation help; Roberto Riveros, for video content; Lisandro Concatti, for social media; and Héctor Muñoz Cantos, for conducting some interviews. I also thank Jesse for his sound feedback on draft chapters. I am grateful to the former Advisory Board—particularly Enrique Azúa, Aquiles Brayner, Caroline Bithell, Daniel Díaz Vera, Rosalía Martínez, and Alicia Salomone—and to the many interns and volunteers who contributed to the project in manifold ways.

I benefited from the expertise and practical support of Juan Pablo González and Daniel Party, and I thank them for their help with some of the most challenging aspects of the research. I wish to recognize others who readily shared their expertise: Fernanda Ortega, Makis Solomos, Marcos Stuardo, Lorena Gacitúa, Cristián Peña, Evelyn Hevia, Peter Kozak, Maxine Lowy, Paz Irarrázabal, Francisco Ugás, Gabriela Torres, and Agustín Gutiérrez.

The moral support, inspiration, encouragement, and practical help of my friends Gabriela Torres, Mauricio Weibel, Lieta Vivaldi, and Roger Golland were vital for finishing the book. I credit my partner James Noble for subliminally influencing my thinking around memory cacophonies when vowing for the importance of chaos. I am forever grateful to my daughter Gabriela Bergmann-Chornik for her wit, charm, positivity, and comments on passages of the book.

I am indebted to various institutions and people who granted permission to use images: Museum of Memory and Human Rights, National Library of Chile, CENFOTO Diego Portales University, Fundación de Documentación y Archivo Vicaría de la Solidaridad, Parque por la Paz Villa Grimaldi, José Giribás, Mario Patricio Cordero, Miguel Lawner, María Fedora Peña, and Adolfo Padilla. I could not have done without my dear friend Aitor Fernández, who kindly shared his expertise to help me select and prepare the images. I am very grateful to Mª Asun Fernández for her generous prayers.

Thanks also to the Museum of Memory for supporting the early stages of the *Cantos Cautivos* project—I fondly remember the attentiveness of Walter Roblero and José Manuel Rodríguez—and to the International Coalition of Sites of Conscience and the British Museum for fruitful collaborations.

I am indebted to the Leverhulme Trust for financing an invaluable three-year period to conduct research for this book. I am also grateful to Chile's Ministry of Cultures, Arts and Heritage, and the National Council of Culture and the Arts for additional funding for the *Cantos Cautivos* project.

And finally, many thanks to you, the readers, for choosing to read this book.

Notes

Preface

1. Beatriz Bataszew Contreras. 2016. "Today I Sing for the Sake of Singing (Hoy canto por cantar)," *Cantos Cautivos*. Accessed April 23, 2023. https://www.cantoscautivos.org/en/testimony.php?query=10685; Ana María Arenas. 2019. "The Clock (El reloj)," *Cantos Cautivos*. Accessed April 23, 2023. https://www.cantoscautivos.org/en/testimony.php?query=10826.

Introduction

1. *BBC Mundo*. 2019. "Protestas en Chile: 'Estamos en guerra', la frase de Piñera que se le volvió en contra en medio de las fuertes manifestaciones." October 22. Accessed February 17, 2021. https://www.bbc.com/mundo/noticias-america-latina-50139270.
2. *Meganoticias*. 2020. "'El derecho de vivir en paz': UDI utiliza letra de Víctor Jara en campaña por el Rechazo." September 7. Accessed May 2, 2021. https://www.meganoticias.cl/nacional/312836-udi-el-derecho-de-vivir-en-paz-victor-jara-rechazo-plebiscito-2020-apruebo-orx05.html. See the special issue on music and sound during the 2019–2020 social protests in Chile edited by Spencer and Bieletto (2020). See also the Museo del Estallido Social, https://museodelestallidosocial.org/.
3. This brief summary seeks to provide readers unfamiliar with Chilean history with a basic understanding of the period. My summary is based on articles from "Política y legislación," *Memoria Chilena*. Accessed January 2, 2023. http://www.memoriachilena.gob.cl/602/w3-propertyvalue-137801.html; "Historia política," *Biblioteca del Congreso Nacional de Chile*. Accessed July 7, 2023. https://www.bcn.cl/historiapolitica/; and on my own lived experience of the late dictatorship and post-dictatorship. For comprehensive histories of these periods, see Stern (2004; 2006; 2010), McSherry (2005), Aylwin (2008), Salazar and Pinto (2010), Corvalán Márquez (2016), and Gálvez Comandini (2021).
4. The Pinochet regime formalized its ideology of *chilenidad* through a Constitutional Act titled "Bases Esenciales de la Institucionalidad Chilena" (Ministerio de Justicia, Chile 1976), according to which the Armed Forces took power to fulfill their duty "to protect the Nation's sovereignty, and the superior and permanent values of *chilenidad*, [. . .] with the aim of preserving the historical and cultural identity of the Fatherland and reconstructing its spiritual and material greatness." The concept of *chilenidad* was previously used during the government of Pedro Aguirre Cerda (1938–1941). As seen in a short documentary titled *¿Qué es la chilenidad?* (What is Chileanness?), commissioned by Aguirre Cerda, the concept was employed to exalt the Armed Forces too (Taulis 1939).
5. This summary of popular music developments is based on my chapter on Chile for the *Encyclopedia of Latin American Popular Music* (Chornik 2013) as well as García (2013), McSherry (2015), entries from *Memoria Chilena* (https://www.memoriachilena.gob.cl/602/w3-propertyvalue-137787.html) and *MusicaPopular.cl* (edited by Rodrigo Alarcón et al., https://www.musicapopular.cl/). For other sources on popular music in Chile and Latin America, see Díaz-Inostroza (2016), González (2017), Rolle et al. (2009), Vila (2014), Torres (1980), Carrasco (1982), Rodríguez Musso (1988), and Pincheira (2023).
6. Díaz and González (2011) compile a "top forty" list of Chilean composers active in the twentieth century, while Bustos (2013) brings women composers' contribution to the fore. See also *Intérpretes y Conciertos Doctos en Chile* database, http://basedeconciertos.uahurtado.

cl/. European music nationalism, impressionism, and formalism were the most important influences on Chilean composers in the 1920–1950s, while serialism gained relevance in the late 1940s; music nationalism became a genuine music *americanismo* in the 1950–1960s (González 2018; Herrera Ortega 2017).

7. Manuel Délano. 2009. "El cantautor Víctor Jara recibirá un funeral 36 años después de su muerte," *El País*, November 28. Accessed January 31, 2022. https://elpais.com/internacional/2009/11/28/actualidad/1259362801_850215.html. When Víctor Jara was assassinated in September 1973, a semi-clandestine funeral was held by his widow Joan Jara and two other people. For studies on historical and current-day carnivals in Santiago and Valparaíso, see Ardito and Puentes (2021) and Bronfman and Álvarez (2022; 2023).
8. Benavente and Party (2022) have produced a rich and detailed musical and choreographic analysis of Los Diablos Rojos by examining seven songs by Víctor Jara that form part of their repertoire. Benavente and Party contend that, beyond social activism and memorialization, Los Diablos Rojos are professional artists with artistic motivations, preoccupations, and objectives.
9. For studies on Jorge Peña Hen, see Carlson (2014; 2016), Castillo Didier (2015), Politzer (2020), and Arraño Astete (2021). Peña Hen is widely credited with being the founder of the first children's orchestra in the Americas. To my knowledge, this claim has not been examined in the light of the long history of children making music in ensembles in the Americas, which goes back to at least colonial times.
10. According to Carlson (2016), Peña Hen's goals of providing access to music for children from all socio-economic backgrounds and making Western art music performance a path out of poverty were later espoused by Venezuela's El Sistema. Geoff Baker (2014) challenges widespread beliefs about El Sistema as a revolutionary social program achieving miraculous social transformations. As with El Sistema, to my knowledge, the social transformations claimed to have occurred because of Peña Hen's program have not been verified by thorough evaluations.
11. Emilio Contreras. 2023. *Biobíochile.cl.* 2023. "Liberan imágenes de biopic sobre Jorge Peña Hen, el 'padre' de las orquestas juveniles en Chile." January 11. Accessed August 15, 2023. https://www.biobiochile.cl/noticias/artes-y-cultura/musica/2023/01/11/liberan-imagenes-de-biopic-sobre-jorge-pena-hen-el-padre-de-las-orquestas-juveniles-en-chile.shtml; *Diario El Día.* 2023. "Más de dos mil personas ovacionaron concierto en homenaje a Jorge Peña en La Serena." July 23. Accessed August 15, 2023. https://www.diarioeldia.cl/region/2023/7/23/mas-de-dos-mil-personas-ovacionaron-concierto-en-homenaje-jorge-pena-en-la-serena-102839.html.
12. NGOs and former imprisonment centers have also collected testimonies of human rights violations occurring during the dictatorship: the Comité de Cooperación para la Paz en Chile, the Vicaría de la Solidaridad, Fundación de Ayuda Social de las Iglesias (FASIC), and Corporación Parque por la Paz Villa Grimaldi, among others.
13. The last census before the coup recorded that the total population of Chile was 8,884,768 inhabitants (Instituto Nacional de Estadísticas 1970: 1). For truth commissions in Chile, victims of serious human rights violations and victims of political violence refer to cases resulting in disappearances or deaths.
14. For the Council of Europe's Parliamentary Assembly (2012), an incarcerated person is a political prisoner when their imprisonment is being imposed in violation of freedom of thought, expression, or assembly.
15. The *Plan Condor* website contains a database of 805 confirmed cases of victims of transnational human rights violations in South America between 1969 and 1981 (https://plancondor.org/en/database-of-victims). Grace Livingstone (2018) has researched the links between the British government and the dictatorships of Argentina and Chile between 1973 and 1982, using declassified documents from British archives. See also Rory Cormac's (2020) study on British covert action in Latin America in the 1960s.
16. See "Nómina de Monumentos Nacionales desde 1925" (May 2020), downloadable from "Monumentos," *Consejo de Monumentos Nacionales de Chile.* Accessed April 21, 2021. https://www.monumentos.gob.cl/monumentos/monumentos-monumentos.
17. Consejo de Monumentos Nacionales de Chile. 2016. "Decreto N° 347 (2016)." Accessed January 18, 2021. https://www.monumentos.gob.cl/servicios/decretos/347_2016; Corporación Parque por la Paz Villa Grimaldi. 2016. "Indignación entre sobrevivientes ante el deterioro del ex cuartel Borgoño de la CNI," *Villa Grimaldi*, October 14. Accessed January 18, 2021. https://villagrimaldi.cl/noticias/indignacion-entre-sobrevivientes-ante-el-deterioro-del-ex-cuartel-borgono-de-la-cni/.

18. *Diario UChile*. 2019. "Venta del centro de tortura 'Venda Sexy' a inmobiliaria genera críticas de agrupaciones feministas." August 13. Accessed December 30, 2022. https://radio.uchile.cl/2019/08/13/venta-del-centro-de-tortura-venda-sexy-a-inmobiliaria-genera-criticas-de-agrupaciones-feministas/; Katia Chornik. 2019. "Sexual Violence, Torture and Chile's Struggle for Historical Memory." *OpenDemocracy*, October 7. Accessed April 22, 2021. https://www.opendemocracy.net/en/democraciaabierta/sale-of-venda-sexy-torture-centre-highlights-chiles-struggle-for-historical-memory-regarding-sexual-violence/; *El Mostrador*. 2024. "'Venda Sexy' como sitio de memoria: Estado concretó expropiación del centro de tortura y exterminio." July 3. Accessed July 7, 2024. https://www.elmostrador.cl/braga/2024/07/03/venda-sexy-como-sitio-de-memoria-estado-cocreto-expropiacion-del-centro-de-tortura-y-exterminio/.
19. For a description and analysis of the wide-ranging consequences of political imprisonment and torture, see also CNPPT (2004: 590–612). An interdisciplinary study conducted by medical doctors, clinical psychologists, and sociologists (Jorquera et al. 2020) examined the causes of death of survivors recognized by truth commissions up to June 2016, by which 9,152 people had died. The median age at death was sixty-eight years, and the main causes were malignant tumors and cardiovascular, respiratory, and digestive diseases (Jorquera et al. 2020: 1173).
20. José Santos Herceg (2019: 11) notes that most writings of ex-political prisoners of the Pinochet regime are unknown. They have not been published by major publishers, and their print runs are extremely limited. Even fewer have been translated, and those published abroad in other languages are not possible to find in Chile. Formats of these texts have included letters, diaries, novels, and short stories, using narrative forms such as epics, journeys to hell, melodramas, confessions, and hagiographies (Santos Herceg 2019: 16).
21. Rosalía Martínez. 2015. "Oración para que no me olvides," *Cantos Cautivos*. Accessed July 24, 2021. https://www.cantoscautivos.org/en/testimony.php?query=10759.
22. Although my work does not draw on behavioral neuroscience or experimental psychology, I wish to mention a body of research dealing with the relationships between music listening and emotions. Falcon et al. (2022) used functional magnetic resonance imaging (fMRI) to investigate the music-evoked (ML) recall of autobiographical memories (AM), suggesting a cortico-ponto-cerebellar network involved in the retrieval of those memories. Janata et al. (2007) coined the term music-evoked autobiographical memories (MEAMs) to refer to spontaneous episodic memories that are elicited during or after music listening. Juslin (2013) noted that when a MEAM occurs, the emotion associated with that memory is also triggered. Scholars have empirically demonstrated that memories evoked by music can generate more vivid and intense emotions than those evoked by other cues, such as famous faces (Belfi et al. 2016) and television (Jakubowski et al. 2021). The above studies are not specific to memories of traumatic events.
23. Society for Ethnomusicology. 2007. "Position Statement on Torture (February 2, 2007)." Accessed December 30, 2022. https://www.ethnomusicology.org/page/PS_Torture; American Musicological Society. 2008. "AMS Board Condemns the Use of Music in Physical or Psychological Torture," *AMS Newsletter* 38 (2), 5. Accessed December 30, 2022. https://cdn.ymaws.com/www.amsmusicology.org/resource/resmgr/files/Newsletter/AMSNewsletter-2008-8.pdf.
24. Carmona Estay et al.'s work won the Museum of Memory's 2021 thesis competition.
25. Illustrating this growth and diversification, Papaeti (2020) compares the number of submissions received for conferences she organized in 2013 (*Music in Detention* at the University of Goettingen) and in 2019 (*Soundscapes of Trauma: Music, Violence, Therapy* at Panteion University, Athens). While the first conference attracted forty proposals (one third of which dealt with Nazi camps), the second attracted eighty submissions (covering a wide range of new topics, geographical areas, and historical periods, with only three papers on Nazi camps). The 2021 international conference *Music, Sound, and Trauma: Interdisciplinary Perspectives* at Indiana University, featuring over ninety papers, is a further testament to the growing interest in the convergence of music, sound, and trauma. The conference included research on a wide range of settings, from wars, dictatorships, terrorist attacks, incarceration centers, migration, rituals, domestic violence, institutions, medical contexts, and classrooms, to opera, theater, and screen.
26. Cultural production dealing with trauma can, and often does, draw on memories of events that the creators themselves did not personally live—or prosthetic memory, borrowing Alison Landsberg's term (2004). An example is Ariel Dorfman's 1990 play *Death and the Maiden*, which

features Schubert's string quartet *Death and the Maiden* played during the torture of one of the characters in a political imprisonment center in (seemingly) Pinochet's Chile.

27. My research approach and methods were approved and overseen by the University of Manchester's Research Ethics Committee (UREC) and adhere to the ethics statements of the Society for Ethnomusicology and the British Forum for Ethnomusicology. A core exclusion criterion for interview participants was to present symptoms of PTSD or other conditions that could be aggravated by interviews. To further minimize risks, I targeted survivors with a previous record of participating in memory and human rights processes and public debates. Stipulated by Manchester's UREC as part of the ethical approval process, former agents are not referred to by their real name but by a pseudonym, except for Álvaro Corbalán, who is a well-known figure in Chile. All other research participants have been given the choice of being referred by their real name, a pseudonym, or "anonymous."
28. The editors of *The Routledge International Handbook of Perpetrator Studies* (Knittel and Goldberg 2020: 7–8) define a perpetrator as "any individual who contributes directly and substantially to genocide (or other mass atrocities)." They acknowledge that while their definition is informed by international criminal law's concepts of genocide, crimes against humanity, and war crimes, it is not strictly limited by legal taxonomies. Knittel and Goldberg's notion is broader than direct perpetrators: it includes categories of complicity yet excludes collective responsibility.
29. For a thought-provoking account of the differences in traditions, practices, politics of citation, and academic writing styles between the Global North and the Global South, see Alfredo González-Ruibal (2021).

Chapter 1

1. Two testimonies on the *Cantos Cautivos* platform—both on the same song—mention that when agents demanded political prisoners to sing, they meant they expected them to snitch on others; some inmates felt additional pressure to collaborate when music was played at blasting volume. Beatriz Bataszew Contreras. 2016. "Today I Sing for the Sake of Singing (Hoy canto por cantar)," *Cantos Cautivos*. Accessed April 23, 2023. https://www.cantoscautivos.org/en/testimony.php?query=10685; Ángeles Álvarez Cárdenas. 2015. "Today I Sing for the Sake of Singing (Hoy canto por cantar)," *Cantos Cautivos*. Accessed May 2, 2023. https://www.cantoscautivos.org/en/testimony.php?query=10772. In political imprisonment centers of the last dictatorship in Argentina, singing also meant grassing on someone—see Gilbert (2021).
2. Alongside France, the USA and Chile were among the main electro-torture users in 1945–1979, according to Rejali (2009: 168–69).
3. Yet in 1984, Patricio Manns composed the "Himno del FPMR" (Anthem of the Manuel Rodríguez Patriotic Front), despite having been a MIR militant until 1979 (Jordán 2010). Generally, militants' practice of aligning musical taste with political militancy became less strict after the coup. For instance, the anthem "El pueblo unido jamás será vencido" (The People United Will Never Be Defeated), written by Sergio Ortega before the coup and popularized by Quilapayún, became relevant to MIR militants, who previously did not identify with songs of the Unidad Popular. "El pueblo unido jamás será vencido" has been sung around the world till the present day in many languages.
4. An allegedly edited recording of Orquesta Cubanacán's performance of "El africano" at the 1986 Festival de Viña del Mar is found at https://www.youtube.com/watch?v=CZDNbXLPwGc. Accessed April 8, 2023. The practice of audiences singing "que se vaya Pinochet" in the chorus continued beyond the dictatorship, as experienced by Wilfrido Vargas and his band when they played "El africano" at the Festival de Viña del Mar in 1994. Camilo Egaña. 2019. "'El Africano', la canción que sedujo a Wilfrido Vargas en un taxi," *CNN*. Accessed April 22, 2023. https://cnnespanol.cnn.com/video/wilfrido-vargas-cancion-camilo-sot/.
5. Tallerweblog (@tallerweblog), "Roberto Carlos y Augusto Pinochet", YouTube, January 14, 2014. Accessed January 6, 2023. https://www.youtube.com/watch?v=Esss7EOAOQo.

6. Mercedes Sosa (1935–2009), known as "the voice of the voiceless," was a celebrated Argentine singer and political activist who rose to fame in the 1960s. Sosa suffered harassment and death threats during the last dictatorship in Argentina, which forced her to flee to Europe. She returned to Argentina in 1982. For studies on Sosa, see Scruggs (2016) and Molinero and Vila (2014).
7. Subsequently, Jiménez remembered this episode in a book titled *Antes de perder la memoria*, jointly written with her friend Teresa Izquierdo (Jiménez and Izquierdo 2015: 67–68). Montes Capó (2022) shows how in *Antes de perder la memoria*, memory becomes a represented space in which music is at once an art, a refuge and a symbol of protection.
8. Cat Stevens / Yusuf Islam did not write "Morning has broken" but reinterpreted a traditional hymn based on a nineteenth-century Gaelic melody, with words by Eleanor Farjeon.
9. Torments and unlawful harassment carry lower prison sentences (from 541 days to five years) than torture and other cruel, inhuman, and degrading treatment (from five years and one day to ten years). Torture and other cruel, inhuman, and degrading treatment were added to the Penal Code as punishable acts through law 20968. Ministerio de Justicia y Derechos Humanos. 2016. "Tipifica delitos de tortura y de tratos crueles, inhumanos y degradantes." Accessed April 6, 2023. https://www.leychile.cl/Navegar?idNorma=1096847. I thank lawyer Francisco Ugás for explaining the different terminologies and sentences used in human rights court cases.
10. Museo de la Memoria y los Derechos Humanos. "Listado de Sentencias Judiciales," *Justicia*. Accessed May 15, 2025. http://interactivos.museodelamemoria.cl/justicia/listadosentencias.php.
11. Examples of this focus are articles, chapters, and special issues such as Birch (2021), Grant (2014; 2020), Friedson (2019), Grant and Papaeti (2013a; 2013b), Johnson and Cloonan (2009), and Cusick (2006; 2008).

Chapter 2

1. *Diario UChile*. 2023. "Corte Suprema manda a la cárcel a 59 ex agentes DINA por la Operación Colombo," March 3. Accessed April 13. https://radio.uchile.cl/2023/03/03/corte-suprema-manda-a-la-carcel-a-56-ex-agentes-dina-por-la-operacion-colombo/. In 2005, Pinochet was charged in connection with Operation Colombo and immediately put under house arrest.
2. For a media piece on *café con piernas*, see John Bartlett. 2023. "'Coffee with Legs: Inside Chile's Risqué and Antiquated Café Culture", *The Guardian*, April 11. Accessed April 11, 2023. https://www.theguardian.com/world/2023/apr/11/coffee-with-legs-chile-cafe-culture.
3. The strategic use of pronouns by interviewees was also observed by Hettie Malcomson (2019: 349) in her study of Mexican narco rap. She notes that all her interviewees, including a former cartel commander and several rappers who had dealt and smuggled drugs, referred to narcos as "they" rather than "we." For Malcomson, this practice creates a distance between the narcos and the speaker; narcos are positioned as the morally flawed "them," in opposition to a more righteous "us."
4. Among other crimes, Corbalán is convicted for his role in Operation Albania (a massacre of twelve FPMR members), the murders of José Carrasco, Tucapel Jiménez, Juan Alegría, and Paulina Aguirre Tobar, and the kidnapping of the last five detained-disappeared of the dictatorship.
5. If Corbalán's claim was correct, the last interview he had prior to mine may have been the interview with the journalist Raquel Correa (2000). That interview mentions an anthem Corbalán composed for the Army's Intelligence School and two cassettes of his music, *Sones militares en tiempo de libertad* (recorded by the Military Academy band) and *Sentimientos de soldado* (recorded by Horacio Saavedra's orchestra, which has regularly performed at Festival de Viña del Mar).
6. Tiltil is known for being the site where, at the time of the War of Independence in the 1810s, the caudillo Manuel Rodríguez Erdoíza was assassinated after being imprisoned by order of Bernardo O'Higgins. O'Higgins was one of the commanders of the military forces that freed Chile from Spanish rule and headed the state and government as Supreme Director of Chile in 1817–1823.

7. See special issue of the *Memory Studies* journal edited by Jonathan Dunnage (2010), devoted to the transmission of memories relating to perpetrators in the context of the Second World War and the Holocaust, the Algerian War of Independence, the left-wing German terrorist movement, and the East German secret police.
8. *The Clinic*. 2013. "AUDIO: El cancionero del ex agente de la CNI Álvaro Corbalán en Punta Peuco," September 9. Accessed July 24, 2021. https://www.theclinic.cl/2013/09/09/audio-el-cancionero-del-ex-agente-de-la-cni-alvaro-corbalan-en-punta-peuco/; Alberto Mayol, Miguel Farías, and Carlos Azócar, presenters. 2015. "Música y política: Álvaro Corbalán, músico, ex CNI y reo," *Radio Usach*, November 26. Música y Política (@MusicayPolitica). "Música y Política: Álvaro Corbalán músico, ex CNI y reo | 26 de noviembre 2015," YouTube, March 27, 2018. Accessed July 24, 2021. https://www.youtube.com/watch?v=ZvJOzB9YcLc.
9. Catalina Batarce. 2018. "'Se me olvidó todo y lo que no . . . también': El mensaje de Corbalán a 45 años del Golpe Militar," *La Tercera*, September 12. Accessed July 24, 2021. https://www.latercera.com/nacional/noticia/se-me-olvido-lo-no-tambien-mensaje-corbalan-45-anos-del-golpe-militar/316829/; Sebastián Mora. 2018. "Álvaro Corbalán envía carta desde la cárcel: 'Se me olvidó todo y lo que no . . . también'", *Televisión Nacional de Chile*, September 12. Accessed March 3, 2022. https://www.24horas.cl/nacional/alvaro-corbalan-envia-carta-desde-la-carcel-se-me-olvido-todo-y-lo-que-no-tambien-2815939.
10. The question of the value of music produced by perpetrators of human rights violations can be linked to debates on the legitimacy of ethical evaluations of art. The most radical views of these debates are moralism (proposing a direct relationship between artistic and moral excellence) and autonomism (denying any connection between art and morality), with various moderate stances in between. In considering Corbalán's music and lyrics, I position myself as a moderate moralist, adhering to Noël Carroll's (1996: 229) view that moral commentary, along with formal comment, is natural and appropriate for certain genres, and it may feature in evaluations of narrative artworks. For an overview of the various views on ethical criticism of art, see Peek (1995).
11. Eduardo Ojeda. 2015. "National Anthem of Chile," *Cantos Cautivos*. Accessed November 5, 2021. https://www.cantoscautivos.org/en/testimony.php?query=10761; Sergio Vesely. 2015. "Song of the Seed and the Plant (Canción de la semilla y la planta)," *Cantos Cautivos*. Accessed March 14, 2021. https://www.cantoscautivos.org/en/testimony.php?query=10754.
12. This brief biography of Corbalán is based on information he provided during our meetings, complemented by Lagos's (2014) contribution to the *Casos de la Vicaría* investigative journalism project. See Salazar (2012) and Insunza and Ortega (2017) for in-depth studies of the CNI and the long list of crimes in which Corbalán participated.
13. For a discussion of music in the context of no-touch torture, see Cusick (2006). *Kubark* methods were used in Project X (1966–1991), a U.S. Army's secret program that developed a counter-insurgency curriculum based on seven Spanish-language training handbooks, targeting South American countries (McCoy 2006: 86).
14. Ignacio Vidaurrázaga Manríquez. 2016. "Crónica personal y aún tibia: el retorno al ex Cuartel Borgoño," *Piensa Chile*, June 10. Accessed February 2, 2023. https://piensachile.com/2016/06/10/cronica-personal-aun-tibia-retorno-al-ex-cuartel-borgono/.
15. *ADN Radio*. 2018. "El día que la Gaviota de Plata se la dieron a un agente de la CNI," February 22. Accessed February 6, 2021. https://www.adnradio.cl/tiempo-libre/2018/02/22/el-dia-que-la-gaviota-de-plata-se-la-dieron-a-un-agente-de-la-cni-3714870.html. Journalists Daniel Campusano, Macarena Chinni, Constanza González, and Felipe Robledo's book *Álvaro Corbalán: el dueño de la noche* (2015) deals with Corbalán's relationships with figures of the Festival de Viña del Mar and television circles in the 1980s. The book is based on fifty-four testimonies of musicians, presenters, and producers who met Corbalán, and is mainly anecdotal.
16. Carolina Mardones. 2016. "CIA asegura que Corbalán ideó plan para asesinar a Aylwin y evitar salida de Pinochet," *BiobíoChile*, April 20. Accessed June 6, 2020. https://www.biobiochile.cl/noticias/2016/04/20/cia-asegura-que-corbalan-ideo-plan-para-asesinar-a-aylwin-y-evitar-salida-de-pinochet.shtml; Biblioteca del Congreso Nacional de Chile. [no date]. "Partidos, movimientos y coaliciones: Avanzada Nacional." Accessed June 6, 2020. https://www.bcn.cl/historiapolitica/partidos_politicos/wiki/Avanzada_Nacional.
17. FOI submitted on December 3, 2019, and replied on December 23, 2019. Museo de la Memoria y los Derechos Humanos. *Justicia*. Accessed May 13, 2023. http://interactivos.museodelamemoria.cl/justicia/listadocondenados.php. See also the summary of some of Corbalán's criminal convictions published by the Centro de Investigación Periodística (CIPER): https://ciperchile.cl/wp-content/uploads/%C3%81lvaro-Julio-Corbal%C3%A1n-Castilla..pdf. Accessed January 18, 2021.

18. Chile's National Institute for Human Rights has been critical of the privileges of Punta Peuco prisoners. *Cooperativa.cl.* 2015. "Punta Peuco: Los 'privilegios' que cuestiona el INDH," September 12. Accessed February 2, 2020. https://www.cooperativa.cl/noticias/pais/dd-hh/punta-peuco-los-privilegios-que-cuestiona-el-indh/2015-09-12/104121.html.
19. *24 Horas.* 2015. "Informe Especial develó los secretos que Álvaro Corbalán escondía en su celda," July 16. Accessed May 30, 2021. https://www.24horas.cl/videos/informe-especial-develo-los-secretos-que-alvaro-corbalan-escondia-en-su-celda-1726865; Verónica Torres. 2012. "Punta Peuco I: la fallida operación de inteligencia de Álvaro Corbalán," *CIPER*, April 18. Accessed May 30, 2021. https://www.ciperchile.cl/2012/04/18/punta-peuco-i-la-fallida-operacion-de-inteligencia-de-alvaro-corbalan/; María José Villarroel. 2020. "Denuncian supuesto acoso de Álvaro Corbalán por mensajes de WhatsApp a funcionaria de Punta Peuco," *Biobiochile.cl*, July 3. Accessed June 2, 2021. https://www.biobiochile.cl/noticias/nacional/region-metropolitana/2020/07/03/denuncian-supuesto-acoso-alvaro-corbalan-mensajes-whatsapp-funcionaria-punta-peuco.shtml.
20. In Spanish, the preposition *en* ("in" in English) is used after the verb "to sit" (*sentarse en la cama*), allowing the double meaning used by Corbalán.
21. "My Way" was popularized by Frank Sinatra in 1969 and is based on the 1976 French song "Comme d'habitude" by Claude François and Jacques Revaux, with new English lyrics by Paul Anka. A version in Spanish was first recorded by the Argentine singer Estela Raval in 1970.
22. In September 2018 (four years after my interviews with him), Corbalán sent a version of this essay to *La Tercera* newspaper, which published a summary and a selection of quotations of the text. These were subsequently republished by other media outlets, including *CNN Chile*, *Televisión Nacional de Chile*, *El Ciudadano*, and *El Desconcierto*.
23. The so-called Theory of the Two Demons (*teoría de los dos demonios*) originated during the transition to democracy in Argentina under the government of Raúl Alfonsín and is often mentioned in the press and political discourses. For an in-depth discussion of the symbolism of this concept, see Franco (2014).
24. Conferencia Episcopal de Chile. 2018. "Comunicado Arzobispado de Santiago. 'Por el bien de la Iglesia', el Papa dimitió del estado del clerical a Cristián Precht." September 15. Accessed July 10, 2022. http://www.iglesia.cl/36798-por-el-bien-de-la-iglesia-el-papa-dimitio-del-estado-del-clerical-a-cristian-precht.html; Felipe Delgado. 2022. "Justicia rechaza solicitud para sobreseer al exsacerdote Cristián Precht por abusos sexuales," *BiobíoChile*, September 29. Accessed October 4, 2022. https://www.biobiochile.cl/noticias/nacional/region-metropolitana/2022/09/29/justicia-rechaza-solicitud-para-sobreeser-al-exsacerdote-cristian-precht-por-abusos-sexuales.shtml.
25. *Cooperativa.* 2011. "Álvaro Corbalán compuso canción por la 'unidad nacional'," July 1. Accessed July 10, 2022. https://www.cooperativa.cl/noticias/pais/dd-hh/alvaro-corbalan-compuso-canc ion-por-la-unidad-nacional/2011-07-01/171035.html.
26. 1980s interview published by *Revista Cosas* cited in *The Clinic.* 2013. "AUDIO: El cancionero del ex agente de la CNI Álvaro Corbalán en Punta Peuco," September 9. Accessed July 25, 2022. https://www.theclinic.cl/2013/09/09/audio-el-cancionero-del-ex-agente-de-la-cni-alvaro-corbalan-en-punta-peuco/; *El Mostrador.* 2015. "Corporación 11 de Septiembre recuerda el Golpe de Estado y distingue al 'Mamo' Contreras por 'por su efectivo combate al terrorismo marxista,'" September 13. Accessed July 25, 2022. https://www.elmostrador.cl/noticias/pais/2015/09/13/corporacion-11-de-septiembre-recuerda-el-golpe-de-estado-y-distingue-al-mamo-contreras-por-por-su-efectivo-combate-al-terrorismo-marxista/; *La Información.* 2019. "La noche que Jesús Quintero entrevistó a Paco de Lucía," September 19. Accessed July 30, 2022. https://web.archive.org/web/20211122102251/https:/www.lainformacion.com/233grados/la-noche-que-jesus-quintero-entrevisto-a-paco-de-lucia/6511908/; Alberto González. 2023. "El obituario de Tito Fernández que confirma polémica amistad con Álvaro Corbalán," *BiobíoChile*, February 15. Accessed February 20, 2023. https://www.biobiochile.cl/especial/bbcl-investiga/noticias/de-pasillo/2023/02/15/el-obituario-de-tito-fernandez-que-confirma-polemica-amis tad-con-alvaro-corbalan.shtml.
27. kaptah62 (@kaptah62). "cancion de alvaro corbalan" [*sic*], YouTube, December 28, 2008. Accessed July 19, 2022. https://www.youtube.com/watch?v=CMx3mKRq4jg.
28. Gabriela Durand. 2015. "To Be Seventeen Again (Volver a los diecisiete)," *Cantos Cautivos.* Accessed May 6, 2022. https://www.cantoscautivos.org/en/testimony.php?query=10738.
29. Gabriela Durand. 2015. "To Be Seventeen Again (Volver a los diecisiete)," *Cantos Cautivos.* Accessed May 6, 2022. https://www.cantoscautivos.org/en/testimony.php?query=10738. It is

not possible to know if Corbalán had a role in the agents' decision to use "Volver a los diecisiete" to torment the imprisoned, yet he expressed aversion to Violeta Parra at least on one occasion. During the launch of his book *Anécdotas de mi General*, Corbalán stated: "From this military mausoleum in Punta Peuco, of living dead already forgotten, from my cell-bedroom, with all the technical problems of a modest disposable radio that is lower quality than Violeta Parra's shampoo [laughter from the audience], I beg you to excuse the quality of the sound." kaptah62 (@kaptah62). "cancion de alvaro corbalan" [*sic*], YouTube, December 28, 2008. Accessed July 19, 2022. https://www.youtube.com/watch?v=CMx3mKRq4jg, 3:16–3:52. Corbalán is likely to be drawing on decades-old smears that Violeta Parra did not wash her hair.

30. YouTube. [no date]. "Community Guidelines." Accessed August 18, 2022. https://www.youtube.com/howyoutubeworks/policies/community-guidelines/. Principle VIII of The Inter-American Commission on Human Rights' "Principles Related to the Conditions of Deprivation of Liberty" (2008: 159) states: "Persons deprived of liberty shall enjoy the same rights recognized to every other person by domestic law and international human rights law, except for those rights which exercise is temporarily limited or restricted by law and for reasons inherent to their condition as persons deprived of liberty." Accessed September 9, 2022. https://www.oas.org/en/iachr/mandate/Basics/principles-best-practices-protection-persons-deprived-liberty-americas.pdf; Ministerio de Justicia. 2020. "Reglamento de establecimientos penitenciarios." Accessed August 18, 2022. https://www.bcn.cl/leychile/navegar?idNorma=123280&idVersion=2020-09-17.

Chapter 3

1. See also the collection of objects created by political prisoners held by the Museo de la Memoria y los Derechos Humanos. "Archivo de Fondos y Colecciones." Accessed December 9, 2022. http://archivomuseodelamemoria.cl/index.php/3499;term/browseTerm.
2. Rosalía Martínez. 2015. "Oración para que no me olvides," *Cantos Cautivos*. Accessed July 24, 2021. https://www.cantoscautivos.org/en/testimony.php?query=10759.
3. "Home," *Julio Iglesias—Official Website*. Accessed October 23, 2022. https://www.julioiglesias.com/pagina.php?cs_id_pagina=5&cs_id_contenido=62. Jesús Quintero's 1987 interview with Julio Iglesias is available at TercerCanal (@tercercanal6242). "Julio Iglesias entrevistado por Jesús Quintero," YouTube, October 7, 2016. Accessed November 2, 2019. https://www.youtube.com/watch?v=x16QuOfmGqQ, 1:37–2:00.
4. Two songs by Redolés, "¿Quién mató a Gaete?" (1996, Who Killed Gaete?) and "Triste funcionario policial" (1999, Sad Police Officer), explicitly deal with torture experiences.
5. It is possible that political prisoners' views on Iglesias were also tainted by rumors about his and his family's support for the Franco regime, which still exist—see, for instance, Jesús Mariñas. 2019. "Julio Iglesias y el retrato de Franco en el cabecero de su cama," *La Razón*, October 28. Accessed December 21, 2022. https://www.larazon.es/gente/julio-iglesias-y-el-retrato-de-franco-en-el-cabecero-de-su-cama-LG25459112/.
6. José Vásquez. 2015. "Julio Iglesias: 'Ya no sé escribir, mi árbol está absolutamente seco,'" *El Mercurio*, October 18, C23.
7. Luis Madariaga. 2016. "Ode to Joy (Himno a la alegría)," *Cantos Cautivos*. Accessed November 5, 2022. https://www.cantoscautivos.org/en/testimony.php?query=10663.
8. Carmen Espinoza and César Montiel, interview by the author, Viña del Mar, April 2022. "Colonia Dignidad | Testimonio de Carmen Espinoza y César Montiel," *Cantos Cautivos*. Accessed December 16, 2022. https://www.youtube.com/watch?v=h4veS_fWsbY. See also Carmen Espinoza Alegría. 2022. "Under my Skin (A flor de piel)," *Cantos Cautivos*. Accessed December 15, 2022. https://www.cantoscautivos.org/en/testimony.php?query=10838; César Montiel. 2022. "Under my Skin (A flor de piel)," *Cantos Cautivos*. Accessed December 15, 2022. https://www.cantoscautivos.org/en/testimony.php?query=10840. A testimony by Alejandra Holzapfel collected by Nancy Guzmán Jasmen (2014: 73) briefly mentions that Iglesias's 1977 song "Soy un truhan, soy un señor" (I Am a Knave, I Am a Sir) was played on record at Venda Sexy at ear-splitting volume during torture sessions.
9. See Gehrta et al. (2018) and other psychology studies cited in the Introduction.

10. The report of the CNPPT (2004) contains numerous mentions of guards' violent behavior toward political detainees. It should be noted that the term "guard" can sometimes be used to play down responsibilities, as in the case of a former DINA agent I interviewed in 2012, who self-identified as a guard (see Chapter 2).
11. Ignacio Puelma. 2015. "Se escucha muy lejos (You Hear It from Far Away)," *Cantos Cautivos*. Accessed November 30, 2022. https://www.cantoscautivos.org/en/testimony.php?query=10698.
12. Sergio Vesely. 2015. "King Ñaca Ñaca (El rey Ñaca Ñaca)," *Cantos Cautivos*. Accessed November 30, 2022. https://www.cantoscautivos.org/en/testimony.php?query=10753.
13. Renato Alvarado. 2020. "King Ñaca Ñaca (El rey Ñaca Ñaca)," *Cantos Cautivos*. Accessed December 10, 2022. https://www.cantoscautivos.org/en/testimony.php?query=10836.
14. The translated lyrics of the "brave soldiers" stanza are: "Your names, brave soldiers / who have been Chile's mainstay / they are engraved in our chests / our children will know them as well. / May they be the death cry / that comes out when we march to the fight / that comes out when we march to the fight / and ringing in the mouth of the strong / they always make the tyrant tremble. / And ringing in the mouth of the strong / they always make the tyrant tremble."
15. In 1980, the Pinochet regime went on to publish an official decree, number 6476, which specified that the lyrics must strictly adhere to the original 1847 version and included specific instructions on tonality (C major), metronome markings (126 / 108 / 126), and the three-times repetition of the line "or the refuge from oppression." Ministerio de Educación Pública. 1980. "Establece texto oficial de la letra y música de la Canción Nacional de Chile," *Ley Chile*. Accessed November 20, 2022. http://www.leychile.cl/Navegar?idNorma=214629&idParte=&idVersion=1980-08-21. When democracy was restored in 1990, the new government published an official decree, number 260, shortening the lyrics and leaving the "brave soldiers" stanza out. Ministerio del Interior. 1990. "Establece estrofas del Himno Nacional, en actos o ceremonias," *Ley Chile*. Accessed November 20, 2022. https://www.bcn.cl/leychile/navegar?idNorma=11640. For a study on the changes to the music and text of the Chilean National Anthem, see Vega (2000).
16. Sergio Vesely. 2015. "National Anthem of Chile," *Cantos Cautivos*. Accessed November 27, 2022.https://www.cantoscautivos.org/en/testimony.php?query=10755.
17. For an outline of the notion of *chilenidad*, see the Introduction.
18. Similarly, a young man called Manuel Segundo Palma Henríquez was arrested and killed by the military in December 1973 for the sole act of singing at the top of his lungs. This case was included in the report of an internal investigation into human rights commissioned in 1976 by the Pinochet regime itself (González 2013).
19. Lucía Chirinos. 2016. "We Shall Prevail (Venceremos)," *Cantos Cautivos*. Accessed November 19, 2022. https://www.cantoscautivos.org/en/testimony.php?query=10690.
20. "Venceremos" was written by Sergio Ortega and Claudio Iturra for the election campaign of Salvador Allende. The words of "L'Internationale" were written by Eugène Pottier during the Paris Commune and later set to music by Pierre Degeyter; "L'Internationale" was the national anthem of the Soviet Union until 1944 and was also adopted worldwide by communist, socialist, social democrat, and anarchist movements. The "Himno de Carabineros de Chile," written by Arturo Arancibia and Francisco Flores, has been in use by the Chilean Police since the late 1920s; an entire stanza of the Police Anthem is directly quoted in LasTesis's "Un violador en tu camino" (A rapist in your path), an anthem against sexual violence that became viral around the world in 2019.
21. Jorge Montealegre Iturra. 2015. "Return, Return (Volver, volver)," *Cantos Cautivos*. Accessed December 5, 2022. https://www.cantoscautivos.org/en/testimony.php?query=10673.
22. Personal email communication with Jorge Montealegre Iturra, December 2022.
23. Luis Cifuentes Seves. 2014. "Lucky Devil (El suertúo)," *Cantos Cautivos*. Accessed December 5, 2022. https://www.cantoscautivos.org/en/testimony.php?query=10654. Jesse Freedman (2022) refers to the lyrics and recording of "El puntúo" and Cifuentes's testimony about this song, found in Luis Cifuentes Seves. 2014. "A Cocky Fellow (El puntúo)," *Cantos Cautivos*. Accessed December 6, 2022. https://www.cantoscautivos.org/en/testimony.php?query=10655. Another *cueca* with humorous and coded lyrics written in Chacabuco over pre-existing lyrics is "Cueca del Filistoque." The piece was not recorded by Chacabuco prisoners in 1974. Yet in 2018, it was reconstructed and recorded by the group Macomba. See Víctor Canto Fuenzalida. 2014. "Filistoque's Cueca (Cueca del Filistoque)," *Cantos Cautivos*. Accessed December 6, 2022. https://www.cantoscautivos.org/en/testimony.php?query=10649.

24. In 1944, before an inspection of the Red Cross, the SS initiated a "beautification" campaign and promoted cultural activities. The SS organized a performance of *Brundibár* for the inspectors and featured it in the propaganda film *Theresienstadt: ein Dokumentarfilm aus dem jüdischen Siedlungsgebiet* (*Theresienstadt: A Documentary Film from the Jewish Settlement Area*). See Rothkirchen (2006: 257) and Joseph Tolz, "Brundibár," *Music and the Holocaust*. Accessed July 2, 2023. https://holocaustmusic.ort.org/places/theresienstadt/brundibar/.

Chapter 4

1. *Emol*. 2013. "Jueces piden perdón por sus "acciones y omisiones" durante la dictadura militar," September 11. Accessed January 28, 2022. http://www.emol.com/noticias/nacional/2013/09/04/618067/jueces-piden-perdon-por-el-rol-que-cumplieron-durante-el-regimen-militar.html; *El Mostrador*. 2013. "Piñera reafirma críticas a la prensa y al Poder Judicial por su actuación durante la dictadura militar," August 31. Accessed January 5, 2022. http://www.elmostrador.cl/noticias/pais/2013/08/31/pinera-reafirma-criticas-a-la-prensa-y-al-poder-judicial-por-su-actuacion-durante-la-dictadura-militar. *Cooperativa*. 2013. "Tohá exigió que Carabineros explique retiro de lienzos sobre detenidos desaparecidos," September 9. Accessed January 5, 2022. http://www.cooperativa.cl/noticias/pais/dd-hh/toha-exigio-que-carabineros-explique-retiro-de-lienzos-sobre-detenidos-desaparecidos/2013-09-09/081412.html.
2. Recollections about the start date of the Tres Álamos choir vary. Jiménez assures it began in April 1976, whereas the *Voces de la Rebeldía* website states it began in late 1975. "Historia," *Voces de la Rebeldía*. Accessed July 21, 2023. https://vocesdelarebeldia.cl/.
3. Bithell's (2014: 222) outline of the main features of community choirs is focused on U.K. choirs. As she indicates, there is no universal definition of community choirs. In Chile, some choirs that define themselves as community choirs, such as the Coro Comunitario de Valparaíso, sing repertoire of the Western classical music tradition.
4. Chapter III of the Second Report on the Situation of Human Rights in Chile of the Inter-American Commission on Human Rights (1976) details the finding of the OAS visit to Tres Álamos camp. Visits to Chile were attempted by the UN Commission on Human Rights' Working Group on Chile (appointed in early 1975), yet the Pinochet administration denied permission and did not cooperate with the investigation. The Inter-American Commission on Human Rights (1976) regrets: "Our working plans have been seriously perturbed by the attitude adopted by the Government of Chile upon receiving our requests for reports. Some requests—a minority of them—have received incomplete replies; most of them, and very important ones, have received no reply whatsoever." Various strategies used by Pinochet's government to interfere with the UN investigation are found in unpublished documents of Chilean Embassy in the UN (1975–1979), housed at the Foreign Affairs Ministry.
5. For Montealegre Iturra (2013: 206–12), communal resilience emerged when political prisoners recognized a common socio-cultural heritage, valued creativity, and developed playful and humorous expressions within a mourning process. The range of positive outcomes described by Jiménez recalls the subversion of the logic of concentration camps noted by de Carvalho (2020: 7) in relation to the *Brundibár* opera at Terezín, performed in a setting of violence, intolerance, and death.
6. Sara De Witt. 2014. "Candombe for José (Candombe para José)," *Cantos Cautivos*. Accessed July 21, 2023. https://www.cantoscautivos.org/en/testimony.php?query=10666.
7. Sibila Sotomayor, one of the four members of LasTesis, spoke on behalf of the collective. The video message was posted on Voces de la Rebeldía (@corovocesdelarebeldia), Instagram, December 20, 2022. Accessed August 7, 2023. https://www.instagram.com/p/CmXp42pDGZX/. In 2020, *Times Magazine* included LasTesis in their 2020 list of the 100 most influential people.
8. Carlos Muñoz. 2015. "The Paper Boat (El barco de papel)," *Cantos Cautivos*. Accessed August 3, 2023. https://www.cantoscautivos.org/en/testimony.php?query=10680. Inspired by the Tres Álamos choir's practice of modifying song lyrics, Cabaluz Gómez and Sosa Valenzuela (2021) devised a classroom activity in which secondary school pupils are asked to collectively create new lyrics dealing with current-day social topics, using music from pre-existing songs. Shirli Gilbert (2005) shows that the practice of modifying song lyrics was widespread in Third Reich camps too. Outside incarceration settings, this practice is often found in football stadiums—see

Katia Chornik. 2018. "How a Cuban Song Became a Football Favourite," *The Economist 1834*, June 14. Accessed August 3, 2023. https://www.economist.com/1843/2018/06/14/how-a-cuban-song-became-a-football-favourite.

9. See Voces de la Rebeldía's website https://vocesdelarebeldia.cl/ and social media accounts https://www.instagram.com/corovocesdelarebeldia/ and https://www.facebook.com/profile.php?id=100063651540617. Marianne Hirsch's first coined the notion of "postmemory" in the early 1990s in relation to Holocaust memories, and later typified it as familial, affiliative, and connective postmemories. The concept has been widely influential and has been applied to cases studies across time and place. As Alloa et al. (2015: 2) note, the emergence of the postmemory notion ties in with a tendency within Memory Studies to grant memory an inter-individual, social dimension.
10. Chacur et al. (2022) note that across publications dealing with different art forms, researchers have discussed reported social benefits that aid interactions with other people, the establishment of social capital, and the construction of social status; researchers have also explored how participation may generate a sense of "family," be a preventive measure against isolation, provide a sense of being part of society, and promote the conservation and dissemination of heritage to the community.
11. "Historia," *Voces de la Rebeldía*. Accessed July 21, 2023. https://vocesdelarebeldia.cl/. This same text is read aloud by members during performances. See video recorded at an event of the Corporación 3 y 4 Álamos. January 30, 2023. Accessed August 8, 2023. https://www.facebook.com/watch/?v=2856945387783173.
12. The Inter-American Commission on Human Rights does not consider the prisoners of the 2019 social revolt as "political prisoners." The use of this term for Mapuche detainees has been disputed too. While secondary school pupils initiated the 2019 revolt, many of those imprisoned are not students and have been indicted for ordinary crimes. Regarding the state's dealings with the search and identification of the dictatorship-era disappeared, and how truth(s) is established, it is not only communities of survivors and relatives of victims who dispute these: Cath Collins (2018) shows that the police, forensic, and legal actors involved in these processes regularly controvert them or judge them insufficient.
13. Regarding self-reparation, I am referring to reparative instances brought about by victims of human rights violations, as opposed to reparations in transitional justice, in which the onus to provide these is upon the entities that committed or failed to prevent human rights violations. See The International Center for Transitional Justice. "Reparations." Accessed July 27, 2023. https://www.ictj.org/our-work/transitional-justice-issues/reparations.

Chapter 5

1. For my analysis of the archival content, I have used an internal database compiling over sixty categories, manually inputted by the team. High-level data about project users comes from website and social media analytics tools (GA4 and Metricool).
2. Ana María Jiménez. 2016. "The Internationale," *Cantos Cautivos*. Accessed August 13, 2023. https://www.cantoscautivos.org/en/testimony.php?query=10697; Julio Laks Feller. 2014. "Partisan Anthem (Himno guerrillero)," *Cantos Cautivos*. Accessed August 13, 2023. https://www.cantoscautivos.org/en/testimony.php?query=10657; María Cecilia Marchant Rubilar. 2016. "We Shall Prevail (Venceremos)," *Cantos Cautivos*. Accessed August 13, 2023. https://www.cantoscautivos.org/en/testimony.php?query=10776. Lucía Chirinos. 2016. "We Shall Prevail (Venceremos)," *Cantos Cautivos*. Accessed August 13, 2023. https://www.cantoscautivos.org/es/testimony.php?query=10690.
3. Alfonso Padilla. 2019. "Cantata Santa María de Iquique," *Cantos Cautivos*. Accessed August 13, 2023. https://www.cantoscautivos.org/en/testimony.php?query=10833. See also Padilla (2016).
4. I view the term "ordinary musician" broadly. As outlined in a call for papers for the 2022 "Ordinary Musicians" conference of the British Forum for Ethnomusicology, various understandings exist: as "hidden" or "amateur" musicians, as those who make everyday contributions to social and community life, and as working musicians who are "ordinary" not necessarily in terms of

ability, but rather in being neither rich nor famous. "Ordinary Musicians." 2022. *British Forum for Ethnomusicology.* Accessed July 30, 2023. https://bfe.org.uk/conf/ordinary-musicians.

5. These centers are Villa Grimaldi, Venda Sexy, Cuartel Central Borgoño, Colonia Dignidad, Calle Pérez Rosales 764 (Valdivia), Cárcel de Valdivia, Campamento de Prisioneros de Pisagua, Campamento de Prisioneros Melinka-Puchuncaví, Campamento Prisioneros Estadio Nacional, Campamento Prisioneros Estadio Regional, Regimiento de Infantería Reforzada N° 3 (Los Ángeles), Comisaría de Carabineros N° 2 (Temuco), and Campamento de Prisioneros Isla Dawson.
6. Roberto Navarrete. 2015. "Oh Saving Victim (O salutaris Hostia)," *Cantos Cautivos.* Accessed December 21, 2022. https://www.cantoscautivos.org/en/testimony.php?query=10760.
7. Eduardo Andrés Arancibia Ortiz. 2019. "The Dance of Those Left Behind (El baile de los que sobran)," *Cantos Cautivos.* Accessed July 31, 2023. https://www.cantoscautivos.org/en/testimony.php?query=10834.
8. Paicavi Painemal. 2017. "The Letter (La carta)," *Cantos Cautivos.* Accessed July 23, 2023. https://www.cantoscautivos.org/en/testimony.php?query=10689; Pedro Humire Loredo. 2015. "Saint Gregory's Tonada (Tonada San Gregorio)," *Cantos Cautivos.* Accessed July 23, 2023. https://www.cantoscautivos.org/en/testimony.php?query=10671. Humire Loredo spoke about his experiences in prison at the launch of the *Cantos Cautivos* project in 2015. At the start of his intervention, he addressed the audience in Aymara language.
9. Luis Alfredo Muñoz González. 2015. "Casida of the Dark Pigeons (Casida de las palomas oscuras)," *Cantos Cautivos.* Accessed July 29, 2022. https://www.cantoscautivos.org/en/testimony.php?query=10678.
10. María Fedora Peña. 2016. "Melody by Jorge Peña Hen," *Cantos Cautivos.* Accessed August 28, 2023. https://www.cantoscautivos.org/en/testimony.php?query=10658; María Soledad Ruiz Ovando. 2015. "Let's Break the Morning (Rompamos la mañana)," *Cantos Cautivos.* Accessed August 28, 2023. https://www.cantoscautivos.org/en/testimony.php?query=10734; Mónica García Cuadra. 2015. "Tacit Song (Canción tácita)," *Cantos Cautivos.* Accessed August 28, 2023. https://www.cantoscautivos.org/en/testimony.php?query=10687.
11. Group email communication from Luis Cifuentes, January 2015. A two-part video of *Cantos Cautivos*'s launch is available on the Museum of Memory's YouTube channel: https://www.youtube.com/watch?v=xYKYKZq9RRc&t=0s and https://www.youtube.com/watch?v=KAUvq9FCjGA&t=0s.
12. Capitalizing on the experience of working on the *Cantos Cautivos* project, Concatti went on to co-develop a testimonial web project on the Falklands/Malvinas War, titled *Malvinas Abril 1982* (https://abril1982.nox.com.ar/). Like *Cantos Cautivos, Malvinas Abril 1982* compiles daily-life experiences within a conflict context, using word of mouth and press coverage to draw potential contributors' attention and combining online crowdsourcing and interviews to collect stories. Yet *Malvinas Abril 1982* collects memories relating to any type of experiences, in contrast with *Cantos Cautivos*'s focus on musical experiences only.
13. I agree with Carolyn Landau and Janet Topp Fargion's (2012) critique of the ingrained ethnomusicological practice of using collected materials for own research purposes only. They argue for "a fairer ethnomusicology, in which access to knowledge—often encapsulated in recordings—is facilitated for all, with ethnomusicologists taking responsibility for their own part in this important process" (Landau and Fargion 2012: 125).
14. The British Museum exhibition *I Object: Ian Hislop's Search for Dissent* (2018–2019), curated by Ian Hislop and Tom Huckenhull, featured a hundred objects addressing acts of creative disobedience, spanning a period of three millennia. *Cantos Cautivos* contributed with a recording of the piece "Doctorcitos," sung in 1974 by Los de Chacabuco, and reconstructed and recorded for the project by a group of Chacabuco survivors and friends—see Luis Cifuentes Seves. 2015. "Little Doctors (Doctorcitos)," *Cantos Cautivos.* Accessed August 13, 2023. https://www.cantoscautivos.org/en/testimony.php?query=10705.
15. The WhatsApp template is found at https://jitter.video/file/?id=TMSZFX046TMJ and was used, e.g., in RED/ACCIÓN (@redaccioncomar), "Mi casa se inunda: sentí en tu celular la desesperación de un vecino inundado," YouTube, November 11, 2019. https://www.youtube.com/watch?v=XXgrt8Db_Vg&list=PLGDsXyyDacT-jdwBrSWojzjkwB6g30Qnf&index=4.
16. A draft bill seeking to sanction historical negationism is currently in process. Victoria Dannemann. 2020. "Chile y los DD. HH.: ¿hay que penalizar el negacionismo?," *Deutsche Welle,* November 9. Accessed November 9, 2023. https://www.dw.com/es/chile-debate-sobre-el-negac

ionismo-dilema-entre-libertad-de-expresi%C3%B3n-y-dignidad-de-las-v%C3%ADctimas/a-55542503.

17. Personal email communication from Lilia Concha Carreño, August 2015.

Chapter 6

1. "Chacal de Nahueltoro," *Memoria Chilena*. Accessed December 2, 2023. https://www.memoriachilena.gob.cl/602/w3-article-92198.html; Pablo Retamal N. and Felipe Retamal. 2023. "El Chacal de Nahueltoro: 60 años de un fusilamiento dramático," *La Tercera*, April 29. Accessed April 30, 2023. https://www.latercera.com/culto/2023/04/29/el-chacal-de-nahueltoro-60-anos-de-un-fusilamiento-dramatico/.
2. See, for instance, the *Scientific Reports* collection of papers published by *Nature*, reporting negative results across the natural and clinical sciences. "Editor's Choice: Negative Results." 2022. *Scientific Reports*. Accessed April 28, 2023. https://www.nature.com/collections/gcifjebabg.

Bibliography

Achilli, Alessandro. 2020. "Individual, yet Collective Voices: Polyphonic Poetic Memories in Contemporary Ukrainian Literature." *Canadian Slavonic Papers* 62 (1): 4–26. doi: https://doi.org/10.1080/00085006.2019.1708532.

Alloa, Emmanuel, et al. 2015. "Figurations of Postmemory: An Introduction." *Journal of Literature and Trauma Studies* 4 (1–2): 1–12.

Ardito, Lorena, and César Puentes. 2021. "Alegría a contracorriente: los muchos carnavales de Santiago." *Contrapulso* 3 (2): 90–108.

Arendt, Hannah. 2006. *Eichmann in Jerusalem: A Report on the Banality of Evil*. New York, NY: Penguin Books.

Arraño Astete, Constanza. 2021. "El Plan Experimental de Extensión Docente de Jorge Peña Hen (1964–1973): aproximaciones a su diseño, implementación y resultados." *Resonancias* 25 (49): 35–60. https://doi.org/10.7764/res.2021.49.3.

Ataria, Yochai, et al., eds. 2016. *Interdisciplinary Handbook of Trauma and Culture*. Cham: Springer.

Aylwin, Mariana, ed. 2008. *Chile en el siglo XX*. 13th ed. Santiago, Chile: Planeta.

Baker, Geoff. 2014. *El Sistema: Orchestrating Venezuela's Youth*. New York: Oxford University Press.

Bareither, Christoph. 2021. "Capture the Feeling: Memory Practices in between the Emotional Affordances of Heritage Sites and Digital Media." *Memory Studies* 14 (3): 578–91. doi: https://doi.org/10.1177/17506980211010695.

Barómetro Político CERC-MORI. 2023. "Chile a la sombra de Pinochet: la opinión pública sobre la "Era de Pinochet", 1973–2023." Accessed June 19, 2023. http://morichile.cl/wp-content/uploads/2023/05/Chile-a-la-sombra-de-Pinochet.pdf.

Barz, Gregory. 2006. "'We Are from Different Ethnic Groups, but We Live Here as One Family:' The Musical Performance of Community in a Tanzanian *Kwaya*." In *Chorus and Community*, edited by Karen Ahlquist, 19–44. Urbana, IL: University of Illinois Press.

Bauer, Susanne. 2009. "The Meaning of Music in a German Sect in Chile: Colonia Dignidad." *Voices: A World Forum for Music Therapy*. Accessed November 14, 2012. https://www.researchgate.net/publication/237693805_The_Meaning_of_Music_in_a_German_Sect_in_Chile_Colonia_Dignidad.

Belfi, Amy M., et al. 2016. "Music Evokes Vivid Autobiographical Memories." *Memory* 24 (7): 979–89.

Benavente, Javiera, and Daniel Party. 2022. "Los Diablos Rojos de Víctor Jara: un análisis coreográfico y musical." *Resonancias* 26 (51): 97–117.

Birch, Alexandra. 2021. "'They Were Drinking, Singing, and Shooting:' Singing and the Holocaust in the USSR." *Journal of Perpetrator Research* 4 (1): 171–91.

Bithell, Caroline. 2014. *A Different Voice, A Different Song: Reclaiming Community Through the Natural Voice and World Song*. New York: Oxford University Press.

Bithell, Caroline, and Juniper Hill, eds. 2014. *Oxford Handbook of Music Revival*. New York: Oxford University Press.

Boyles, Jude, and Christine Adcock. 2013. "Stone Flowers." *Healthcare Counselling & Psychotherapy Journal* 13 (4): 32–39.

Brauer, Juliane. 2016. "How Can Music Be Torturous?: Music in Nazi Concentration and Extermination Camps." *Music & Politics* 10 (1). doi: http://dx.doi.org/10.3998/mp.9460447.0010.103.

Bronfman, Paulina, and Ricardo Álvarez. 2022. "Youth *Comparsas* in Valparaíso (Chile): Artivism, Performativity and Repertoire of Ecological Political Action." *Youth and Globalization* 4: 259–79.

Bronfman, Paulina, and Ricardo Álvarez. 2023. "*Banda Dignidad*: Carnival, Artivism and Liminality in the Context of the Chilean Social Outbreak of October 2019." In *Music and Resistance: From 1900 to the Present*, edited by Igor Contreras Zubillaga and Helena Martin Nieva. Turnhout: Brepols.

Bustos, Raquel. 2013. *La mujer compositora y su aporte al desarrollo musical chileno*. Santiago, Chile: Ediciones Universidad Católica de Chile.

Cabaluz Gómez, Lylian Paz, and Sara Valentina Sosa Valenzuela. 2021. "Voces de la Rebeldía: hacia una didáctica de música y memoria." Memoria para optar al título de Profesora de Música, Music, Universidad Metropolitana de Ciencias de la Educación.

Campusano, Daniel, et al. 2015. *Álvaro Corbalán: el dueño de la noche*. Santiago, Chile: Ceibo Ediciones.

Carlson, Alexandra. 2014. "Inundating the Country with Music: Jorge Peña, Democracy, and Music Education in Chile." *Journal of Historical Research in Music Education* 36 (1): 65–78. doi: https://doi.org/10.1177/153660061403600105.

Carlson, Alexandra. 2016. "The Story of Carora: The Origins of El Sistema." *International Journal of Music Education* 34 (1): 64–73. doi: https://doi.org/10.1177/0255761415617926.

Carmona Estay, Naomi, et al. 2021. "Memoria y educación musical: selección y análisis de fuentes patrimoniales de los archivos del Museo de la Memoria y los Derechos Humanos (1973–1975) para la creación de material didáctico para las clases de música en primero medio." Memoria para optar al título de profesor y profesora de música, Universidad Metropolitana de Ciencias de la Educación.

Carrasco, Eduardo. 1982. *La nueva canción en América Latina*. Santiago, Chile: CENECA.

Carroll, Noël. 1996. "Moderate Moralism." *The British Journal of Aesthetics* 36 (3): 223–38. doi: https://doi.org/10.1093/bjaesthetics/36.3.223.

Caruth, Cathy. 2014. "Disappearing History: Scenes of Trauma in the Theater of Human Rights." In *Knowing the Suffering of Others*, edited by Austin Sarat, 170–200. Tuscaloosa: The University of Alabama Press.

Cassidy, Sheila. 1977. *Audacity to Believe*. Cleveland: Collins World.

Castillo Didier, Miguel. 2015. *Jorge Peña Hen (1925–1973): músico, maestro y humanista mártir*. Santiago, Chile: LOM Ediciones.

Central Intelligence Agency. 1963. "Kubark Counterintelligence Interrogation." *The National Security Archive*. http://nsarchive.gwu.edu/NSAEBB/NSAEBB122/CIA%20Kubark%201-60.pdf.

Centro de Derechos Humanos. 2022. "Informe anual sobre derechos humanos en Chile." Edited by Judith Schönsteiner. Santiago, Chile: Universidad Diego Portales.

Chacur, Karima, et al. 2022. "Older Adults' Participation in Artistic Activities: A Scoping Review." *European Journal of Ageing* 19: 931–44. doi: https://doi.org/10.1007/s10433-022-00708-z.

Chornik, Katia. 2003. "Captive Tango: Music in Nazi and Chilean Concentration Camps." Master's thesis, Royal Academy of Music and University of London.

Chornik, Katia. 2013. "Chile." In *Encyclopedia of Latin American Popular Music*, edited by George Torres, 90–92. Santa Barbara, CA: Greenwood.

Chornik, Katia. 2014. "Música y tortura en centros de detención chilenos: conversaciones con un ex agente de la policía secreta de Pinochet." *Resonancias* 34: 111–26. doi: https://doi.org/10.7764/res.2014.34.7.

Chornik, Katia. 2019. "Voces de la Rebeldía and Los Diablos Rojos de Víctor Jara: Remembering Chile's Violent Past through Music and Dance." *Filigrane: Musique, Esthétique, Sciences, Société* 23. doi: https://doi.org/10.4000/12i82.

Chornik, Katia, and J. Patrice McSherry. 2017. "The Power of Captive Songs: Music Can Help Recover the Historical Memory of Political Detention in Chile and Latin America." *LSE Latin American and Caribbean Blog* (blog), March 20. Accessed March 20, 2017. https://blogs.lse.ac.uk/latamcaribbean/2017/03/20/the-power-of-captive-songs-music-can-help-recover-the-historical-memory-of-political-detention-in-chile-and-latin-america/.

Cifuentes Seves, Luis. 2020. *Dilo, antes que sea demasiado tarde*. Santiago, Chile: Cuarto Propio.

Cizmic, Maria. 2021. "Reflections on Music and Trauma in Ariel Dorfman's *Death and the Maiden*." Music, Sound, and Trauma: Interdisciplinary Perspectives conference, Zoom.

Cobussen, Marcel, and Nanette Nielsen. 2012. *Music and Ethics* Farnham: Ashgate.

Collins, Cath. 2018. "Transitional Justice 'From Within:' Police, Forensic and Legal Actors Searching for Chile's Disappeared." *Journal of Human Rights Practice* 10 (1): 19–39. doi: https://doi.org/10.1093/jhuman/huy003.

Collins, Cath, et al. 2020. "Informe anual sobre derechos humanos en Chile 2020." Centro de Derechos Humanos UDP. Accessed January 5, 2021. https://derechoshumanos.udp.cl/cms/wp-content/uploads/2020/12/12_Abrira%CC%81n_las_grandes_alamedas_-_Justicia_Memoria_y_No-Repeticio%CC%81n_en_tiempos_constituyentes.pdf.

Comisión Asesora para la Calificación de Detenidos Desaparecidos, Ejecutados Políticos y Víctimas de Prisión Política y Tortura. 2011. "Informe de la Comisión Nacional sobre Política y Tortura." Santiago, Chile: Ministerio del Interior.

Comisión de Verdad y Justicia [Paraguay]. 2008. "Informe Final." Accessed December 12, 2023. https://www.derechoshumanos.net/lesahumanidad/informes/paraguay/Informe_Comision_Verdad_y_Justicia_Paraguay_Conclusiones_y_Recomendaciones.pdf.

Comisión Nacional sobre la Desaparición de Personas [Argentina]. 1984. "Nunca Más." Accessed November 9, 2021. http://www.enmanosdenadie.com.ar/wp-content/uploads/2013/03/nunca-mas-conadep.pdf.

Comisión Nacional sobre Prisión Política y Tortura. 2004. "Informe." Santiago, Chile: Ministerio del Interior. Accessed November 4, 2020. https://bibliotecadigital.indh.cl/handle/123456789/455.

Comissão Nacional da Verdade [Brazil]. 2014. "Relatório da Comissão Nacional da Verdade." Accessed November 9, 2021. http://cnv.memoriasreveladas.gov.br/.

Comisión Nacional de Verdad y Reconciliación. 1991. "Informe." https://cedocmuseodelamemoria.cl/informe-rettig/.

Comité para la Prevención de la Tortura. 2021. "Resumen Ejecutivo del Informe Diagnóstico de caracterización y vulneraciones a los derechos humanos en el área Penitenciaria." Accessed November 9, 2021. https://mnpt.cl/wp-content/uploads/2022/03/Resumen-Ejecutivo-Area-Penitenciaria-1.pdf.

Contreras, Manuel. "Manuel Contreras: 'Los detenidos desaparecidos están en el Cementerio General.'" Interview by Daniel Matamala and Mónica Rincón. *CNN*, September 10, 2013. Accessed July 18, 2020. https://www.youtube.com/watch?v=NIZZediL1Gw.

Corbalán Castilla, Álvaro. 1998. *La verdad está enferma*. Santiago, Chile: self-published.

Corbalán Castilla, Álvaro. 2008. *Anécdotas de mi General: las que viví y . . . las que me contaron*. Santiago, Chile: Asesorías Comunicacionales.

Corbalán Castilla, Álvaro. 2014. "Saludo del Teniente Coronel (R) Álvaro Corbalán Castilla, en el Aniversario de la gesta heroica del 11 de Septiembre de 1973" (unpublished manuscript), typescript.

Corbalán Castilla, Álvaro. 2018. *Las respuestas de Corbalán*. Santiago, Chile: Editorial Once de Septiembre.

Corbalán Castilla, Álvaro. 2019. *Belleza y sentimiento de los poemas de mi madre*. Santiago, Chile: self-published.

Cormac, Rory. 2020. "The Currency of Covert Action: British Special Political Action in Latin America, 1961–64." *Journal of Strategic Studies* 45 (6–7): 893–917.

Cornejo Ulloa, Francisca. 2023. *Lolita Lola. Memorias Sonoras de Ex Prisioneras Políticas.* Santiago, Chile: Palabra Editorial.

Cornejo Ulloa, Francisca. 2020. "Memorias sonoras de mujeres ex presas políticas durante la dictadura militar chilena en la Cárcel del Buen Pastor de Valparaíso." Tesis para optar al Título de Antropóloga Social, Universidad de Chile.

Corporación Nacional de Reparación y Reconciliación. 1996. "Informe de calificación de víctimas de violaciones de derechos humanos y de la violencia política." https://cedocmuseodelamemoria.cl/wp-content/uploads/2011/12/Informe_CNRR.pdf.

Correa, Raquel. 2000. "Álvaro Corbalán, desde Punta Peuco Dos, ex CNI condenado a cadena perpetua cuenta su historia." *El Mercurio*, August 6, D24–26. Accessed July 18, 2020. http://www.bibliotecanacionaldigital.gob.cl/visor/BND:353384.

Correa, Raquel. 2011. "Entrevista de Tomás Mosciatti a Raquel Correa (tercera parte)." Interview by Tomás Mosciatti. November 30. Accessed November 3, 2022. https://www.youtube.com/watch?v=XbSwjBFkVI4.

Corvalán Márquez, Luis. 2016. *Los partidos políticos y el golpe del 11 de septiembre: contribución al estudio del contexto histórico.* Santiago, Chile: Editorial USACH.

Cusick, Suzanne. 2008. "You Are in a Place that is out of the World . . . : Music in the Detention Camps of the Global War on Terror." *Journal of the Society for American Music* 2 (1): 1–26.

Cusick, Suzanne G. 2006. "Music as Torture / Music as Weapon." *Trans: Revista Transcultural de Música* 10. Accessed April 5, 2019. http://www.sibetrans.com/trans/a152/music-as-torture-music-as-weapon.

Cusick, Suzanne G. 2013. "Towards an Acoustemology of Detention in 'the Global War on Terror.'" In *Music, Sound and Space: Transformations of Public and Private Experience*, edited by Georgina Born, 275–91. Cambridge: Cambridge University Press.

Davis, Colin, and Hanna Meretoja, eds. 2020. *The Routledge Companion to Literature and Trauma.* Abingdon: Routledge.

Dayan, Peter. 2011. "L'absence de la polyphonie dans les romans de George Sand." In *George Sand: Intertextualité et Polyphonie II*, edited by Nigel Harkness and Jacinta Wright, 93–109. Bern: Peter Lang.

de Carvalho, Vinicius Mariano. 2020. "Restaging *Brundibár*: An Exercise in Resistance and an Antidote to Intolerance." *Arquivo Maaravi: Revista Digital de Estudos Judaicos da UFMG* 14 (26): 139–48. doi: https://doi.org/10.35699/1982-3053.2020.21744.

Defensoría de la Niñez. 2022. *Estudio de análisis del enfoque de derechos humanos de niños, niñas y adolescentes en el currículum educativo* . Santiago, Chile: Defensoría de la Niñez. Accessed September 30, 2023. https://www.defensorianinez.cl/estud_y_estadi/estudio-de-curriculum/.

Department of Justice [Canada]. 2019. "The Impact of Trauma on Adult Sexual Assault Victims: How Trauma Affects Memory and Recall." Accessed December 12, 2022. https://www.justice.gc.ca/eng/rp-pr/jr/trauma/p4.html.

Díaz-Inostroza, Patricia. 2016. *Yo no canto por cantar: cantares de resistencia en el Cono Sur.* Santiago, Chile: Ediciones Memoriarte.

Díaz, Rafael, and Juan Pablo González. 2011. *Cantus Firmus: mito y narrativa de la música chilena de arte del siglo XX.* Santiago, Chile: Amapola Editores.

Dunnage, Jonathan. 2010. "Perpetrator Memory and Memories about Perpetrators." *Memory Studies* 3 (2): 91–94. doi: https://doi.org/10.1177/1750698009355672.

Durán Pardo, Claudio. 2003. *Autobiografía de un ex-jugador de ajedrez.* Santiago, Chile: Lom Ediciones.

Elon, Amos, ed. 2006. "Introduction." In *Eichmann in Jerusalem: A Report on the Banality of Evil*, edited by Hannah Arendt, vii–xxiii. New York: Penguin Books.

Embajada de Chile en Naciones Unidas, Grupo Allana. 1975–79. "Statement Made by Chairman of the Ad Hoc Working Group on Chile." In *Oficios, memorandos e informes secretos, confidenciales y reservados del Ministerio de Defensa, contenidos en el Fondo*

Ministerios, Instituciones y Particulares del Archivo General Histórico del Ministerio de Relaciones Exteriores de Chile.

Falcon, Carles, et al. 2022. "Soundtrack of Life: An fMRI Study." *Behavioural Brain Research* 418. doi: https://doi.org/10.1016/j.bbr.2021.113634.

Faúndez, Ximena, et al. 2014. "Transmisión y apropiación de la historia de prisión política: Transgeneracionalidad del trauma psicosocial en nietos de ex presos políticos de la dictadura militar chilena." *Terapia Psicológica* 32 (3): 201–16. Accessed July 2, 2019. http://teps.cl/index.php/teps/article/view/42/45.

Feld, Claudia, and Valentina Salvi, eds. 2019. *Las voces de la represión: declaraciones de perpetradores de la dictadura argentina.* Buenos Aires: Miño y Dávila Editores.

Fernández L'Hoeste, Héctor, and Juan Carlos Rodríguez. 2020. "Introduction: In and Out of Digital Humanities: Nations, Networks, and Practices in Latinx America." In *Digital Humanities in Latin America*, edited by Héctor Fernández L'Hoeste and Juan Carlos Rodríguez, 1–20. Gainesville, FL: University Press of Florida.

Fiedler, Klaus, and Karolin Salmen. 2021. Major Theories in Social Psychology. In *Oxford Research Encyclopedia of Psychology.* doi: https://doi.org/10.1093/acrefore/9780190236557.013.810.

Fifer, Julian, et al., eds. 2022. *The Routledge Companion to Music and Human Rights.* Abingdon: Routledge.

Fisher, Atarah, and Avi Gilboa. 2016. "The Roles of Music amongst Musician Holocaust Survivors before, during, and after the Holocaust." *Psychology of Music* 44 (6): 1221–39.

Franco, Marina. 2014. "La 'teoría de los dos demonios:' un símbolo de la posdictadura en la Argentina." *A Contracorriente: una revista de historia social y literatura de América Latina* 11 (2): 22–52. Accessed September 5, 2021. https://core.ac.uk/download/pdf/159288872.pdf.

Freedman, Jesse. 2022. "Memories of Captured Song: Exploring Shifting Memories and the Legacies of Music-Making in Chilean Detention Centers through the 'Cantos Cautivos' Testimonial Project." *Music & Politics* 16 (1). doi: https://doi.org/10.3998/mp.2339.

Friedson, Steven M. 2019. "The Music Box: Songs of Futility in a Time of Torture." *Ethnomusicology* 63 (2): 222–46.

Gálvez Comandini, Ana Carolina, ed. 2021. *Históricas: movimientos feministas y de mujeres en Chile, 1850–2020.* Santiago, Chile: Lom.

Garcia da Silva, Thiago Loreto, et al. 2016. "Event Centrality in Trauma and PTSD: Relations between Event Relevance and Posttraumatic Symptoms." *Psicologia: Reflexão e Crítica* 29:34: 1–7. doi: https://doi.org/10.1186/s41155-016-0015-y.

García, Marisol. 2013. *Canción valiente, 1960–1989: tres décadas de canto político y social en Chile.* Santiago, Chile: Ediciones B.

Gehrta, Tine B., et al. 2018. "Psychological and Clinical Correlates of the Centrality of Event Scale: A Systematic Review." *Clinical Psychology Review* 65: 57–80.

Gilbert, Abel. 2021. *Satisfacton en la ESMA: música y sonido durante la dictadura (1976-1983).* Buenos Aires: Gourmet Musical.

Gilbert, Shirli. 2005. "Music as Historical Source: Social History and Musical Texts." *International Review of the Aesthetics and Sociology of Music* 36 (1): 117–34. Accessed June 4, 2013. https://hrcak.srce.hr/en/file/95031.

González-Ruibal, Alfredo. 2021. "Scholars from the Global South Must Be Helped to Make a Splash." *Times Higher Education*, October 28. Accessed December 30, 2021. https://www.timeshighereducation.com/opinion/scholars-global-south-must-be-helped-make-asplash.

González, Juan Pablo. 2017. *Des/encuentros en la música popular chilena 1970-1990.* Santiago, Chile: Ediciones Universidad Alberto Hurtado.

González, Juan Pablo. 2018. *Thinking About Music from Latin America: Issues and Questions.* Lanham: Lexington Books.

González, Mónica. 2013. "El informe secreto de Pinochet sobre los crímenes." *Centro de Investigación Periodística (CIPER)*, September 10. Accessed February 10, 2016. http://ciperchile.cl/2013/09/10/el-informe-secreto-de-pinochet-sobre-los-crimenes/.

Grant, M. J. 2013. "The Illogical Logic of Music Torture." *Torture Journal* 23 (2): 4–13.

Grant, M. J., and Anna Papaeti. 2013a. Special issue "Music and Torture | Music and Punishment." *The World of Music (New Series)* 2 (1).

Grant, M. J., and Anna Papaeti. 2013b. "Thematic Issue on Music in Detention." *Torture Journal* 23 (2). Accessed December 12, 2023. https://irct.org/wp-content/uploads/2022/11/Volume-23-No.-2-1.pdf.

Grant, M. J. 2020. "Understanding Perpetrators' Use of Music." In *The Routledge International Handbook of Perpetrator Studies*, edited by Susanne C. Knittel and Zachary J. Goldberg, 206–17. Abingdon: Routledge.

Grant, Morag Josephine. 2014. "Pathways to Music Torture." *Transposition: Musique et Sciences Sociales* 4. doi: https://doi.org/10.4000/transposition.494.

Gutman, Yifat, and Jenny Wüstenberg, eds. 2023. *The Routledge Handbook of Memory Activism*. Abingdon, Oxon: Routledge.

Guzmán Jasmen, Nancy. 2014. *Ingrid Olderock: la mujer de los perros*. Santiago, Chile: Ceibo Ediciones.

Guzmán, Nancy. 2000. *Romo, confesiones de un torturador*. Santiago, Chile: Editorial Planeta.

Herrera Ortega, Silvia. 2017. *Tradición, vanguardia y ruptura: el serialismo dodecafónico en Chile*. Valparaíso: Ediciones Universitarias de Valparaíso.

Hevia Jordán, Evelyn. 2020. "Reflexiones en torno a la escucha activa de historias de vida de sobrevivientes de la represión política: las experiencias de hacer entrevistas biográficas." In *Archivo Oral de Villa Grimaldi: patrimonio ciudadano de testimonios y memorias*, edited by Omar Sagredo Mazuela and Isidora Salaberry Pavone, 95–124. Santiago, Chile: Corporación Parque por la Paz Villa Grimaldi.

Hislop, Ian, and Tom Hockenhull. 2018. *I Object: Ian Hislop's Search for Dissent*. London: Thames & Hudson; The British Museum.

Hood, Mantle. 1960. "The Challenge of 'Bi-Musicality.'" *Ethnomusicology* 4 (2): 55–59. https://www.jstor.org/stable/i237973.

Instituto Nacional de Derechos Humanos. 2015. "Diagnóstico de la inclusión de la educación en derechos humanos en el currículum escolar chileno al año 2015." Accessed January 4, 2016. https://bibliotecadigital.indh.cl/items/d91594c8-287c-460a-b0d6-c922f45f45ab/full.

Instituto Nacional de Estadísticas. 1970. "Población total país: XIV Censo de población y III de vivienda." Santiago, Chile.

Insunza, Andrea, and Javier Ortega, eds. 2017. *Los archivos del cardenal 2. Casos reales*. Santiago, Chile: Editorial Catalonia.

Inter-American Commission on Human Rights, Organization of American States. 1976. "Second Report on the Situation of Human Rights in Chile." Accessed June 27, 2023. http://www.cidh.org/countryrep/Chile76eng/toc.htm.

Jakubowski, Kelly, et al. 2021. "Phenomenological Differences in Music- and Television-Evoked Autobiographical Memories." *Music Perception* 38 (5): 435–55. doi: https://doi.org/10.1525/mp.2021.38.5.435.

Janata, Petr, et al. 2007. "Characterization of Music-Evoked Autobiographical Memories." *Memory* 15: 845–860. doi: https://doi.org/10.1080/09658210701734593.

Jara, Joan. 1998. *Victor: An Unfinished Song*. London: Bloomsbury.

Jelin, Elizabeth. 2002. *Los trabajos de la memoria*. Madrid: Siglo Veintiuno.

Jensen, Meg. 2019. *The Art and Science of Trauma and the Autobiographical: Negotiated Truths*. Basingstoke, Hampshire: Palgrave Macmillan.

Jiménez, Ana María, and Teresa Izquierdo. 2015. *Antes de perder la memoria*. Santiago, Chile: Editorial Cuarto Propio.

Johnson, Bruce, and Martin Cloonan. 2009. *Dark Side of the Tune: Popular Music and Violence*. Farnham: Ashgate.

Jordán, Laura. 2010. "Cantando al MIR y al Frente: cita y versión en dos canciones militantes de Patricio Manns." *Actas del IX Congreso de la IASPM-AL*: 367–76. Accessed February 2, 2017. https://iaspmal.com/index.php/2016/03/02/actas-ix-congreso/.

Jorquera, María José, et al. 2020. "Estudio descriptivo de mortalidad en sobrevivientes de tortura y prisión política en el período de la dictadura militar en Chile, 1973–1990." *Revista Médica de Chile* 148 (12). https://scielo.conicyt.cl/scielo.php?script=sci_arttext&pid=S0034-98872020001201773.

Juslin, Patrik N. 2013. "From Everyday Emotions to Aesthetic Emotions: Towards a Unified Theory of Musical Emotions." *Physics of Life Reviews* 10 (3): 235–66.

Karagodin, Maxim. 2019. "Remembering Pinochet Online: The Chilean Diaspora in the United States' Reclamation, Contestation and Archival of Digital Memories." Master of Arts, Interdisciplinary Latin American Studies, Lateinamerika-Institut, Freie Universität Berlin.

Karagodin, Maxim. 2022. "Digitally Archiving Collective Memories in the Chilean American Diaspora." *Virtualis* 13 (25): 34–53. doi: https://doi.org/10.46530/virtualis.v13i25.410.

Karmy Bolton, Eileen, et al. 2011. "¿Roja, militar, apolítica? Notas sobre cumbia y politicidad." *Tiesos pero cumbiancheros*. Accessed January 29, 2016. http://www.tiesosperocumbiancheros.cl/?p=139.

Keaney, Emily, and Anni Oskala. 2007. "The Golden Age of the Arts? Taking Part Survey Findings on Older People and the Arts." *Cultural Trends* 16 (4): 323–55. doi: https://doi.org/10.1080/09548960701692696.

Knittel, Susanne C., and Zachary J. Goldberg, eds. 2020. *The Routledge International Handbook of Perpetrator Studies*. Abingdon: Routledge.

Lagos, Andrea. 2014. "El agente del corvo de oro." In *Los archivos del Cardenal 2: casos reales*, edited by Andrea Insunza and Javier Ortega, 9–20. Santiago, Chile: Catalonia.

Landau, Carolyn, and Janet Topp Fargion. 2012. "We're All Archivists Now: Towards a More Equitable Ethnomusicology." *Ethnomusicology Forum* 21 (2): 125–40.

Landsberg, Alison. 2004. *Prosthetic Memory: The Transformation of American Remembrance in the Age of Mass Culture*. New York, NY: Columbia University Press.

Lazzara, Michael J. 2006. *Chile in Transition: The Poetics and Politics of Memory*. Gainesville: University Press of Florida.

Lazzara, Michael J. 2014. "El fenómeno Mocito (las puestas en escena de un sujeto cómplice)." *A Contracorriente* 12 (1). Accessed October 17, 2015. http://acontracorriente.chass.ncsu.edu/index.php/acontracorriente/article/view/1301.

Lessa, Francesca. 2015. "Justice Beyond Borders: The Operation Condor Trial and Accountability for Transnational Crimes in South America." *International Journal of Transitional Justice* 9 (3): 494–506.

Livingstone, Grace. 2018. *Britain and the Dictatorships of Argentina and Chile, 1973–82: Foreign Policy, Corporations and Social Movements*. Cham, Switzerland: Palgrave Macmillan.

Lutowicz, Analía. 2012. "Memoria sonora: una herramienta para la construcción del relato de la experiencia concentracionaria en Argentina." *Sociedad y Equidad: Revista de Humanidades, Ciencias Sociales, Artes y Comunicaciones* 4: 133–52.

Madariaga, Carlos. 2020. "El 'Estallido social' y la salud mental de la ciudadanía: una apreciación desde la experiencia PRAIS." *Revista Chilena de Salud Pública* 23 (2): 146–56. doi: https://doi.org/10.5354/0719-5281.2019.56475.

Malcomson, Hettie. 2019. "Negotiating Violence and Creative Agency in Commissioned Mexican Narco Rap." *Bulletin of Latin American Research* 38 (3): 347–62.

Matamala, Felipe. 2021. "Trauma transgeneracional: cómo la violencia del Estado en el 18/O puede reabrir las heridas de la dictadura." *Ciper Académico*, 6 January. Accessed November 15, 2023. https://www.ciperchile.cl/2021/01/06/trauma-transgeneracional-como-la-violencia-del-estado-en-el-18-o-puede-reabrir-las-heridas-de-la-dictadura/.

McCoy, Alfred. 2006. *A Question of Torture: CIA Interrogation, from the Cold War to the War on Terror*. New York: Owl Books.

McSherry, J. Patrice. 2005. *Predatory States: Operation Condor and Covert War in Latin America*. Lanham, MD: Rowman & Littlefield.

McSherry, J. Patrice. 2015. *Chilean New Song: The Political Power of Music.* Philadelphia: Temple University Press.

Mertens, Donna M. 2018. "Ethics of Qualitative Data Collection." In *The SAGE Handbook of Qualitative Data Collection*, edited by Uwe Flick, 33–48. London: SAGE.

Ministerio de Justicia [Chile]. 1976. "Acta Constitucional N° 2 Bases Esenciales de la Institucionalidad Chilena." *Biblioteca del Congreso Nacional de Chile*, September 11. Accessed November 15, 2023. http://www.leychile.cl/Navegar?idNorma=6655.

Ministerio de Salud [Chile]. 2006. "Norma técnica para la atención de personas afectadas por la represión política ejercida por el Estado en el período 1973–1990." Accessed November 15, 2023. https://www.vicariadelasolidaridad.cl/catalogo/norma-tecnica-para-la-atencion-de-personas-afectadas-por-la-represion-politica-ejercida.

Minsburg, Raúl. 2015. "El recuerdo del que escucha." *Revista Afuera: Estudios de Crítica Cultura* 15. Accessed October 2, 2015. http://revistaafuera15.blogspot.com/p/musica-en-dictadura-y-memorias-sonoras.html.

Molinero, Carlos, and Pablo Vila. 2014. "A Brief History of the Militant Song Movement in Argentina." In *The Militant Song Movement in Latin America: Chile, Uruguay, and Argentina*, edited by Pablo Vila, 193–228. Laham: Lexington Books.

Montealegre Iturra, Jorge. 2013. *Memorias eclipsadas: duelo y resiliencia comunitaria en la prisión política.* Santiago, Chile: Editorial Asterión.

Montealegre Iturra, Jorge. 2018. *Derecho a fuga: una extraña felicidad compartida.* Santiago, Chile: Asterión.

Montes Capó, Cristian. 2022. "Singing as a Refuge in Times of Trauma." In *Refugees, Refuge and Human Displacement*, edited by Ignacio López-Calvo and Marjorie Agosín, 163–76. London: Anthem Press.

Mooney-Somers, Julie, and Anna Olsen. 2016. "Ethical Review and Qualitative Research Competence: Guidance for Reviewers and Applicants." *Research Ethics* 13 (3–4): 128–38. doi: https://doi.org/10.1177/1747016116677636.

Moscoso Urzúa, Valeria. 2013. "Caracterización de la escala de gravedad de síntomas del trastorno de estrés post-traumático en personas afectadas por terrorismo de Estado en Chile: un acercamiento a la evaluación del daño." *PRAXIS: Revista de Psicología* 24: 89–114.

Natale, Eleonora. 2022. "Researching Violence and Everyday Life in the 1970s: An Ethnographic Approach to the Argentine Military Family." *Bulletin of Latin American Studies* 41 (3): 450–64. doi: https://doi.org/10.1111/blar.13293.

Neustadt, Robert. 2011. "Reading Spanish American National Anthems: "Sonograms" of National Identity." *Music & Politics* 5 (1). doi: http://dx.doi.org/10.3998/mp.9460447.0005.102.

Nora, Pierre. 2002. "Reasons for the Current Upsurge in Memory" (blog), April 19. Accessed November 9, 2021. https://www.eurozine.com/reasons-for-the-current-upsurge-in-memory/.

Nowak, Manfred. 2022. "Music Torture in the 'War on Terror.'" In *The Routledge Companion to Music and Human Rights*, edited by Julian Fifer, Angela Impey, Peter Kirchschlaeger, Manfred Nowak and George Ulrich, 325–31. Abington: Routledge.

Organization of American States. 1985. "Inter-American Convention to Prevent and Punish Torture." Accessed June 27, 2025. https://www.oas.org/juridico/english/treaties/a-51.html.

Organization of American States. 2008. "Principles and Best Practices on the Protection of Persons Deprived of Liberty in the Americas." Accessed September 9, 2022. https://www.oas.org/en/iachr/mandate/Basics/principles-best-practices-protection-persons-deprived-liberty-americas.pdf.

Padilla, Alfonso. 2016. "La música en una cárcel de la dictadura chilena." In *Com som! Sem som . . . : Liberdades políticas, liberdades poéticas*, edited by Heloísa de A. Duarte Valente and Simone Luci Pereira, 237–50. São Paulo: Letra e Voz.

Panico, Mario. 2019. "Questioning What Remains: A Semiotic Approach to Studying Difficult Monuments." *Punctum* 5 (2): 29–49. https://doi.org/10.18680/hss.2019.0021.

Papaeti, Anna. 2013. "Music, Torture, Testimony: Reopening the Case of the Greek Military Junta (1967–74)." *The World of Music (New Series)* 2 (1): 67–89.

Papaeti, Anna. 2020. "On Music, Torture and Detention: Reflections on Issues of Research and Discipline." *Transposition: Musique et Sciences Sociales* 2. doi: https://doi.org/10.4000/transposition.5289.

Parliamentary Assembly, Council of Europe. 2012. "The Definition of Political Prisoner." Accessed September 19, 2022. http://assembly.coe.int/nw/xml/XRef/Xref-XML2HTML-en.asp?fileid=19150.

Pavlovic, Milijana. 2013. "Alma Rosé and the Lagerkapelle Auschwitz." Colloque "Musique et camps de concentration," Conseil de l'Europe, Strasbourg.

Peek, Ella. 1995. "Ethical Criticism of Art." *Internet Encyclopedia of Philosophy*. Accessed November 22, 2021. https://iep.utm.edu/ethical-criticism-of-art/.

Pettan, Svanibor, and Jeff Todd Titon, eds. 2015. *The Oxford Handbook of Applied Ethnomusicology*. New York: Oxford University Press.

Pincheira, Rodrigo. 2023. *Como una ola*. Concepción: Nuevos Territorios.

Politzer, Patricia. 2020. *Batuta rebelde: Jorge Peña Hen, una biografía (1928–1973)*. Santiago, Chile: Lumen.

Polti, Victoria. 2014. "Memoria sonora, cuerpo y bio-poder: un acercamiento a la experiencia concentracionaria en la Argentina durante la última dictadura cívico-militar." XI Congreso Argentino de Antropología Social, Rosario. Accessed August 20, 2020. http://cdsa.aacademica.org/000-081/1560.

Rebolledo, Javier. 2012. *La danza de los cuervos: el destino final de los detenidos desaparecidos*. Santiago, Chile: Ceibo Ediciones.

Rebolledo, Javier. 2013. *El despertar de los cuervos: Tejas Verdes, el origen del exterminio*. Santiago, Chile: Ceibo Ediciones.

Rejali, Darius. 2009. *Torture and Democracy*. Princeton: Princeton University Press.

Reynolds, Frances. 2004. "Conversations About Creativity and Chronic Illness II: Textile Artists Coping with Long-Term Health Problems Reflect on the Creative Process." *Creativity Research Journal* 16 (1): 79–89. doi: https://doi.org/10.1207/s15326934crj1601_8.

Richard, Nelly. 2001. "Las confesiones de un torturador y su (abusivo) montaje periodístico." *Revista de crítica cultural* 22: 14–19.

Ritter, Jonathan. 2012. "Complementary Discourses of Truth and Memory: The Peruvian Truth Commission and the Canción Social Ayacuchana." In *Music, Politics, and Violence*, edited by Susan Fast and Kip Pegley, 197–222. Middletown, CT: Wesleyan University Press.

Rodríguez, Clelia O. 2017. "How Academia Uses Poverty, Oppression, and Pain for Intellectual Masturbation." *RaceBaitR* (blog), 6 April. Accessed November 15, 2023. http://racebaitr.com/2017/04/06/how-academia-uses-poverty-oppression/#.

Rodríguez Musso, Osvaldo. 1988. *La Nueva Canción Chilena: continuidad y reflejo*. Havana: Casa de las Américas.

Rolle, Claudio, et al. 2009. *Historia social de la música popular en Chile, 1950–1970*. Santiago, Chile: Ediciones de la Universidad Católica.

Ronström, Owe. 2014. "Traditional Music, Heritage Music." In *The Oxford Handbook of Music Revival*, edited by Caroline Bithell and Juniper Hill, 43–59. New York: Oxford University Press.

Rothkirchen, Livia. 2006. *The Jews of Bohemia and Moravia: Facing the Holocaust*. Lincoln: University of Nebraska Press.

Salazar, Gabriel, and Julio Pinto. 2010. *Historia contemporánea de Chile*. 5 vols. Santiago, Chile: Lom.

Salazar, Manuel. 2012. *Las letras del horror. Tomo II: la CNI*. 2 vols. Santiago, Chile: LOM Ediciones.

Santos Herceg, José. 2019. *Lugares espectrales: topología testimonial de la prisión política en Chile*. Santiago, Chile: Colección Idea, 2019.

Schönsteiner, Judith, ed. 2022. *Informe anual sobre derechos humanos en Chile.* Santiago, Chile: Centro de Derechos Humanos, Universidad Diego Portales.

Scruggs, T. M. 2016. "Singing Truth to Power: Mercedes Sosa, 1935–2009." *NACLA Report on the Americas* 42 (6): 4–5.

Sereny, Gitta. 1995. *Into That Darkness: From Mercy Killing to Mass Murder.* London: Pimlico.

Sharman, Adam, et al., eds. 2017. *MemoSur / MemoSouth: Memory, Commemoration and Trauma in Post-Dictatorship Argentina and Chile.* London: Critical, Cultural and Communications Press.

Spencer, Christian, and Natalia Bieletto, eds. 2020. "Volver a creer. Música, sonido y escucha en el movimiento social chileno (2019–2020)." *Boletín Música* 54. Accessed February 5, 2021. https://proyectosonec.org/documento/volver-a-creer-crisis-social-musica-sonido-y-escucha-en-la-revuelta-chilena-2019-2020/.

Stern, Steve J. 2004. *Remembering Pinochet's Chile: On the Eve of London 1998.* Durham, NC: Duke University Press.

Stern, Steve J. 2006. *Battling for Hearts and Minds: Memory Struggles in Pinochet's Chile, 1973–1988.* Durham, NC: Duke University Press.

Stern, Steve J. 2010. *Reckoning with Pinochet: The Memory Question in Democratic Chile, 1989–2006.* Durham, NC: Duke University Press.

Stone, Philip R., et al., eds. 2018. *The Palgrave Handbook of Dark Tourism Studies.* London: Palgrave Macmillan.

Sutton, Julie P., ed. 2002. *Music, Music Therapy and Trauma.* London: Jessica Kingsley.

Taulis, Emilio, director. *¿Qué es la chilenidad?* (Laboratorios Taulis, 1939). Accessed January 15, 2018. https://cinechile.cl/pelicula/que-es-la-chilenidad/.

Theocharis, Angelos. 2019. "Polyphonic Memory and Narratives of Resilience in Svetlana Alexievich's *Secondhand Time.*" *Journal of Languages, Texts, and Society* 3: 185–206.

Toltz, Joseph. 2004. "Music: An Active Toll of Deception? The case of Brundibár in Terezín." *Context* 27/28: 43–50.

Torres, George, ed. 2013. *Encyclopedia of Latin American Popular Music.* Santa Barbara, CA: Greenwood.

Torres, Rodrigo. 1980. *Perfil de la creación musical en la Nueva Canción Chilena desde sus orígenes hasta 1973.* Santiago, Chile: CENECA.

United Nations. 1984. "Convention Against Torture and Other Cruel, Inhuman or Degrading Treatment or Punishment." Accessed June 27, 2025. https://www.ohchr.org/en/instruments-mechanisms/instruments/convention-against-torture-and-other-cruel-inhuman-or-degrading.

Valdés, Hernán 1974. *Tejas Verdes: diario de un campo de concentración en Chile.* Barcelona: Ariel.

Vega Durán, Osiel. 2000. *Himno Nacional de la República de Chile: antología de versiones vocales e instrumentales.* Santiago de Chile: División de Cultura del Ministerio de Educación y Sociedad Chilena del Derecho de Autor.

Vila, Pablo, ed. 2014. *The Militant Song Movement in Latin America: Chile, Uruguay, and Argentina.* Lanham: Lexington Books.

Vukliš, Vladan, and Anne J. Gilliland. 2022. "Archival Activism: Emerging Forms, Local Applications." *UCLA Previously Published Works.* doi: https://escholarship.org/uc/item/112790sz.

Waxman, Rebecca. 2020. "'It Was Like a Space of Resistance:' Functions of Music for Female Political Prisoners During the Pinochet Dictatorship." Master of Music, Musicology, The University of Edinburgh.

Waxman, Rebecca. 2021. "'It Was Like a Space of Resistance:' Functions of Music for Female Political Prisoners During the Pinochet Dictatorship." *MUSIC.OLOGY.ECA* 2. doi: http://journals.ed.ac.uk/music-ology-eca/article/view/6479/8787.

Weibel Barahona, Mauricio. 2019. "Manual de periodismo de investigación: ética / narrativa / investigación / seguridad." Paris and Montevideo: UNESCO.

Wilson, Jacqueline Z., et al., eds. 2017. *The Palgrave Handbook of Prison Tourism.* London: Palgrave Macmillan.

Wright, Thomas C., and Rody Oñate Zúñiga. 2007. "Chilean Political Exile." *Latin American Perspectives* 34 (4): 31–49. doi: https://doi.org/10.1177/0094582X07302902.

Websites

https://abril1982.nox.com.ar/
https://www.adnradio.cl/
https://www.amsmusicology.org/
https://archivommdh.cl
http://basedeconciertos.uahurtado.cl/
https://www.bbc.co.uk/
https://www.bcn.cl/
https://beta.creativememory.org/
https://bfe.org.uk/
https://www.biobiochile.cl/
https://www.cantoscautivos.org/
https://ciperchile.cl/
https://cnnespanol.cnn.com/
https://www.cooperativa.cl/
https://www.diarioeldia.cl/
https://www.dw.com/
https://www.economist.com/
https://www.elciudadano.com/
https://www.eldesconcierto.cl/
https://www.elmostrador.cl/
https://elpais.com/
https://www.emol.com/
https://www.ethnomusicology.org/
https://gulag.cz/
https://holocaustmusic.ort.org/
https://www.ictj.org/
https://www.iglesia.cl/
http://interactivos.museodelamemoria.cl/
https://www.julioiglesias.com/
https://www.lainformacion.com/
https://www.larazon.es/
https://www.latercera.com/
https://www.bcn.cl/leychile/
https://www.meganoticias.cl/
https://www.memoriachilena.gob.cl/
https://www.memoriasdeexilio.cl/
https://memoriaviva.com/
https://www.monumentos.gob.cl/
https://museodelestallidosocial.org/
https://www.musicapopular.cl/
https://www.nature.com/
https://www.oas.org/
https://www.opendemocracy.net/
https://piensachile.com/
https://radio.uchile.cl/

https://www.theclinic.cl/
https://www.theguardian.com/
https://villagrimaldi.cl/
https://vocesdelarebeldia.cl/
https://www.24horas.cl/

Index

For the benefit of digital users, indexed terms that span two pages (e.g., 52–53) may, on occasion, appear on only one of those pages.